The Coombes Approach

A companion website to accompany this book is available online at:

http://education.rowehumphries.continuumbooks.com

Please type in the URL above and receive your unique password for access to the book's online resources, which include additional colour photographs and a detailed map of the school grounds.

If you experience any problems accessing the resources, please contact Continuum at: info@continuumbooks.com

Also available from Continuum

The Coombes Approach

Learning through an experiential and outdoor curriculum

Susan Rowe and Susan Humphries

continuum

Continuum International Publishing Group

The Tower Building	80 Maiden Lane
11 York Road	Suite 704
London SE1 7NX	New York NY 10038

www.continuumbooks.com

British Library Cataloguing-in-Publication Data
A catalogue record for this book is available from the British Library.

ISBN: 978-0-8264-4044-0 (paperback)
     978-1-8553-9743-9 (hardcover)
     978-1-8553-9759-0 (PDF)
     978-1-8553-9729-3 (ePub)

Library of Congress Cataloguing-in-Publication Data
Rowe, Susan.
Coombes approach: learning through an experiential and outdoor curriculum / Susan Rowe.
   p. cm.
   Includes bibliographical references and index.
   ISBN 978-0-8264-4044-0 (pbk.) – ISBN 978-1-85539-743-9 ( ) – ISBN 978-1-85539-759-0 ( )
1. Experiential learning.   2. Outdoor education.   3. Holistic education.   4. Coombes County Infant and Nursery School.   5. Early childhood education–England–Case studies. I. Humphries, Susan. II. Title.

LB1027.23.R69 2012
371.39–dc23
                         2011040414

Typeset by Newgen Imaging Systems Pvt Ltd, Chennai, India
Printed and bound in India

DEDICATION

We wish to state that this book rests on the work of our colleagues, parents and governors who have shared the responsibilities and vision with us. Hopes and aspirations have been worked out together and any successes are the results of cooperation with these generous people.
The children we teach have influenced our direction at every point and this book is dedicated to them and to all the adults who shared the passion.

Contents

Preface

This book describes the ethos, values and work of The Coombes School from its opening in 1971 until January 2010 when the Headteacher, Susan Rowe retired because of ill-health. Susan Humphries, the founding Headteacher has continued to offer her services to the school on a voluntary basis since then.

The book describes the route taken by one school to create a child-friendly curriculum where basic human needs are recognized. Other schools are on their own similar journey. Every school is distinct in its approach and we make no claims that we are doing anything better than other schools.

Acknowledgements

We owe grateful thanks to one of our parent group, Fiona McLean, a professional photographer, for the black and white images in this book.

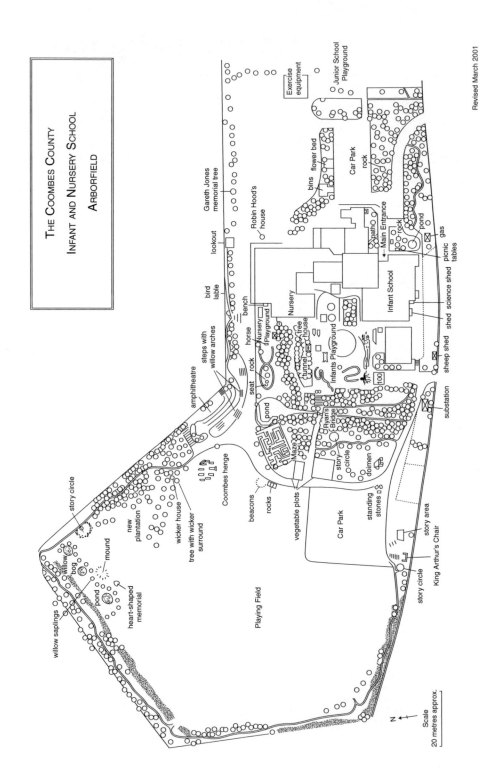

THE COOMBES COUNTY
INFANT AND NURSERY SCHOOL
ARBORFIELD

Revised March 2001

THE SCHOOL GROUNDS

School Timeline

1971	Opening of The Coombes County Infant School
	Tree planting programme and playground development start
1975	First pond installed
1976	Wild flower planting starts
1977	Deliveries of autumn leaves for soil improvement start
1978	Series of all-weather pathways started
	First wooden badges made and presented to the children
1979	First lambs reared at school
1980	Changes to topology of the landscape start
1986	Boardwalk pond dug: amphitheatre started
	First deputy headteacher retires
1987	Links with Learning through Landscapes start
1989	School name changed to The Coombes Infant School
1991	Opening of the Nursery Unit and school name changed to The Coombes Infant and Nursery School
	Joint winners of the Jerwood Award: building of addition to nursery, creation of enclosed nursery garden and a new school library
1996	BBC Open University Production *A School For Our Time* filmed
2002	Retirement of founding Headteacher Susan Humphries
2003	Deputy Headteacher Susan Rowe appointed as headteacher
	Susan Humphries continues to work in school on a voluntary basis and as Environmental Consultant and Governor
2007	Formal Collaboration with neighbouring Junior School – taking joint action on all professional matters
2008	Amalgamation of the two schools to form the Coombes CE Primary School
2010	Unexpected retirement of Headteacher Susan Rowe due to ill-health

1 Introduction and ethos

This book is about a group of teachers who taught in a state school from 1971 to 2010. Like similar professionals in other schools, our group wanted to teach in a way that would help children to thrive socially, emotionally and spiritually as they progressed through the required National Curriculum and National Strategies.

In the book we describe how we developed a pattern of education where learning is experienced as relevant and joyful. We turned to the natural world for inspiration because it could offer breadth and depth of knowledge in a holistic way. In this multi-sensory, ecologically renewing situation it seemed we could learn more about ourselves while engaged in caring for our part of the planet. The cultivation of the school grounds and their purposes for play and formal learning is a radicalizing force through many chapters. The regular use of the outside largest classroom celebrates learning in a community of many living things.

We advocate educating children in a society where the adults are the conscious role models. The children see the adults drawing on each others' talents in a way that suggests interdependence, respect and care and they absorb the messages implicit in this culture.

There is no perfect way to teach but we can all improve the conditions in which children learn.

History

Our school opened its doors to children aged 5–7 years old in 1971. Prior to this, the children had been taught in a school on the same site for 5–11 year olds. A rapidly increasing pupil population, partly the result of an expanding British army garrison nearby and partly the result of new house building in the area, meant that additional classroom space was required and our then local authority, Berkshire County Council, took the decision to open a separate Infant School adjacent to the Junior School and separated by a playground and car park. The sports pitch was on land beyond the Infant School and because there were no distinctive features along the route to it, a pathway was defined simply by use. Within the first few weeks the grass had ceased to exist: heavy wear reduced the surface to clay and mud. There is a good deal of pragmatic learning in situations such as these and pathways started to figure in our development of the site.

Susan Humphries was appointed headteacher of the Infant School when it was opened in the Spring term of 1971, with the builders completing their work at one end of the school with classes starting in the finished section. During that term, interviews were held to appoint a deputy headteacher and when the school re-opened in September of that year, Wyn had joined it as Deputy Head, a post that she held until her retirement in 1985. They appointed three new teachers to join the two who had transferred from the Primary School. Among the early appointments were two newly qualified teachers who are still on the staff group today: Carol our ICT specialist and Gill our music specialist.

In 1990, a nursery unit was added catering for children aged 4 years. This offered part-time nursery education to 26 children in the morning sessions and another 26 children at the afternoon session. At the age of 5, nursery children transferred into full-time education in the Infant department. Most of our children would transfer from the Infant/Nursery School at the age of 7 to the neighbouring Junior School.

Teaching style

From the first term our work centred on building relationships and quickly led us to work collaboratively. The six classes worked in two teams with three teachers in each using cross-curricular thematic learning approaches. Our choice was to meet all the children from time to time, exchanging groups, sharing ideas and systematically teaching together. We knew that what the children experienced from the method was likely to be incorporated in their behaviour. We saw the job of teaching as one where the children influenced the teachers rather than being submissive to them. There was a dynamic in their whole system of exchanges that we have held to through the history of the school and its gradual expansion.

The staff were keen to be active researchers believing that change was inevitable and desirable but that we wanted to initiate much of it. There was also another priority, that is, working in the way that we did, we were going to be able to react to government requirements with a degree of independence. A further aspect was motivational – by working in novel ways we could make room for the dreams of individuals. Above all, we needed to use our combined skills to produce innovation and evidence for changing the practice in this school.

Work with other institutions

We talked to tutors in the Education Department of Bulmershe College of Higher Education about our intention to create an evolving school, that is, one that would not become stagnant. We hoped that they would encourage student teachers to get involved with the children's projects and that in return we could further the work of any individuals planning small- or large-scale pieces of research. Most of the students' needs did not require a lot of extra work but one or two opportunities that came to us from the college were quite intense. In every case we recognized the gains for the children and students and the value for us as teachers. Probably the most influential result was to stir our professional creativity and inventiveness.

One piece of work made possible by the Reading University Reading Centre was to anglicize and trial the introduction of a new reading scheme: Reading 360 published by Ginn. Wyn led the assessment with help from the whole team. The typically North American phrases were removed, spellings were altered where necessary and stories were toned up for greater appeal. Working on this reading scheme raised many questions among us and answered a few in terms of the commercial interests involved in educational material and how we all respond to marketing pressures.

The mathematics tutors at Bulmershe College of Higher Education at the time were Peter Seaborne and Christine Haigh and they brought Logic Blocks to our attention and introduced their use to the children. Wyn and Sue, another teacher at the school, led us all in staff workshops with the materials so that we faced parallel challenges to those the children were meeting with the blocks. As a result we were all guided towards an understanding of the theory of sets where logical manoeuvres are worked on sets of things. This demonstrated practical knowledge of the universal set, subsets, the empty set and disjoint sets where objects have nothing in common. Teachers from many other schools came to watch the use of the Logic Blocks and listen to the children voicing their mathematical conclusions.

On the basis of the rapport between school and college, four lecturers came at different times to spend a term working alongside a class teacher. This was insightful for both who came to have more knowledge of each other's roles. As part of their training, many student teachers visited the school and saw the open organization and cross-professional demonstrations as a spread of ideas to which they wanted access. This situation drew them into the Coombes team when vacancies arose and it tended to support the open ethos of the school.

Our continuing thematic work was being developed inside and outside the buildings and the children spent many hours being taught outside in the natural world. Their important connection to other forms of life and to a planting programme drew interest from the founder member of the Learning through Landscapes Trust, Merrick Denton-Thomson. At this time, Susan Humphries became a trustee of this organization and with help from all the teachers makes a contribution to shaping landscapes for other schools. The outcome of this goes well beyond the 20 years of regular meetings of the Trust because it increases our confidence in designing our own spaces and starting new work in them.

We had excellent training in working as advisors for Independent Television schools programmes.[1] This work lasted for 10 years and many of the science programmes were filmed either in whole or in part at our school. Notes for teachers were written in collaboration with a Headteacher colleague at a school in Nottinghamshire. Graham Sellors, the Producer and his Directors made more than forty programmes for schools in six series. The scientific principles illustrated in the programmes used children and their teachers learning about recycling, the irreversible effects of heat, life in ponds, incubating eggs, uses of materials, seed to seed cycles, birth, growth and death, water, earth, air and other important scientific concepts. We measure the success of that work from a process begun that is still reaping rewards. In going public with our work we believed that the introduction to it would grow on in different ways in our own and in other schools. All the National Curriculum Science for 5–8 year olds was covered in action-based projects and the minute examination of ideas, method and results took our own work forward.

Early publications

Tending to the ideas we believe in drew us to writing about them. The first stimulus was from Usborne Books. Wyn became advisor for their series of primary maths books and there was a companion large picture book. Other opportunities to write followed the television work and our approach to teaching science was commissioned and published by Colin Forbes of Forbes Publications in 1993.[2] Our artist was one of our parent group, Carol Holliday, and she sketched on site to capture the active participation of children gaining power through experimentation. The two books were child-based for both children and teachers. Text flowed through illustrations, and the books were big. Carol managed to reveal layers of perception about our teaching style from hours spent with her children in school. Two other books followed, with line drawings by Carol. These were about social and cooperative exercises that we used in school.

Jerwood Award and links with the Open University

Our developing work shaped our professional growth and has a bearing on the symbolic and practical levels of our current thinking. In 1991, the school was presented with a Jerwood Award and secured £50,000 to turn some more of our dreams into reality. We built a large porch and storage cupboard at the entrance to our nursery unit and we created a library that had a sense of luxury about it: the shelves were made of pine planking, the carpet was a thick wool pile, there were spotlights to highlight temporary exhibitions and a door that swung open from the centre. There was sufficient space for a class of children and we got the contrast in atmosphere so that this space could give everyone a shift in mood when they used it.

In 1996, Professor Peter Woods of the Open University was using the Jerwood Award scheme as a research tool to identify schools with creative practices. He made a sustained programme of visits to The Coombes and decided to explore the characteristics of our developing project work. The school was the subject of an Open University and BBC film that is still being used regularly for teacher training.[3] Subsequent books were written by Peter and his team, aimed at professional development in which the Coombes was the main example.[4]

Every detail of our history has left traces on us. The continuity of processes started by events such as those described earlier has no boundaries. The desire to be directly involved in research, the conviction that we as teachers can never be self-sufficient and the pleasure of doing something together as a group of teachers is professionally reaffirming.

Collaboration and amalgamation

Back in 1991, the two schools – The Coombes Infant and Nursery School and Arborfield, Newland and Barkham CE Junior School – shared a site, but operated as two separate institutions that had developed in very different ways. We sought regular opportunities to work together, but the teaching styles and curriculum delivery in the two schools remained dissimilar. At the end of 2006, the headteacher of the Junior School retired, and a decision by the governors of both schools as well as the local authority, now Wokingham Borough Council, was taken to enter into a year of formal collaboration, with the Infant School headteacher taking over the leadership of both schools. This collaboration preceded the September 2008 amalgamation of the two schools into a new Primary School serving children from 3 years to 11 years. We had turned full circle and were once again one school with the indispensable addition of the nursery unit.

We now have almost 540 pupils on roll (52 part-time places in the Foundation Stage 1 – the Nursery; 90 children in Foundation Stage 2 – the Reception group; 180 in Key Stage 1 – the Infant department; and 250 in Key Stage 2 – the Junior department) and we anticipate around 600 pupils by 2011. If the population estimates are correct, our numbers may still rise although plans for a lot of additional housing in our area could mean the building of a new school on the south side of our catchment area and our pupil numbers could change predictions at a stroke. We are facing many challenges, not least the size of our school; at present this is a contrast to the numbers of the past. We are fortunate to have a staff group that is proactive, resilient and optimistic for the future. Much of what we have learned since 1971 is underpinning the development of our new school and the style of education and setting we offer will be based in large part on our educational experiences of the previous 30 odd years. We plan to be part of a system which is at the cutting edge of education and we accept that we must take risks and always stay vulnerable. We know that risks accompany innovation and that growth and change are integral elements of school-based research, professional dedication and the sharing of authority.

The Coombes School has become known for its innovatory and creative way of working while keeping a broad and balanced curriculum and for the way in which the outdoor landscape of the school has been transformed into its largest classroom. There is much interest from fellow professionals as we take on the challenge of working with older children but we have experienced mentors among the staff group and we learn from each other. We demonstrate that we think we are in the job for the children and that what is important is to be with them as much of the time as possible. We spend a lot of time examining our people skills and we all consider that this people-first philosophy is the bedrock philosophy for all of us. Our school rule that 'we care for each other' sums up our intentions.

Style of working: Our educational philosophy

Teaching is about the transmission of cultural values. Generally, a child is much more capable of achieving meaningful and rewarding relationships when working cooperatively and much more limited when experiencing the isolation of competition or when required to think creatively and deductively in isolation. Since our school opened we have built a learning community on the basis of collaboration and cooperation and in which social aspects of learning are at the core.

Over the years, the adult group at The Coombes has developed a style of working in the context of some powerful shared beliefs. The journey to this point has had its painful and difficult moments, in the manner of all relationships in a group trying to reach a consensus feeling. This is as true today as it was when the school opened. Directives from central and local government as well as a plethora of national educational initiatives, strategies and white papers have been a ceaseless priority and have sometimes been at odds with our empirical knowledge of our job. Our guiding principal is to support national and local initiatives and to be proactive rather than reactive in meeting their requirements, while continuing to explore our purpose in working with individuals and groups of children.

Our core belief is that education is about offering children and ourselves as the adult group, authentic experiences through which we can start to understand ourselves and our relationship with the world around us. There is a wide gulf between reading about or seeing Shrove Tuesday/Mardi Gras celebrations on TV and being directly involved in one. The tool to knowing is simple experience. Making the pancake batter in class, bringing the batter to the hall and feeling that you are being treated as a customer in a pancake parlour or creperie is a sensory experience. The choice of cooked pancakes, the atmosphere thick with the buttery frying smells, the entertainment as teachers flip the pancakes to each other from pan to pan and the teacher waiter service provide clear and simple messages.

There is considerable national pressure today to raise children's standards in writing. We believe that we should improve children's writing by giving them genuine experiences to write about – this is the body of a good novel or biography and the lifeblood of a good read. The significance of such moments is not merely about developing writing skills or recording of quantities as a mathematical exercise, it is about the power of sharing and about linking the past to the future. There is a maxim that states 'how do I know what I think unless I hear myself say it?' The frequently used starting point is shared talk that produces more ideas around the experience or focus.

Note making is another shared activity when post-it pages with children's impressions are stuck on the windows. The corner stone of our practice is relationships so the manner of speaking and the way we collect comments is a continuation of this idea. Swapping thoughts and ideas in pairs and working in changing partnerships helps the views of everybody to come across and is instructive for citizenship. The contexts for learning should be more about discovering basic values than giving the teacher peace of mind about test scores.

The pleasure principle

Teaching and living through the pleasure principle concerns the working mind of every human being. If a person or group of people can express themselves joyfully, kindly and creatively, then they are more able to share knowledge and be less afraid of mistakes. Living within a culture based on kindness helps us to express ourselves and take risks in our own unique way. A nurturing culture is about keeping peace with each other, using mediation and talk to resolve argument, studying the effect of our behaviour on our group, and promoting democratic practices. Self-awareness is an important part of good communication and such beliefs must be lived rather than formally taught.

We are all in constant training to uphold this frame of mind and success stems from the adult group's attitudes towards each other to validate the model for teaching the children. The adult group has to shape its own behaviours towards each other so that the children catch the attitudes and the tone. The ways in which teachers work together, in which they greet each other and in which they treat each other, the children, parents and visitors, give powerful messages about the quality of morale and education in the school. People tend to be receptive to positive images and tend to mirror what they meet in their day-by-day setting.

The treadmill to raise scores on children's academic performance presents as a fault line running through our philosophy and reflects today's trend in education. Monotonous drills to improve children's writing for the standardized tests tends to result in famine for the imagination and an anxiety driven scheme of work. Some anxiety might be worthwhile especially if it is directed towards the framework of testing and scoring as a whole, but this is not the case. If we teach to tests and targets there is a danger that we could end up only teaching what can be measured. That would be a disaster for the future generation.

We have to teach about the value of friendship, about making relationships, about playing and working cooperatively because these practices affect the society we are aiming to build. Competition and measurement have the effect of dragging down enjoyment but in the current educational climate much of what we have to do is premised on competition and measurement as is our academic reputation. We constantly struggle to ensure a balance in all that we do, and to keep at the heart of our work a culture of nurture, kindness and compassion.

If we take the view that a school is a microcosm of a fair society, our culture will not allow sexism, racism or the oppression of any child. Neutrality about these issues will not be good enough. We must help everyone to hold up the golden rule in his or her own behaviour as a matter of course and make it a daily experience. Our school of thought is to live by a single rule for all: 'we care for each other'. 'Each other' is our global term for all living things as well as humankind and equally we care for the animals and plants that are a part of our ecosystem.

Environmental development

We feel that our brief as a group is to reverence the natural environment and view ourselves as a tiny part in the web of life. Regenerating the landscape of the school and being involved in its evolution seemed a complex and attractive project through which we could define our ethics. The building of the Infant School in 1971 had been the cause for the destruction of arable farm land and our teachers were committed to raising our children with a deep respect for the land and its natural systems and a sense of connection to every other form of life. We felt that we could return something to the land that had been harmed by intensive farming and damaged by the building of the school.

During staff meetings, our talk turned towards holistic education in which community and the earth were joint beneficiaries, and we determined that whenever we could manage it, we would teach out of doors. We would also hold in mind the balance between outdoor and indoor education, and we would take what happened inside the classroom outside into the environment while bringing the outside environment into school – indoors and outdoors could be complementing each other for optimum value.

Children's thoughts often turn to the outdoors. They spend a considerable portion of their school lives in the playground, and what happens there will affect their behaviours and expectations indoors. The outside setting of the school is just as important as the indoor one, and needs the same careful thought and provision. Learning about nature by planting trees and wild flowers is an activity that stresses cooperation and responsibility for the environment and these are implicit messages about a wider world. The children need to go outside to interact with each other in a bigger and freer space. A school garden and playground planned to support good social play can mean that the children test the code of ethics of responsible, caring and cooperative behaviours in a hospitable setting that makes sense of this view.

We as teachers need to reflect on the quality of the outdoor environment at school, by watching children interact with each other as they play and work outside. This is the key to assessing the quality of the outdoor provision and it should be followed by a discussion with colleagues on how the school landscape could be more effectively used and developed. Teachers can also set the tone for social and cooperative behaviours out of doors through a means by which they formally use what is on offer there.

In our experience it is possible to alter children's perception of the outdoor environment by the way in which it is used to support the curriculum. A bleak playground can be made more inviting to the children if memorable learning adventures are regularly set there. Planning for treasure hunts, making the playground a chalkboard for the children's drawings, adapting it as an arena for street theatre or concerts means that the children see the spaces as possible scenarios for many activities. The schemes build positive perceptions that play into the children's cultural memories. Later when the association between place and event is recalled it can produce an empowering feeling of knowing and belonging to the place.

Revisiting our beliefs

Life is not just about plain survival; it should give us a taste for looking inward and looking outward, a commitment to work and to caring for ourselves and each other. With the amalgamation of the Coombes Infant/Nursery School with the neighbouring Junior School, the enlarged adult group is having to revisit and examine these founding philosophies, to validate our practice against our statements of belief, and to ensure a consensus of core values that will guide the work of our new Primary School.

There is a high level of exchange between the teachers. The struggle to do the job well is the central issue and the children need to perceive shared leadership and modelled democracy. We role play the risks we take and put our personal limitations on show. Sometimes we model problem solving together and argue with each other about decisions in front of the children. At other times, we act out a story with a message or sing directions to each other and to them. For the children to gain knowledge and understanding of their adults, the process needs to have the realistic edge of adult interaction. We admit mistakes, we point out the necessary elements of risk taking in the everyday work, and we vary our means of presentation to each other and to the children. We acknowledge that we do not always get along with each other, or get on well together all the time.

Acceptable risk taking

Being in a school where things happen means taking risks. We gamble on thorough preparation and knowing our community to build up shared skills projects. One of our beliefs is that our children need to have regular experience of other animals as part of their education. This is a reason for raising sheep in the school grounds and is part of studies about mammalian life cycles. Other contexts for meeting animals stem from regularly planned visits of horses and dogs, racing pigeons and kittens to be used to support diversity. All animals act spontaneously and can register negative signals from another animal group so a child with an adverse reaction to the smell of a goat or to a frequently excreting horse can provoke an irritable reaction from the animal such as biting or aggressive nudging. As teachers we assume that careful preparation of the children through explaining body functions and briefing everyone about respect for other living things will adjust behaviours to the occasion. At presentation times we carefully watch the conduct of all the living things brought together so that we can anticipate problems. Every now and then we are made aware of the thin line we tread. On one occasion, a shire horse stood on a teacher's foot as his finer points were being described. He removed his foot and the teacher stoically said nothing at the time. On a different occasion a camel became obsessed with our Nursery teacher and to such an extent that we could not get it to do anything but obsessively follow her.

Retrospectively, these moments are amusing but they might indicate matters of health and safety that could affect the experience of the whole group and our commitment to this way of working. We need to be bold in our professional judgements and watch ourselves being bold in case we become too bold. Once the experience is over the children need to be in on the stories that have happened. How else can we become a place of never-ending interest and how can and do we learn from the shortcomings?

Organization of teaching and learning

For many children, the pleasure is taken out of learning when they have long periods of sitting at a table practising skills. An active body supports an active mind contributing to learning and good health. As well as physical movement, we believe that a changing setting can help concentration and stimulate effort. Confining children to one classroom and one teacher also seems to us to be restricting. In staff meetings, we discussed the accepted pattern of teaching and instead settled on a routine that would mean that the teachers would run a programme in which they worked in teams to help the children experience more depth and opportunities in the curriculum. We were looking for greater levels of performance from the adults and children by increasing the feelings of pleasure and satisfaction day by day. We planned that the children would start the day with their class teacher, but that after registration the children would have a timetabled move to another teacher and classroom.

Movement around class bases has the effect of giving children a familiarity with the whole building, of letting them experience a range of teaching styles and personalities and of adding the risk of moving from the known to the slightly less well known.

Designing the teaching space, deciding where things should go and collecting subject-specific resources gave a real sense of specialism to each of the classrooms. Adopting this secondary school style of organization was something new to us all, and could have proved to be problematic for very young children (5–7 years old). The children's responses were encouraging: even our very youngest and newest pupils adapted quickly to moving about the school and working with different adults and we noted how the children themselves looked after each other and kept a protective eye on the less-confident children. When the children arrive in class for their focused activities in language and mathematics, the teacher knows that they are in a group related by age and of a particular level.

The levelling of the groups is a fluid arrangement agreed in discussion between the teachers. There is an element of ability banding, but maturity and confidence levels also play their part in determining a particular group for a particular child. One of the great strengths of this system is the ability to be very focused on differentiation. The pattern we have now adopted for four mornings a week is of dividing a year group of children into three groupings for literacy and mathematics work: a supported group, a core group and an extended group. The teacher is able to differentiate the teaching and learning for the children in an already differentiated group.

Critics might suggest that this organizational style could result in children not being challenged by more able peers, and missing out on peer-group teaching of more able with less able. This has been only a minor part of what we observe. Within their differentiated groups, the children teach each other, support each other and nurture each other. For the rest of the day the children are taught in mixed ability age groupings, as well as in vertically grouped classes. For 1 day a week, the children remain in their class groups all day and a modified timetable operates. We believe that there is a good balance between mixed ability, mixed age and ability group teaching and that the children thrive in their range of groups.

Throughout life, each of us will belong to many groups, and our place in them is crucial to our emotional health and social well-being. Our school is not going to be remotely similar in action to television contests where winners collect laurels in different forms each week. Real education is the long haul about becoming the best you can be as a human being in various networks of human relationships.

Teaching strategies

We agreed that our teaching strategies would alternate sitting, listening, writing, reading and mathematical exercises with short physical bursts that would sometimes focus on cognitive tasks. The children might go outside to work on collecting related words taped to or hung from trees, or search for rhyming couplets pegged on lines across the pathway. Very often they write their tables or number bonds with charcoal on the pathways, and use large chalks to practice their writing on the playground: they might be asked to create number lines using rubber-backed carpet tiles which have numbers painted on them. These large-scale cognitive tasks involving gross motor skills help the children to develop concepts and to consolidate their understanding of them.

At other times, we take the children out to skip or to march or to dance. Such periods of short intensive physical activity have the effect of releasing endorphins and upping oxygen levels to the brain. The other side to this more physically expressed work is that when the children are moving about, they can contact and relate to each other instinctively. Learning in a social context becomes more typical and this substantially helps another of our prime objectives. Opportunities to work together in this way make for pleasurable associations between learning, mastering tasks and making friends. We never stop needing this all through our lives.

When the school first opened, we adopted this kinaesthetic style of teaching and learning with children aged 5–7 years old. We are also using these techniques with younger children (3–5 years) and older children (7–11 years) and finding them equally successful. Teachers talk anecdotally about taking the children out for a break or a run about after a concentrated session, and we all know the benefits of this. What we have found is that short energetic bursts within a session can lead to increased concentration, children keeping on task and there is better performance of tasks alongside better behaviour. Physical invigoration is as important for the adult group as it is for the children, and our teachers feel the benefits of kinaesthetic and energetic tasks for themselves.

The activities we planned for the outside such as detecting and gathering up paired words that the teachers have hung in the trees, collecting individual words set around the edge of the playground to make a well-known phrase or proverb or poem, collecting adjectives to describe leaves, running the world's 'longest sentence' across the playground, all these exercises require cooperation and a supportive setting. Using the playground to turn a story into drama with lots of physical action and fresh language produces the story with a new perspective. We decided that in order to improve our teaching programme, we would need to prepare the outdoor spaces in much the same way as preparing the resources for teaching inside the classrooms.

Children need knowledge about the shape and timing of a session as it helps to overcome any anxiety about a change of scene. As part of our aim to help the children to feel comfortable, we include an outline of the work to be covered as an introduction to a lesson. Any resources set up outside and left in certain areas remain undisturbed by other groups of children using the site, and it is common to see several different activities being undertaken in the playground by different groups at any one time. Our children have learned to respect the preparations made for them by their adults, and they respond sensitively to them.

Evaluating our work

We set our intentions to teach as best we can and to understand the process of learning better, but we are always questioning the ways in which we translate theory into action and are regularly adapting our teaching strategies and styles. We learn from each other's successes and failures, and we continue to experiment. At the end of a learning adventure, we analyse it as a group together and reflect on the experiences the children have had. We brainstorm fresh ideas and changed ways of doing the familiar. Our teaching as a result is constantly questioning and searching for depth and we recognize that we are in the process of continued reform.

A multi-sensory approach

We are advocates of a multi-sensory approach. It seems obvious to us that energy and pleasure in learning and teaching flow from an approach that appeals to all of our senses. Gentle exercise is incorporated into the curriculum so that it assists the skills programme with aspects of motor skills. Tai Chi movements and postures, walking the floor area by only treading in the centre of the tiles, lying on the floor to read, going outside, all these add a kinaesthetic element to the children's learning. In the playground, working in a change of air with more oxygen to breathe and different smells to sniff, all help us to enjoy variety and refocus on cognitive tasks. When taking advantage of the outdoor learning opportunities, the multi-sensory approach never stops evolving. The breezes, the cool and warm spots, the smell of trees in bloom, the sounds of birds, the noise of traffic, the change of surfaces to walk on are some of the variables that make a richer textural world.

Inside the classroom, the multi-sensory experiences continue. For instance, the children sing the alphabet, they dance the alphabet, they eat the alphabet ('c' for cornflake or crisp), they engage in activities connected with the alphabet (washing the windows on Wednesday with warm water), they model letters with their bodies, they 'smell' the alphabet ('a' for angelica, 'b' for bay, 'c' for curry plant) and we try to match as many letters to plants growing in our gardens as we can. When using all their senses, the children start to internalize the learning. It becomes a part of them and it can be fun. By combining elements of visual learning, auditory learning and kinaesthetic learning, we can make our teaching interactive for all the children in the group and we can meet their individual learning styles.

Social context

School is the first full-blown society that a child enters. Vygotsky's[5] theories of the social context of learning suggest that the child should experience this transition as moving into an open system in which his parents or carer continue to play a major part. In this open system, the crucial nurturing factors of love, understanding, support and belief in the child should always be cherished and apparent. The regular presence of parents, grandparents and governors working alongside the children and sharing the teaching–fostering role has benefits for us at many levels. There is more support for tasks and more support for the quality, attitudes and awareness for everyone. The adults get insights about the value system at work and can get in touch with their own creativity and the creativity of the children. We are working towards maximum learning opportunities and want to represent a learning group. As a group of adults, we are a principal learning resource for each other in the art of living, learning and developing individual as well as group potential.

Learning needs to be experienced as a pleasure because of its integration with good mental and physical health. There are many necessary struggles to acquire useful skills whether they are focused on mathematics or interpersonal elements. Some of the processes are challenging and negative and the most brilliant teacher cannot awaken a feeling of pleasure in all the children about all aspects of the curriculum. We want our children to find courage enough to try hard to overcome obstacles and naturally their best resource is the inner self.

Our programme seeks to build up the child's awareness of their inner being through the stimulation of pleasure in learning and joy in working cooperatively. The most transforming knowledge is gained first-hand in a social context and through a variety of inside and outside activities. In the early years, how children learn to work as a group, to develop friendships, to respect each other, to tolerate difference, to share resources, to nurture each other will all be vital in ensuring their future successes as well-rounded adults. We are educating our children for an uncertain future and our first responsibility is to give them the tools and the practice to become socially adept, to show kindness, to be patient, to be empathetic, to be able to work together, to be an effective member of a team. These responsibilities in our opinion outweigh the passing on of banks of knowledge or the teaching of more intellectual and abstract skills.

In societies all over the world, there are disaffected young people and adults who find social interaction difficult and who lack empathy with each other. Some of these young people and adults are likely to be products of educational systems that failed them. The skills we need to develop as nurturing, socially mature adults have to be practised from the very earliest years and again and again through life.

Social and cooperative activities

We have designed our own system of social and cooperative exercises that we use with the children[6] and that we are planning to refine and develop as we work with older children in our primary school. The activities are non-competitive and they encourage the sharing of space, turn taking, patience, helpfulness, observation, negotiation, compromise and collaboration. The ability to work as a successful member of a team is a competency greatly prized in the workplace and in institutions such as schools and we need to ensure that the children get plenty of opportunity to practise the skills of working together, to develop self-esteem and to be effective group members. Our aim has been to raise the level of cooperative consciousness in our children and to help them to understand that all human beings can and must learn from each other. It is a struggle to break down the competitive barriers that breed fear and suspicion among groups unaccustomed both to a cooperative ethic and to sheltering all members. The common ground that gives children fun when working in teams and in groups of varying size and that fosters newcomers, has to be made explicit because it involves essential life skills.

Thematic teaching and learning

Enjoyment in the educational process stems from involvement in carefully structured, multi-sensory experiences that follow a theme. In our judgement, thematic teaching is well suited to learning in a social context and to active participatory engagement, and we shall describe some of our themes in Chapters 7 and 8. Carrying our beliefs into action has meant finding models of education where important messages are conveyed as practical situations are explored. We see thematic teaching as a useful key for unlocking fresh energies, creativity and lots of interaction with each other. We think that more levels of intelligence are satisfied when we occupy the children's minds, bodies and hearts by following themes that need lots of personal interaction with each other, and lots of interaction with a range of materials and resources. Learning through these themes is integrated learning that relates the gathering of knowledge to several perspectives. A satisfactory theme stimulates the emotions and has practical elements; it draws everybody towards a felt knowledge and an experiential approach. Choosing a theme and fixing the orientation for it depends on decisions reached by the teaching groups who discuss it thoroughly during planning meetings. Thematic teaching is well established and has proven its worth but we dare not develop all our teaching around a single system. The staff group offer a comprehensive approach with emphasis on broad, whole-person development. Enjoyment for the children is realizable when there is also a balance between passive and active learning, between quiet sitting and reflection and bursts of physical energy.

Observing children

Since our school opened, we have watched children at work and at play and made some observations that have influenced our teaching and learning styles. We are committed to developing independent learners in our community who will go on to become life-long learners. We have noted that the children learn by watching each other and working with each other – by mimicking and then through mimicking gaining confidence in their own abilities. This happens in our classrooms and outside where the children are given the time and opportunity to be together, to work together and to talk together. There are advantages when we give the children time and opportunity for peer teaching and peer coaching.

Our thoughts on developing independent learners were confirmed through the research of David Whitebread[7] and his colleagues at Cambridge University. In a long-term study of children in Foundation and Reception classrooms, the researchers noted that very young children learned effectively by watching one another and without the intervention of adults, and that quite often, the most effective response that the teacher could give to a child asking for help was to refer them to another child who had greater competence or expertise. The researchers noted that sometimes when an adult became involved in an activity the children were more inclined to say that they could not do something. If they were working with another child, they were less likely to question their own ability and they copied the other children around them instead. We are convinced that these sorts of teaching strategies also work well with older children as well as with the very young, and as our new primary school grows and develops we shall be testing the strategies with the older children.

The influence of Howard Gardner

In all our work with children, we have been mindful and respectful of difference. At the heart of our educational philosophy lies the belief that every child has a unique potential; perhaps mathematical, scientific, musical, physical or artistic. Over the years we have endeavoured to meet each child's individual needs and aptitudes and enable each of them to make the best of his/her special gifts. We have done this through a broad and varied curriculum, taught whenever possible by experts, and through a wide variety of teaching styles. The work of Howard Gardner[8] influenced us greatly when it was published in 1983, and has continued to influence us. Gardner's eight intelligences (linguistic, logical-mathematical, musical, bodily kinaesthetic, spatial, interpersonal, intrapersonal, naturalist) form the bedrock for our constantly developing curriculum and like Gardner we believe that we need to plan for and teach for all types of intelligence in order for the children and adults to be able to live life well. We also do our best to provide for the spiritual/moral development of the child and the adult group. Traditionally, schools have been expected to concentrate on linguistic and the logical-mathematical intelligences, but we are convinced that we should be developing the whole range of intelligences in order to equip our children for the best possible future. One former pupil who has become a talented horticulturalist and successful business-man remarked recently that 'it all started for me when you took me outside to plant sunflowers'.

Following chapters of our book will focus on how we operate as an adult group working together, how we plan our curriculum coverage, how we plan for the spiritual, moral and ethical development of us all in the school family, how we created and use our soft and hard outdoor landscape, how we teach science, how we have set up a pattern of school traditions which binds us together and on wider educational issues. The photographs that accompany the text will give some flavour of the range of our activity and of our imaginative and experiential teaching and learning programme.

Notes

1. Central Independent Television Alive and Kicking; All Year Round.
2. S. Humphries and S. Rowe. *The Big Science Book: All about Living.* Forbes Publications: London, 1993; S. Humphries and S. Rowe. *The Big Science Book: Materials and Forces.* Forbes Publications: London, 1993.
3. A School for our Times? Produced by Rosemary Hill for the Open University, 1996.
4. P. Woods. 'Talking about Coombes: Features of a Learning Community', in J. Retallick, B. Cocklin and K. Coombe (eds), *Learning Communities in Education.* Routledge: London, 1999; R. Jeffrey and P. Woods. *The Creative School.* RoutledgeFalmer: London, 2003.

5. L. Vygotsky. *Mind in Society: The Development of Higher Psychological Processes*. Harvard University Press: Cambridge, MA, 1978.

6. S. Rowe and S. Humphries. *Playing Around: Activities and Exercises for Social and Cooperative Learning*. Forbes Publications: London, 1994.

7. H. Anderson, P. Coltman, C. Page and D. Whitebread. Developing Independent Learning in Children Aged 3–5. Paper presented at 10th Conference of European Association for Research on Learning and Instruction, Padova, 2003.

8. H. Gardner. *Frames of Mind: The Theory of Multiple Intelligences*. Fontana Press: London, 1993 (a second edition following the original 1983 book).

2 Leadership style and organization

Leadership style

The leadership style at our school is based on democratic principles and elements of leadership are distributed among the whole staff group. Since the school opened in 1971 we have operated in this way although there has always been a headteacher and a deputy head. Following amalgamation, we restated our principles and the leadership style is still based on elements of leadership being distributed among the whole staff. Until January 2010, the school operated with a headteacher, deputy headteacher and two assistant headteachers, one based in each section of the school. In accordance with our earlier statement we attempted to strike a balance between the scale of responsibilities of a larger school and a more modern sentiment about power sharing. We believe that it is essential that the whole teaching team feel equal in every respect to each other, and that this principle extends to the ancillary staff group. The adults may vary in the length or type of their educational experience and their employment years at our school but by itself this should not imply any sort of seniority in our staffing structure. Visitors to the school have commented that there are many equal partnerships at work among the staff, child and parent community. The intergenerational aspects encourage a sense of family atmosphere and tend to produce a restructuring of the hierarchical dimensions from which schools have often suffered. Every school is distinct in the way that it develops a particular pattern of leadership and our approach has resulted in a school where there is little hierarchy and where there is an understanding that leadership is fluid and a work in progress. The particular responsibilities of the deputy head and assistant head lie in deputizing for the headteacher in her absence, in being exemplars of good teaching, in leading the group through the cycles of performance management, in taking the lead role in assessment, pupil tracking and data analysis and in working proactively for the future of the school.

In every school, some of the most creative teachers have little appetite for leadership and do not want to be dominated by those who strive for power and the use of it. They see a move away from the classroom to be a move where the losses will be greater than the gains. Organizational power exercised without the full participation of this group undermines their role and the status of being a class teacher. We believe that being a teacher in the classroom should have the highest standing. Our school needs to achieve its goals with the power of every teacher directed towards the children and each other.

Becoming a leader is not solely for those who are paid more or for those who seek to lead. The role is for everyone at different times. We gift leadership to each other recognizing that there are many fields of skills and the insights to match them. Probably there has to be a formally established headteacher to help the group reach agreement on the aims and shared perspectives of the school, although the headteacher role is changing dramatically and there are more instances of shared headship or collaborative work between a number of schools with only one nominal leader.

Emotional intelligence integral to each member of the group would suggest that every person needs to influence his or her fellow professionals as well as teach the children. When we can engage in discussion about our priorities with passion and humility and with the children at heart and in mind we are co-teaching each other and deepening our personal awareness. These ideas are premised on each of us being aware of our natural egotism, acknowledging it and striving for a state of co-dependency where power is a revolving dynamic.

Inevitably there are times when groups of people get set against each other. In the case of our schools' amalgamation, some necessary building work could have been an opportunity to transform our school and the way we could work together. Our needs were for flexible teaching spaces, a purpose built library, a welcoming reception area, a refinement of the external appearance of the school for an aesthetic quality and a control on the spread of the footprint of the building. Initially, the emphasis from our local authority was on a participatory approach to design with views expressed to them from the teachers through the headteacher and from the governors. Hundreds of hours of consultation followed. Ultimately the plan has been carried in such a way as to allow easy expansion at minimum cost.

During Michael Heseltine's period of Secretary of State for the Environment from 1979 to 1981, he said that 'Future generations will judge the quality of our contribution by the quality of the architecture we leave behind.' He urged caution on public authorities about applying short-term expediency to redevelopment schemes. It would seem that the rhetoric and the practice are as far apart as they ever were. This is not to say that any other headteacher or Chair of Governors would have fared any better but it does mean that when everything has been tried and resolution is impossible, the right response is a steadfast return to other business.

Communication

The increase in pupil numbers and numbers of staff resulting from the amalgamation in 2008 has brought with it some challenges that we are discussing as a whole staff group and one of these is effective communication. Obviously the best communication is through the involvement of all 'being in the know' and we have been reluctant to set up small groups to work separately from the whole team on bedrock issues. A major problem is that these working parties can exercise power on behalf of other people and that membership of them can lead to feelings of disenfranchisement in others. We believe that management divides can spring up quickly and result in more rigidly hierarchical control. The charmed circle can be a restriction of movement and growth for the whole group.

The basis of effective communication for us is the full staff meeting that all teachers attend weekly and to which ancillary staff and governors are welcome. During these meetings, we explore areas of common concern, calendar issues and anticipated visitors and we also undertake professional development work and training. The meetings take place in classrooms as well as in the larger hall spaces. This has the added advantage of conveying to our teachers the importance of the classroom spaces; it is in the latter after all that our key work is undertaken daily at the coalface.

A mixture of meetings for small and large groups result in proposals for what should be planned for the children's needs. One of these smaller sessions is for regular team meetings, one for Foundation Stage and Key Stage 1 and the other for Key Stage 2. These separate sessions consider planning for the coming week or half term, key stage issues which do not impact on the other key stage, on organization, on particular children and matters of mutual interest. There is a highly social feel to the gatherings that is more difficult to attain with the whole group meetings when sheer numbers make it necessary to run it as a more formal period. Both types of forum are aimed at maximizing success for the children and issues are taken between one and the other meetings.

Equality and cooperation

The freedom to disagree with those who are perceived to have greater educational experience or status is a crucial element in our meetings. Members of staff should feel able to state genuinely held views without being labelled as someone who is trying to undermine the group. Interest and involvement increase at meetings where there is some provocative conversation. It is important that we consider divergent proposals because ultimately a better working practice may come through them. Every teacher values cooperation in the classroom and knows that teachers must act together if the school is to function well, but arguments must be inserted into the meetings if they are to have a life.

All organizations need a sort of dynamic tension within them because people nurse their own goals as well as nursing goals agreed by the group. When a merger of the Infant and Nursery School and the Junior School was proposed there were teachers in both schools who were not in favour of the amalgamation. Two members of the Junior School teaching group eventually opted to get further professional experience in other settings at the end of the year of collaboration. This masked their discomfort; they did not welcome a change in leadership styles or in practice. Four teachers in the Infant setting had reservations and these reservations were clearly stated: the size of the amalgamated school; a check in the progress of certain ambitions (the settling down period in such mergers is approximately 2 years and could be longer) and quite understandably energies have to be directed towards the new situation; sidelining those ambitions, the need to have Church of England status and a reluctance to have church involvement and dogma; the wide difference in philosophy, ethos and practice between the two separate schools.

We held to the majority view that was in favour of an amalgamation and the majority of the parent group was pro-amalgamation. We pulled together to resolve our differences and reach a consensus. For us, this was democracy in action. Our basic ideals often work counter to our more egotistical selves. Now we are a very large staff team, and our systems for working together are being trialled, evaluated and modified with experience.

It is not an easy time trying to pull two disparate groups together and there is natural and healthy disagreement. However it is worth all the effort that we are all putting in and our collective, cooperative ethic is a persuasive do-it-to-yourself guide. In reality amalgamation was not the transparent and negotiable decision it appeared to be. Local authority planners had already declared for amalgamations of adjoining schools and at some point in the schools' futures it would have brought it about. It was better to realize the changes with a high level of purpose and with the obvious wish of the parents being fully exercised.

Flattened management structure

We are keen to avoid a linear management system structure. We believe that elements of leadership should and do rotate and that leadership should be distributed among the whole group and not to just a few. The type of flattened management structure that we propound is intended to give positive power to everyone with more roles to play as coaches, mentors, training providers, team leaders, leaders of workshops for staff or parents, consultants and experts in a field. The groups and roles experience should shift and there are no watertight compartments into which people can be trapped. Members of our team will put themselves forward for particular roles or be asked to undertake a specific responsibility. Three members of staff (two teachers and a support assistant) have taken assessment, pupil tracking and analysis of statistical data as areas of responsibility; these would conventionally be undertaken by a teacher with a management role. Two more members of staff have taken a special interest in continuing professional development and mentorship coordination for trainees. Again, these are areas more usually given to colleagues setting strategic direction and looking at value for money. Another group including teachers and support assistants has developed an interest in solutions orientated working and undertook professional training together over 3 days; they are now advocates for new skills in our setting and are working to bring them to other areas. Yet another group is looking at the Primary National Strategy and implementing its recommendations in our school.

Members of our team encourage each other to follow diverse interests and to be project leaders for a particular theme. When Jo, our Art Coordinator, thought that the children's spontaneity needed a fillip, she talked to colleagues about clay as the best medium for realizing the unexpected. She argued that children need the artist's studio experience to get dirty, take risks and feel the buzz that comes from personal discovery. Ultimately this led the whole school through a 2-week project centred on clay. Jo persuaded a former parent who is a professional artist to work as an artist-in-residence at school during the project and to co-lead the children's and adults' exploration of clay as a medium. She sourced a large and beautiful custom-made marquee to act as a studio and another parent put up the marquee with the help of Malcolm our caretaker, a grandparent and a parent. Prior to this she asked one of our governors to lead the excavation and shifting of large quantities of clay from the seam in our own school field. Another parent promised his small digger to lift the clay from the ground.

At the same time, Patrick recognized that by looking at the uses of clay we might build with it and make something functional. Carol and Jane said that clay could be a means for children to work on reverse print-making from patterns made in slip clay. In this adaptive way, the group formulated a plan and an informal compact was the result. Fundamentally, teachers extend the original ideas pushing them to contain new aspects of learning. It helps the initiating idea to be experienced in combination with others and leads to more interesting results.

The types of leadership described are enriching – they touch on self worth and dedication to the group. All members of the team have similar opportunities to become the leader when they feel it is right for them and the task suits their particular strengths and abilities. Trainees working with us comment on how liberating it is to be in a school where they feel able to contribute to the commonwealth and the rewards of leadership are seen to be shared. Howard Gardner suggests that there is 'an inappropriateness of the corporate top-down model for schools'[1] and he promotes a school culture based on respect and ethical foundations where emotional and interpersonal intelligence count highly.

Decision-making

Visitors to the school ask how we ever reach decisions if we have such a flattened management structure. Our response is that the decisions we make are based on consensus – that there is full discussion and that everyone has the opportunity to have a voice and to be heard. It takes us longer on occasion to reach a decision, but we do not perceive this to be any sort of bad thing. Of course there are occasions when an instant decision has to be made, and this usually falls to the headteacher. Our way of working is not always comfortable. It calls for honesty and mutual trust since discussions can sometimes reveal marked differences of opinion. Disagreement is not in any way harmful to the group. To be able to hear both sides of an argument or to reflect on opinions very different from our own is constructive. On issues where there are polarities of view, we usually look for areas in which compromise can be made to bring the two views together.

The process is time-consuming: it requires a lot of discussion and sometimes we put a topic on hold for a week or so in order that everyone has the opportunity to reflect and reconsider. The decisions we reach are based on the consensus of the group and once reached, everyone will adapt to them. We try to evaluate the decisions that we have made over time and discuss successes and failures and their impact. Again, this calls for honesty of approach and a critical analytical style of working together.

A day of reckoning generally arrives for any problem not hammered out already or foreseen. Criticism from members of the group who see defects in the school turns a spotlight on our problems. Such challenges set off discussion and re-evaluation and are always worthwhile. Disagreement is never a destructive force unless it is about mistaken self-interest and even then, the problem raised has to be acknowledged. A bigger difficulty arises from complacency because this leads to stagnation.

The emergence of a school that is frequently visited by other professionals was an option open to argument in the early years of the school's history and echoes of this debate still influence us today. The then headteacher and her deputy were visiting the University of Delaware each summer to run in-service workshops at the invitation of Dr Carol Vukelich. She proposed return visits so that US teachers could be part of a British version of early years' education. Schools in the United States closed in June and the difference allowed a 2-week practicum in the United Kingdom. Our teachers were broadly opposed to this because they felt pushed at the end of the summer term and they cited parent interviews, concerts and many other pressures. It was easy to reach a decision. At the next meeting, the matter appeared again when Sue, one of the teachers, said that it was illogical to reject visitors if we were running an open school. She spoke about the value to other professionals of being involved in end-of-term traditions and about her wish to be out of the mould and repetitive programmes. She talked about being starved of professional opportunity in her previous job and to feeling threatened. This initiated an aftermath and a heated division of opinion followed. One teacher walked out of the meeting. Carol and Gill talked of the less obvious but keenly felt aspects that had shaped general concerns. These misgivings involved visiting fellow professionals not working for the good of our children. The behaviour of visitors was quoted where some of them had considered themselves beyond the classroom etiquettes. It appeared that our teachers wanted protocols drawn up to strengthen the existing system. The sole aim of visits was to collect educational benefits for their own studies through being of service to our children first and working for the good of the group. The meeting concluded with a twist where some teachers decided to host visitors and others would not be involved.

Our immediate concern was mediation between teachers and children who would not get to know the visitors and the teachers who wanted to be in the scheme. The steps agreed were that children not having contact with the visitors in their classroom would meet them during PE, dance, music and games. In meeting and relating to overseas visitors social opportunities for all the children could be realized. Mediation can prepare for the longer future where the right to dispute is upheld and compromises can follow.

We adopted three agreements that stemmed from this divergent meeting. In the first we agreed to be much more active in judging the worth of a proposal before accepting or opposing it. Any scheme in draft would be considered across two meetings or more that would allow proper time for consideration. This was in spite of some schemes being able to be reviewed and dispatched on the spot. Later and with much business to get through these discrepancies were resolved. The second agreement was about a change of heart following a decision. It was felt by some teachers that there should be a halt on the time in which individual scruples could short-circuit group decisions. In future, when we appeared to be of the same mind we would have a deal about the time allowed for calling this decision into question. Its length could be set to suit the circumstances.

The third and perhaps most fundamental agreement was to define visitor roles. The optimistic faith we had felt about visitors making connections with the children would not be taken for granted. We would expect more from the visitors and ask them to sit with the children to research from a child's view. All of this may help to explain why and how we found ourselves developing a certain style in order to have ethical viability. These meetings all make clear how beliefs affect action.

Our two school journeys towards amalgamation were equally tense ones. Many people had very strong views that were openly expressed and both groups spent long hours of discussion before deciding to press ahead. Time spent on hearing each other out and on understanding and empathising with differing points of view has meant that the first 2 years of our new school have been purposeful. Of course there are areas in which some of us disagree with each other, and there always will be in any workplace. It is by breaking down the barriers to communication and by involving everyone equally in the process of change that as a group we have been able to travel a long way. An issue that we found particularly challenging was that of school uniform. At the Infant/Nursery School there had been no uniform while at the Junior School there had been a consistently enforced policy for uniform. The views of the children, the staff groups, the parent groups and the governors were very divided in both settings. We entered into a long period of consultation and discussion about the culture we wanted to promote: non-authoritarian, practical, tolerant and advertising individuality. Questionnaires were issued to all the groups in order that we could get as true a picture as possible of the range and strength of opinion. The final decision of our governors was a compromise – we adopted a non-compulsory uniform consisting of sweatshirts, polo-necked shirts, fleeces and waterproof jackets. We also issued a clear dress code for those children and parents who preferred to avoid any uniform. Predictably the decision had a mixed reception – some would have preferred there to be no uniform option at all and others wanted a full uniform to be worn by all the children. One parent removed a child from the school because our decision was open to interpretation – the meaning we had intended.

Giving children a voice

We are exploring the ways in which we give our children a voice in their school community. We are constantly engaged in dialogue with the children and seek their views. The children have many opportunities to talk with the adult group in the course of the day and they are always listened to. Many schools have developed a School Council comprising children as well as staff and governors; the children are elected by their peers and serve for varying periods of time. A School Council had operated at our Junior School, but since the amalgamation of our two schools we have been looking at other ways in which we might get all the children from youngest to oldest, contributing to the running of the school and in the setting of its tone and ethos. We have to ensure that everyone has the chance to be heard and to express an opinion. It may well be that we go down the route of expecting all Key Stage 2 children in their final year at our school to be school councillors.

Giving parents a voice

The parent group should have a significant voice in school, and over the years at the Infant School a series of Parent Forum meetings was devised. Parents were invited to come to school in the evening and to critique the way the school was operating. Rather than take general points, we aimed to explore life in a child's day at school. By using the timetable we would 'live' through a day and as we identified the parts we invited parents to comment and question. The greatest value would be put on what the children had reported but we would also answer questions and give explanations. Given this context it was worth allowing an evening for each class group in order to maximize the new information we hoped to get. Comparisons were frequently made about parents' personal school experiences and the here and now experiences of their children. We always sit in a large circle so that everyone is visible, speakers are talking to the group and not just to the teachers. This is in contrast with a lecture delivery that might be perceived as undemocratic. The parents were asked to give honest, critically constructive feedback to the staff group and their ideas and opinions were minuted by each class teacher. Summaries of the meetings were published and posted around the school. Much of what the parents talked about helped the staff group and governors to refine the annual School Improvement and Development Plan and the parents had direct impact on how the school worked. In later years we set up meetings for the parents in pairs of classes. The parents were encouraged to be honest about how they viewed our school, and they knew that they were having a direct impact on how the school went into the future.

During the amalgamation process, the Parent Forum meetings were suspended. The parents were being asked for their views at a range of meetings and through questionnaires and we were concerned about the rapidly growing number of evening meetings. We planned to resume the Forum because it makes use of the parent social network and genuinely refers to parents' and teachers' needs. Three separate meetings are planned for each Key Stage with an additional meeting for the Foundation Stage. We believe that it is in this type of direct, face-to-face contact that we can truly begin to understand how our parent group perceive the school. We need to learn from what they have to tell us. The views of the parents will be summarized and published throughout the school and on our learning platform.

Open door policy

The school's leadership style is based on transparency and equality, democracy and consensus. It reflects our open door policy where parents, other family members, governors and visitors have access to us and can work alongside us. Due care is of course given to health and safety and safeguarding duties and an apparently relaxed stance is actually anything but that. We are aware of who is in school with us, where they are and what they are doing. Strangers are questioned and the children themselves are alert to newcomers to whom they have not been formally introduced. Our open door policy is an essential ingredient of a doctrine based on handling situations effectively. Schools are about people and people should be viewed in human terms. When doors are locked and access for all is only by the keypad entry systems, the general effect of such precautions is to be redolent of reformatory behaviours and practices, and we are anxious to make our school as un-prison-like as we can. We work in an open community where people are welcomed to work alongside us. Of course there is an element of risk in this approach, but it is risk that has been most carefully considered and that is constantly being reviewed. Crime in school settings concerns us, but we do not believe that locked doors or only partially opening windows will do anything to keep out those with an evil intent – windows can be smashed and locks forced. The result of locking the children inside the school building is to keep out the parents and to imply that there is harm lurking outside. The facts are incontrovertible – children are most at risk from people in their own families and from those who are well known to them.[2] Our open door policy is also discussed in Chapter 9.

Parental involvement

Parents bring their children in the mornings into the school buildings and classrooms, and many of them choose to stay for a while. We do not have a formal building opening time but ask that unaccompanied children are not left with us before 8.30 a.m. (20 min before the start of registration at 8.50 a.m.). Parental access has real benefits for us all. The many who come to the classes are always happy to hear a reader other than their child, to undertake a small task for the teacher setting up the classroom, or just to talk with other parents. Similarly at the end of the school day, parents are encouraged to come to the classrooms to meet their children. There can be problems with noise, especially if pre-school children are not properly supervised but on the whole, these disadvantages are outweighed by the positives that accrue from parents being encouraged into school.

Many parents spend longer periods in school with us and they become invaluable participants in the education process. Our teaching and support group know how best to get direct involvement in activities and how to encourage them to consider their own future careers. Many of our well-trained support staff started their school experiences with us as helping mums or dads and some of our teaching group had a similar start to their professional career.

Grandparent and extended family days

Each term, we hold a grandparents and family day, usually preceding the half-term break. On these days, we make the features compatible with family-oriented learning and we have always been advocates of this style. We have evolved techniques that allow the classes to rotate through workshops determined by the nature of the topic and often our intention is to present challenges that require additional help. Attendance at these days should satisfy adult expectations as a learner as well as being a social instrument by improving interaction between adults and children. The staff group monitor the distribution of activities and seek feedback from the family visitors. We believe that education is a family matter and trust that these days help us move in the direction that puts the family at the heart of our school community. Of course there is significant change to the usual school routine but the benefits of this programme outweigh the difficulties. This series of days is described more fully in Chapter 9.

Our governors

Our governors give strong commitment to the school. Most of them spend regular time working with us and being involved in our schemes. Two governors regularly attend our staff meetings and provide feedback to the whole governing group. We perceive our governors to be critically supportive members of our team and their views and advice are always listened to. Governors usually commit time and support to a particular area of school life and they serve on relevant sub-committees or working parties. They also offer their own individual talents and expertise to the school community. The Foundation (Church) Governors, of whom there are three offer effective links with our local churches. Governors understand the work and goals of the school and channel this awareness of our goals into the community. What really matters to us is that our governors position themselves in such a way as to help us to do more than we might have expected to do. There is always a waiting list to become a governor and parents in particular are keen to join this group that argues and questions on behalf of the children.

Vocation

There is a feeling among many of our staff group of vocation. Motivation and high self-esteem leads to a deepening sense of vocation and helps us to have a greater personal investment in our chosen profession. Consultation on and full participation in every aspect of the life of the school also cements our feelings of vocation. Most of us perceive teaching as a way of life, an expression of belief and a statement of intent for the future. Like most teachers, we tend not to count the hours we spend in the school or at home on school-related business, and notions of work–life balance, although important, are not our drivers.

Vocation is a cohesive force for us, and the focus is always 'with children at heart and in mind'. We demonstrate that we think we are an axis for the children and that it is crucial to be with them for as much of the school day as possible. We spend a lot of time examining relationships and we all think that this 'people first' philosophy is fundamental. Our school rule, 'we care for each other' says it all.

An integrated curriculum: A case study of sheep

We have found that an integrated curriculum approach is instructive and enjoyable for us all. It enables us to go deeper into topics than would be possible with separate subject teaching. Studies based on the four sheep owned by the school illustrate this approach. The sheep are part of the outdoor setting and are moved around the grounds in mobile fencing or they are pastured in one of two small fenced paddocks. One of these slopes beside the school and the other one slopes beside the entrance to the playing field. Both small paddocks have been planted by the children with fruit trees and these are protected by park-type tree-guards. Grass in these areas and in the margins of the playing field is rotationally cropped by the sheep with benefits to the ground of being aerated, manured and kept short to favour the spread of violets, primroses and cowslips that the teachers and children have added year by year. At some point during the spring and autumn the sheep are grazing either under trees in blossom or under trees in fruit. This combines to make the area strikingly attractive. The sheep are always a strong presence in the grounds. They act as a hub of interest involving the life of another species. Sheep watching and touching can have a restorative and spiritual quality for many children and adults.

A peripatetic shepherd checks the health of the animals from time to time and he brings a ram to stay with the flock for 6 weeks. This is arranged so that mating might be seen incidentally but it is talked of in a very relaxed way: the children understand that if the sheep are to have lambs, the mating must happen first. Births are planned for the period following Easter because lambs are vulnerable to frost and cold rain. In making this life cycle visible, we try to minimalize the risks so the ram is not introduced to the sheep until December and most births will take place in late April or May. The birth of lambs usually happens early in the morning but children have often been around when one of our lambs is born. After 2 or 3 days following birth and providing they have bonded well with their mothers, the lambs are taken into the classroom for short periods to be weighed, cuddled and enjoyed at close range.[3] Not all pregnancies result in a successful birth and death is a fact of life and sensitively explained in these terms. The children are reminded about the unbroken series of births and deaths among the sheep that speak of the continuity of life and that for us dates back 28 years to the time the school adopted two orphan lambs. We view parts of this story in photographs that remind us all of the recurring patterns.

Early man understood that fleece and hair cut or combed from animals in late spring would grow back in time to protect the animals in winter. Human ingenuity and needs combined to shear and collect hair and fleece, separate it so that the fibres would lie parallel and then twist the strands together to make workable lengths. Other skills were developed that involved hooking, weaving and knitting to produce width, length and firmness from these pieces. The value to the children is in actively participating as the processes are linked and in making their own meaning from this research-based approach. To extend the meaning, the children will also follow some deconstructing activities that correspond with the fabrication processes. Unpicking loosely woven cloth, unwinding discarded hand-knits and separating felt means deconstructing and analysing drawn from evidence in the children's hands. The undoing is a way of making discoveries that can be deeply satisfying and it needs to be thought of as a reverse flow.

Shearing

Our shepherd brings in a ram of his own to shear before our Textiles Day and he also shears three of our small flock. On this occasion, he uses old-fashioned hand shears rather than electric ones. This organization makes it possible for two classes at a time to see detail in the shearing and watch from closer quarters. Shearing is a very physical exercise for the shepherd and he must talk about his tools, the order in which he moves his shears along the line of the animal's body and so on before he starts. He needs to prime the children for the sight of blood spots because it is easy to nick the skin of the sheep. He also explains to the children that the sheep will probably evacuate because this is also common. We have cleaning cloths, dustpan and brush and a bucket of water on hand.

Morris the shepherd points out that the fleece should be kept as clean as possible and that once he has started to shear the sheep he will not stop until the job is finished. One of the team will help him with any details that need attention. The school animals are not easily phased by crowds of children but there are degrees of tension about being sheared. Morris shows the purple antibiotic spray used for the treatment of any cuts. He tells the children that they can measure his success as a shearer if he can remove the fleece by following its contours and not breaking it. The fleece will be laid out on the pavers so that a plan of the animal's body is the result. Before the sheep come into the area, we ask the children to keep as still and quiet as possible.

The shearer's hands move along the sheep's body in a fluid movement and the fleece ripples off showing the creamy underside of the wool growing closest to the body. Before shaking the fleece out to demonstrate his skill, Morris attends to any blood spot. The sheep is confused by its sudden lost of weight and we can clearly see its bony framework. We are always taken aback by how slight the sheep are under their coats. The children are thoughtful during this time and there are many empathetic moments; the children frequently comment that they feel sorry for the sheep.

Morris explains that the sheep need relief from the flies that breed in their long wool and he talks about the benefits of being freed of their long coats during summer. The sheep is then led away and we do any necessary tidying up. After this Morris shakes out the fleece for examination: as one child summed up, 'That's a flat pack of the sheep.' Some children draw around the outline of the fleece with charcoal before Morris gathers it up and ties it together using the neck wool as an integrated tie so that the fleece remains intact for the market. We throw the fleece to one another to verify its functional shape and it is passed around so that all the children can assess the feel and weight of the bundle. Later on, the charcoal outline will be measured and may be transferred to a sheet that is stretched and pressed over the charcoal outline.

In the classroom the fleece is weighed and divided between the two classes who watched it sheared for washing, carding, dyeing and other experiments. In this way the children refer to the demonstration with specific regard to history, maths and science and they use the new words they have learned. This sequence is followed two classes at a time, including the youngest nursery children. The nursery children often wash their wool on that same day: they mix soap flakes into warm water and they squeeze and rub the wool in one of the water trays. Another water tray is used for rinsing and then the clumps of wool are pegged on a line to dry.

Working with the fleece

Older children also wash the fleeces by hand to free the wool of some of its lanolin and dirt and they put them on bushes to dry in the time-honoured way. We own several sets of carders and the children use these to disentangle the woollen fibres in preparation for the textile-making workshop. In the classrooms, the children have informal moments to card fleece when it is convenient for them.

Membership of the carders group is ad hoc and supported by parents and visitors joining in for the odd 10-min session. It is a job made pleasant by group talk and work and often includes humming or singing. Pulling a set of two wire combs against each other creates a lot of friction and it could be a dreary chore to tease out the fibres unless you feel motivated by the social context. In textile terms, teasing, carding, picking and combing mean ridding the fleece of knots and seeds and rearranging its fine threads so that they are in line with each other. The adults may talk to the children about metaphors and their relationship with working with fleece: 'Stop picking on me!', 'I'm teasing out the problem', 'You're teasing me', 'This is a knotty problem'. These are sayings that have their roots in the past and they relate to the preparation of fleeces – a time-consuming job in the early days.

Carol and Judy do many experiments with the children to dye fleece using plants from the school gardens. We grow woad for this purpose and we also extract dyes from mint, stinging nettles, beetroot, green walnuts, spinach and onion skins (available in our gardens). We buy plums from the supermarket as our damsons are not in season at the time we work with the fleece; in the past damsons were grown in large quantities throughout the country for their pigment. The dyes are fixed in the fleece using vinegar or alum. All the colours obtained are muted but later, when the wool is woven or knitted the stripes of different tones combine well.

The research to collect plant pigment began by sandwiching specimens in absorbent paper and then squashing the plant under rolling pins. Flowers barely left any stain on absorbent paper – green walnuts stained brown on hands, clothes and fleece showing their worth immediately. Onion skins released their pigment into fleece when the two simmered in a preserving pan. The yellow extract was the second-most reliable plant pigment that we discovered, although plums and beetroot were also potent staining agents. Again, we set the dyes with vinegar. Samples of every result tested on clumps of fleece were mounted on lines after being rinsed as a test of colour-fastness. Carol and Judy captioned the display with the names of the sheep, the origins of the dyes and the names of the children who had done the research work.

From fleece to cloth: Textiles day

The relationship between the stages of production from sheep to cloth has many aspects. The children have seen sheep shearing, handled the cleaning of the fleeces, managed carding and collected and tested dyes. We move on to work with our volunteer craft experts. If we follow the Jack o' Newbury tale we shall start shearing the last remaining sheep on our Textiles Day. In this case, it will be done in the centre of the playground with electric clippers instead of the hand shears that slow down the process. The chosen sheep is brown with white markings: its fleece will be versatile in pattern making and it will be easier to identify during processing and much more complex to sort.

All the children stand around the edge of the playground and get a distant view of the action. The previous shearing demonstration delivered the teaching points and the children know that the fast modern method will stand as a comparison. Morris shears much more speedily this time and after a few minutes the sheep is led back to pasture by children from one class who will stay to feed and water it and make sure that it settles down. The fleece is sorted by parents who have another class of children to help them with this and with the carding. Spinners work with another class and as the carded wool is delivered they give all the children a brief turn on the spinning wheel or with the distaff. Eventually the spun wool is passed to knitters, weavers and crochet workers paving the way for a new group of children to participate.

Most of the extensive practical work is done in the open air as it was when cloth production was a rural industry. There is some circulation space between the weavers, spinners, carders, knitters, crochet workers and the felt maker but artists sharing this open studio are able to call across the space or catch a piece of the action going on among the children or co-workers. In this community, artistic parents and visiting artists are demonstrating the pleasure that comes from making things. We believe that knowledge of this kind is as vital to the children as elements of the National Curriculum. It is teaching about perseverance and it can also make a contribution to understanding sustainable development and suggest potential future skills. It might also speak of human relationships and how they thrive under joint responsibilities.

Once the latest sheep wool has passed through the first stage and while the craftspeople are waiting for it, the fleeces prepared earlier by the children have been fed into the system. The experts are now plugging fleece into canvas to become a wall hanging and two are making a fleece rug. Other prepared fleeces are going through the traditional route. Children are sketching, watching and taking turns. They rendezvous in the classroom to record their hands-on history, make predictions, and deconstruct weaving and knitting. Teachers and children follow a schedule that helps groups to circulate between the craft workshop, the sheep pen, the display of sheep-related items – from shears and teasels to tapestries, felt and clothes and they visit the lines of dyed wool samples in the science area that they have had a hand with. The most vital element in this day is the craft workshop with its participatory requirement: every child is putting together a personal repertoire of experiences.

At the end of the day it clinches the process to see two or three token articles produced from the morning's shearing. Knowing that the children were part of at least two sequences but have seen them all and talked about them with the craftspeople is key to the experience. The children carry small plastic bags so that samples of untreated and carded fleece, spun thread, knitted cloth can be systematically pocketed and taken home to share and discuss.

Further extensions

We introduce the children to one small area of the origins of the English language and reflect on how language has built up over years of history. We look at the number of metaphors we derive from wool to see how basic and accessible wool is and always has been. Those with unswerving ideological leanings are said to be 'dyed in the wool' and when we are too trusting it is easy to 'pull the wool over our eyes'. Psalm 72 speaks of God as filling every cell: 'He shall come down like the rain into a fleece of wool, even as the drops that water the earth'. When our thinking is muddled we say it is 'woolly' and if we daydream we can be described as 'wool gathering'. Words derived from the processing of wool to create types of cloth also boosts our everyday language: phrases such as 'weaving a tale', 'a warped individual', 'being fleeced', 'homespun entertainment' and 'spinster' are figures of speech that reflect the symbolic and practical importance of sheep and wool.

We also collect the fables, parables, poetry and story that are connected to wool and sheep and we incorporate them in our work. Fortunes have been made from the backs of sheep and the Jack of Newbury tale is an historic incident that demonstrates this. In the story, a wealthy aristocrat laid a wager claiming that it was not possible to be clothed in a suit that had doubled as sheep's clothing on the same day. Jack of Newbury rose to the challenge and with the townspeople acting as witnesses he had the sheep sheared at dawn. A determined workforce organized by Jack fitted the aristocrat with his new clothes before sunset on the same day. We outline the story emphasizing the processes and friends from local crafts guilds, parents and children help to manufacture something that can be worn by the end of the school day. Over the years we have produced knitted and woven scarves and small pram blankets.

When we follow this scenario, the experiences themselves are the rationale for doing the work but they also raise the need for the specialized language. The why and wherefore of the depictive phrases, 'looking sheepish', 'making sheep's eyes', 'trimmed down to size' become clearer following the shearing of sheep because the animals are noticeably thinner when they are 'fleeced' and quite giddy with weightlessness.

The weaver uses the shuttle to pass a weft thread backwards and forwards between the warp threads and while he or she does this, a spare shuttle is passed round the group. The teacher mentions the shuttle bus that travels between the park and ride centre and the town of Reading. The to and fro shuttle has given its name to vehicles going backwards and forwards over distance. We also think about the phrase 'on tenterhooks': newly produced wool was attached to hooks stretched across large frames – these were known as tenters.

The experience of cross-curricular and integrated curriculum work on a topic like sheep is an example of work that matters to us all. The children are learning in the context of a teaching and learning community and all the adults exchange ideas with them and with one another because they are still en route to becoming better in their field. The basis for learning is the sharing of problems and skills, a curiosity about everything and plenty of opportunities for consolidating social skills and working cooperatively. Many subject areas are covered and the children are partaking at every stage. In this set up, artistic parents and visiting craftspeople are co-leading each other and us. It is a demonstration about the pleasure of sharing – progress is interdependent and there is much to learn in this.

Notes

1. H. Gardner. *Five Minds for the Future*. Harvard University Press. Cambridge, MA, 2007.
2. See statistics on child abuse and children at risk figures available from Child Line at: www.childline.org.uk, from the NSPCC available at: www.nspcc.org.uk/inform/research and from central government at: www.statistics.gov.uk/hub/child and www.direct.gov.uk
3. Following these activities, the children always wash their hands thoroughly in soap and water. We also position warning notices for any pregnant mothers before and after lambing as they will need to avoid contact with the sheep for a week or two.

3 The outdoor classroom – the soft landscape

It is worth bearing in mind that creativity needs to work in any number of ways so that its effects are present everywhere. The traditional landscape of a school certainly needs creative re-thinking if it is to become a model for environmental awareness and responsibility. 'Think global: act local' needs to start with the toddler and become a way of thinking all through life. Education is about giving children a system of values that will have real relevance to their future lives. This cannot be done by instruction alone because a child internalizes values through interaction with other human beings, with other living things and in the way a community expresses itself. Every child needs to grow up feeling an active member of a group that has creative powers and environmental principles.

Trees – dreaming of a school set in a wood

When we opened the Infant School in 1971, we stood on the bottom line both environmentally and aesthetically. This was something of a benefit because we could clearly see a number of ethical and responsible ways to involve the children. It was they who asked for trees. Their urge to climb and hide was couched in this way and it provided us with a valuable start to an arboretum project. Our first response to this signal was to bring into the playground eight huge hardwood tree trunks. Children needing to climb used the fallen tree trunks to scramble along and because some were positioned over others, there was height and breadth to the structure. At some points, there were open spaces to drop. The tree trunks in the playground matched the children's needs for climbing and hiding.

We started a tree-planting programme, but many of the young trees which the children planted died. The topsoil was so thin and the clay layer so cold, that we needed to repeat the planting year by year. We learned a lot by doing this. The children believed in the idea of planting a wood around the school and they collected acorns and other seeds and brought self-seeded trees from their home gardens to continue the project. Some of us thought that we should change our policy of simply planting by going further and altering the nature of the land itself.

Young trees in a woodland have a strong link to the parent stock through the soil that contains so much leaf and woodland material. With this idea in mind, we organized deposits of leaf litter from our local Council. These were delivered from October to January directly from the road sweeping vehicles that had cleared local rural areas. In a beautiful and commonsense way hundreds of metric tonnes of autumn leaves ended up being spread on our school grounds. This had the effect of improving the soil as the leaves decayed into rich humus. It became a key concept of our sustainability teaching and the result was to simulate soil conditions in a woodland. This programme ran for 10 years and only changed when permission to unload on our site was revoked by the Council for 'safety' reasons. The benefits to the land of having these vast amounts of leaves redistributed on it made all the difference to the heavy base soil. In the children's vegetable and flower areas the leaves were mixed with the base soil and over time, the plots became freer draining and easier to work.

While leaf litter was such a dependable source for the foundation of our woodland garden scheme, the pathways around the area were being overworked, impacted and sterile tracks. We asked for help from the tree surgeons and companies that maintained the hedgerows in the local area to donate their wood chippings so that we could apply these to the path surfaces. This treatment made sustainable and porous covering for all the paths and was another example of recycling. We kept the school's back gate open for deliveries and metric tonnes of woodchip poured into the project (and is still coming to this day). In their present state, our older trees are now shedding enough leaves to feed the soil with a thin cover.

Different groups of fungi then play their part in breaking down the decaying material. This fungal element is regarded by foresters as crucially important in the soil as well as fundamental to the process of decomposition. When leaves and woodchip are laid on the ground, their presence encourages these essential organisms that fruit as mushrooms and toadstools. The effects are most noticeable in the autumn, but there is evidence of these organisms in spring and summer too. Sometimes, we get extraordinary mushroom/toadstool rings, a wide variety of fungi forms and colours as well as the recognizable common fungi such as Wood Blewit, Penny Bun, Inkcaps, Chanterelle and Field Mushrooms. Children and teachers never collect these fungi for tasting but if there are a great number of fungi fruiting at any time, they are occasionally gathered for spore printing. The caps are placed gills-down on white paper under a loose cover of cling film and then left overnight. During this time, the spores are released and the wonderful patterns can be fixed with hair lacquer or spray glue.

The soil fertility is influenced by the living organisms in it and from the action of earthworms and moles. In their different ways, worms and moles mix the soil from the lower levels with the plant matter on the surface and serve to aerate the ground.

Willow

More than any other species, the willow contributed to the development of the idea of a school within a wood. Many of our first plantings were of willow, because this wood is fast growing and because the children could plant hundreds of them as sticks pushed into the ground. They make few demands in terms of soil conditions, the stick cuttings cost nothing and within 2 years they can be lush with growth and hosting aphids. This is a step-by-step approach to building a natural community where the numbers of beetles and birds multiply in response to the availability of food and shelter.

Willow has been our pioneer species serving to protect other slower growing species, checking and directing our movement around the grounds and providing copious amounts of material for weaving and experimenting. Rooting lots of willow in a bank of earth or on the flat can make an interlocking system of roots below ground and stems above ground. This is a particularly useful resolution for landscaping newly built banks or stabilizing worn-down playground edges. When the willow grows, its roots act to anchor soil so that it does not wear away. Above ground, the lateral branches can be woven so that their continuing growth produces a living hurdle. If small children find weaving willow in situ difficult because the branches tend to spring apart, garden ties can make the experiments achievable. We have grown tunnels, arches, domed shelters and a giant figure from willow and so far have always found craftspeople in the community to advise and inspire when we needed help with traditional willow weaving methods. Native species of willow in our grounds include weeping willow, crack willow, white willow and pussy willow or sallow. Our children like willow because its young shoots can be woven into floppy garlands for Easter or Midsummer's Day. Crack willow is cut to make bundles of ten sticks and single sticks, and these are used in our classrooms as maths resources for teaching place value.

There is an implicit connection between what the children are doing with the willow and what their ancestors would have been doing in the past when using this material. There is also an underlying implication about sustainability and the renewal of resources: the regenerative properties of willow are well known and understood. Willows are also hosts to a huge number of insects. Many of them will feed on other trees as well, but a large number of them use willow exclusively. No other tree except oak supports more life, and in this country virtually all moth larvae depend on willow.

We place white sheeting underneath a tree and shake the branches. The children are then able to examine the range of living things which fall onto the sheet to get some idea of the wealth of life the tree supports. The sheet used for inspection is gathered up later, by which time most creatures have made a safe return to their habitat. Creatures brought indoors for further study are returned to the original habitat at the end of the teaching session, and the children understand the importance of this liberation.

The planting is a part of taking thoughtful action to improve local conditions. During their time at school, the children will have had several opportunities to be a tree planter and they get real pleasure from seeing their trees flourish.

One of the unforeseen consequences of putting nature back in the school site is a rabbit population that exploits the tangle of briars, nettles and scrub. The children love to see the rabbits, but they eat the crops from the children's gardens and de-bark the young trees. All our young trees must now have guards and our gardens have fences and nets for protection. This is part of our story: it is freedom, change and affection for the natural world.

Eco-gardens are better places to learn about the dynamics of life and offer opportunities that closely mown grass or formal flowerbeds do not. Our gardens provide us with a range of species for study and fun, with the emphasis being on native trees and shrubs.

A few native trees are grown as Christmas trees and these are Cupressus Leylandii. The advantages they give of fast growth, pyramidical form and close-packed flattened branches make them the best choice for decoration and there is no anguish when they are cut down. Ecologically they have no value and they are probably the most exclusively planted conifers in gardens: the children assume that these were planted for this very purpose. Ideally, we would cut Norway Spruce but our experience is that these are slower growing and do not have a reliable spread. In early December, we harvest the Christmas tree for the school hall and each class of children takes turn to bring it indoors.

Mistletoe

Mistletoe has been planted throughout our school woodland but so far it has only germinated on the apple trees. In February when the berries are ripe, all the children gather in turn to pick two berries each. The children then press the berries into the bark of the deciduous tree they have chosen and there is a 1 per cent likelihood of germination. At this point we have 17 successful strikes to remind us of the mythology and beauty surrounding this plant. The inspiration for this tradition comes from the legends surrounding the mistletoe plants, and we use Padraic Column's version of Baldur's doom from 'The Children of Odin' as an example of the power in retelling an ancient story cycle.

Holly and other evergreens

Holly is an excellent tree for birds and insects. Holly needs cross-pollination before it can berry and only female trees produce fruit, but staff at garden centres will advise about the necessary male tree. The appeal of evergreens is the sense of continuity they bring and hollies can also come in a range of striking foliages. We walked four classes of our children to the local garden centre and when we did a quick poll about their choice of plants, two thirds of the children wanted topiary designs in the school gardens. In the garden centre some of the hollies and bay trees had been formed around frames to become spheres on spheres, birds, rabbits and mushroom shapes. We met the children's unlikely choice by training willow stems into the giant figure where children can help with the shaping. Topiary features such as the intricate geometric designs of holly (the children's top choice) are very awkward to maintain and need more formal settings than ours.

Ivy

Ivy can make dense leafy patterns and good ground cover. It is one of the two larval food plants of the Holly Blue butterfly. In spring the female lays eggs beside the flowers of holly and the butterflies that came from these larvae after pupation lay their eggs on common ivy at the budding tip. Later the larvae feed on the flowers and the fruit before over-wintering in the pupa state. Ivy is a must in a wild garden being one of the best wildlife plants that produces nectar in late autumn when nectar is scarce. It is also a great provider of nesting sites and hibernation cover. We prune ivy for the evergreen garland which is the central Christmas decoration of the Infant School hall every year, and ivy growing on the ground is easy for children to collect.

Log piles

We make log piles with dead wood around the gardens and as the wood rots it becomes ideal for fungi and for wood-boring insects and adds to the wildlife value of our woodland. These piles are hibernating sites for some creatures and living space for others such as nocturnal ground beetles that live at the bottom of the heap.

We teach the children about the system in which we exist: that plants are the foundation for all the life on our planet and ultimately that all living things depend on the plants. This teaching depends on being able to see the interaction between species: staying in the garden to watch insects collect pollen, studying sparrows and finches collecting seeds from the heads of sunflowers, identifying newts' eggs on the oxygenating plants. All species are parts of a whole in which each makes a contribution to others: we all fit together.

Shelter belt

Surrounding the school playgrounds, sports field and car park is a framework of trees which shelters the children from the wind and sun. The whole landscape gets its perspectives from these trees that have value individually and collectively. As a shelter-belt the trees reduce the wind speed and filter some of the sounds and traffic fumes from the B3349 road (School Road). None of the trees are more than 36 years old and tree planting is a focus for some work every year. Management of the trees is very light, but some are inevitably sacrificed when there are changes to the school building. The building has needed extensions and is in the throes of building work at the time of writing. Another major re-landscaping task will be needed when the new buildings are finished and when trees are replaced it will mean that different children get to experience planting for a new purpose. In the more distant future groups of trees will reach maturity at different times due to the practice of yearly planting. Developmental stages need to be represented and to those who planted them, every tree is significant. Some trees in our collection are more impressive because of their age and size but in terms of a growing arboretum the stock is young and needs time to prove its value.

Woodland management

Coppicing hazel and cutting back some alder, hornbeam, oak and silver birch may seem rather drastic but we do this on a rotational basis. The children use the poles from the re-growth of these trees and the conditions in the woodland change every time trees are cut. As a result of cutting, a single stem produces several leaders which mature as a clump to shelter many more insects and birds. We also prune a few trees to produce low spreading growth and we cut some to encourage forking. Centuries ago this was the way that trees were shaped for house and ship-building.

The upkeep of our woodland area depends upon light management since we aim to mimic ancient woodland where there is some layered growth. Willow needs yearly cutting and shaping otherwise it overtakes everything nearby. Originally we had a lot of clear ground to cover and the children planted willow cuttings in the intended woodland areas as statements of our intention. These cuttings quickly established and helped us by building up a green mantle in which there were numbers of slower growing trees.

In the first years, the children cut off the willow tips with classroom scissors: a practice that they very much enjoyed. When the willows had set the woodland in motion we thinned them out to reduce the competition. Willow remains an important subject for us providing frameworks for banks, a shelter and a tunnel but these require fixed routines for trimming and shaping and this is hard work.

There are a few trees in our gardens that have been used for experiments carried out with the children. The trees have main-stem branches that have been tied so that the branches grow in a curve. A healthy tree can be stressed to produce unusual growth forms. Another way we do it is by tying socks on a branch and filling the socks with stones. At a later date the sock is cut off and the branch develops with a kink as it returns to its natural direction. We add variety here and there by tying trees together: ash is well suited for this experiment because it grows energetically in our clay soil. Walking through or standing in the centre of a tree can work if the main stem is cut so that the tree grows two or three central stems. We felt that pruning for special effects was particularly valuable. In due course, the woodland develops with many special features, a few through experiments such as the ones described but mostly through the spread of plants and animals.

Fruit trees

When we started our environmental initiative we built up our stock of trees so that the children would have examples of all the native trees. We moved slightly beyond this so that we could include trees such as cedars, medlars, mulberries, quinces, olives, figs and walnuts. Our trees refresh us with their beauty and with their fruit. Apple trees grow into small trees that flower with lovely fragrant blossom. In the autumn the children collect the fruit with their teachers and make toffee apples, tarts, pies and crumbles that

are shared with everybody. Seventeen trees were planted for this purpose and three crab apples were added to the mix to help with pollination. The children also pick and eat apples directly from the trees so that they can experience fruit at optimum freshness (we use no herbicides or pesticides). The aim of being able to eat locally produced food becomes a practice with some likelihood of being remembered. There are several varieties of apple grown in the gardens and we use these to sample taste, rank the apples' appearance and check the flavour and the pip count. This is a school research exercise with a focus on personal decision-making. The intention is to improve knowledge of the product and uphold personal taste and personal perspectives. Every year, we transform one of the classrooms into an apple barn.

The children taste six or seven varieties of apple, sample fresh apple juice and apple blossom honey and they listen to stories based on apple such as Adam and Eve, the Golden Apples of the Hesperides, Iduna and the Golden Apples and Atalanta's Race.

Pears and their grafting stock, the quince, are in our woodland orchard as further examples of blossom and fruit to smell and enjoy. These trees do not fruit reliably: the weather conditions in their flowering period determine the crop. The fruits are cut up for tasting so that samples can be available to everyone. The etiquette for tasting is that nobody may eat until every person in the group is served. These experiences add to our sense of community and increase our appreciation of the trees around us.

Plums are also grown for their blossom and fruit. Most of our trees have been grown from plum stones and they tend to be self-fertile. They crop well with a fruit full of flavour when eaten directly off the tree or cooked immediately after picking. These plums tend to degenerate a few hours after picking, but the fun and the learning is centred on finding the plums, helping others to find them and then sitting down together and enjoying eating them. The greengage is awkward as it fruits in mid-August when the children are on holiday, parents and teachers harvest the fruit and freeze or jam it so that we can taste it from the spoon when school starts again in early September. At first taste our damsons are so acidic that they set teeth on edge but they do sweeten after the first cold nights. By this time many have fallen, but we also pick all the fruit we can reach and make pies or jam with it.

Fruit on our cherry trees is ready to eat at the beginning of July. Sometimes we are fortunate enough to pick and eat with the children but this fruit is a favourite of birds who are drawing on the wealth in our gardens and we do not begrudge them it. Our two fig trees are being trained up south-facing walls. Their productivity depends upon the weather but we have enjoyed some success with them. Each fig can be cut into four portions so that some of our classes have a chance to taste home-grown fresh figs.

Snowdrops and hazel

In the last days of January and through most of February many people go to see the snowdrops in bloom in some of the old churchyards and private parks. There should be opportunities for this sort of gentle pleasure in schools because it is an important experience that can illustrate the profundity of the natural world. Snowdrops bloom and scent at a quiet time of year, the bulbs multiply and the flowers seed when there is little competition from other species. Block planting them as woodland bulbs among young hazel trees gives the bulbs both protection and nutrients. A path runs round this layout giving a good view of the snowdrop drifts and on a sunny day, the fragrance is incredible. The success of this is not so much about size, but more about aspect, woodland situation and a yearly plan where the children fit in a few more snowdrops in the green (at the point of blooming and just after) while the rest of the plants are clearly visible. Our hazel grove is surrounded by a low wooden fence to keep human feet away from these fragile plants.

Wild flowers

Many primroses, violets and cowslips bloom on the bank at the front of the school. By selective weeding of the bank we prevent these flowers from being swamped by strong plants such as brambles, docks and teasels. The aim is to make the bank appear as natural as possible with the spring flowers growing in association with grasses and low growing trees. We never pick these flowers, but we do encourage the children to finger them gently because at close quarters there is so much to discover. The density of these flowers also adds to their appeal: it means that in spring the bank is almost a solid block of yellow with the violets a very sharp contrasting colour.

There are plenty of reasons to follow a planting method that highlights wild flowers blooming together in a dense mass. In this plan we can divide clumps of primroses with the children and avoid treading on later flowering types so that maintenance is easier, the impact on the senses is greater, the children pay more attention to the flowers and the concentration of insects is much more noticeable. Our aim is to have a series of botanical attractions with blocks of flowers expressing the relationship of the plants to the seasonal cycle so that through the year the plants evolve: growing, blooming, seeding and dying back. It is an illustrated calendar and as the flowers bloom in their order they nourish and sustain insect life.

Daffodils

A key annual event for the children is picking the flowers that they have grown for Mother's Day at the end of March. In the autumn every child in the school plants at least two narcissus bulbs: a school tradition that dates back to 1972. The cumulative efforts from this yearly planting produce large stands of daffodils that are built up by not being allowed to go to seed. The hardy bulbs bloom in groups of yellow across the school grounds and enable the children to be certain of their Mother's Day bouquets. We talk to the children about the importance of being a planter: for some plants like the narcissus, planters also have pickers' rights.

Bluebells

Bluebells grow prolifically through the older part of our woodland that we named Bluebell Wood to honour this beautiful flower. A central pathway keeps damage to the plants at a minimum and we teach the children to study the bluebells from this pathway. We also have Spanish or Garden Bluebells growing at the front of the school at a good distance from the native species. Both sorts of bluebells are loved for their colour, shape and scent but if we pick bluebells to study or draw we only take the culti-vated variety from the front garden, and never the native bluebells in Bluebell Wood. A substantial amount of native bluebell seed was scattered through the woodland when a friend of the school sadly died and it was then that we first opened up the woodland pathway. As a result of this, the area has become a real delight and we are careful to stress that all such flowering woodlands must remain as un-disturbed as possible in order to protect them and in the light of the Countryside Code. Simple long-term changes such as providing the children with a bluebell wood on site is a practical way to help them to appreciate the countryside and the variety of life it holds. There are no instant fixes for countryside restoration but there are many benefits aesthetically and spiritually that the long-term commitment is worthwhile.

Other wild flowers

A flower-picking opportunity arises when dandelion, buttercups, daisies and clover bloom in the school grounds. We negotiate with the grass-mowing workers from the Local Authority to avoid cutting the margins of the playing field because once the flower heads are chopped off the grass is robbed of its special features. Following time-honoured practice these common flowers are picked to see 'how much you like butter' or they are de-petalled in the ritual of 'he loves me, he loves me not' or 'tinker, tailor, soldier, sailor, rich man, poor man, beggar man, thief': in the old tradition, dandelion seed heads are blown off, the number of breaths needed to clear the seed head said to determine the time of day. The children also use the flowers to make daisy chains and bracelets or crowns.

The teachers challenge the children to make repeating patterns with the flowers, such as four clovers, three buttercups, two dandelions, ten daisies. The children then repeat the pattern and extend it. Teachers and children also work with these flowers in the style of the artist Andy Goldsworthy, enhancing a small area of grassland by adding extra flowers in a variety of patterns. This is often a small group activity: the results that are ephemeral are captured by camera. In reorganizing these little patches of grassland the children are learning something about plant communities and experiencing age-old pastimes and traditions in one of the cheapest and most effective ways.

We alert children to flower and plant communities by walking the pathways with them and searching the open land of the school playing field. Here, the hazards, problems and expense of a field trip away from the school site with a large group of children do not exist. The school grounds are the main botanical resource. When walking the school grounds, we pause and reflect whenever we come across small animals, birds or insects. We do the same for flowering plants in groups or as single specimens: this gives us time to study the characteristics, think about the plant's value in the food chain or its medicinal uses. At flowering time the plants are at their most attractive and invite our notice.

Wild and cultivated (garden) plants mingle in the school gardens to make a never-ending seasonal clock. The diversity suits children and wildlife alike and there is always something worth going out to enjoy. Combining elements of the old countryside, the park and the back garden in our scheme helps the children to get pleasure and learning from their surroundings. Our garden is a model for conservation and sustainability. Different ground levels produce environments for damp-loving plants or for plants that prefer well-drained ground. Acid-loving plants grow well in ground topped regularly with bark mulch and others prefer the clay typical of our region.

Flowers in the grassland react badly to weed killers and pesticides and part of our management policy is to prohibit this treatment. We are also uncertain about the possible consequences to children (in spite of the manufacturers' assurances). On the whole we feel that such plants as nettles, ragwort and dock are a necessary part of the diversity of life, as are aphids, slugs and rats or mice. Since there is a relationship between all living things, we aim to care for our school grounds so that it is an exemplar of this truth.

Our pond areas support wildlife and the kinds of plants in them are part of our nature reserve. Kingcups and yellow flag iris, water lilies, water forget-me-not and meadowsweet help the butterflies, bees and other insects and are perching places for dragonflies and damselflies.

Sometimes we plant field poppies in association with flax or wheat and they are often present among the sunflower crop. They take advantage of disturbed ground and once there has been a concentration of them, they tend to appear all over the place in subsequent years.

We absorb a lot of information through the nose and some plants when in bloom become a focus of interest because of this. Lavender and lilac both release strong scent and they are two smell 'themes' which frequently occur in a large number of supermarket items ranging from polishes to toiletries. Two lilac bushes grow in the front gardens and there are several lavenders which provide flower-heads for the children to cut and put into bowls. When the children rub the lavender heads between their fingers, the oil is released and the children can relate a range of products to the plant source.

Mint, bay, rosemary, ransoms (wild garlic) and wild strawberries grow in the school grounds as well as yellow archangel, red deadnettle and big communities of celandine. There are masses of other flowers and plants; honeysuckles are particularly enjoyed by the children and they are all landscape features that provide a food source for wildlife and an important habitat.

Raised beds

Some of our planting is done at eye-level in raised beds. The framework for these is reclaimed timber, and ledges around the beds make good seating or temporary writing desks. Lots of recording is done out of doors and a system of raised beds puts flowers and vegetables and the insects on them at the children's eye level. One such bed is very bold. Shaped like a large boat, it has telegraph poles as masts and a netting 'sail' for climbing plants. Soil in this bed is never waterlogged and it provides a warm microclimate because it catches lots of sunlight. Delicious tomatoes, beans, peas, mange-tout and courgettes are grown by the children as well as flowers. This raised bed was a solution to the problem of a class of children and their teacher wanting a garden as close to the classroom as possible. When parents collect their children at the end of the school day, many sit around this garden to exchange news with each other and enjoy a social time as they wait for their children to join them. There are other raised gardens which give the same benefits and the children plant and harvest pumpkins, gourds, potatoes and flowers from them: the soil warms up quickly and the container gardens are easier to tend than gardens at ground level.

Sunflowers

Every year, the biggest cultivation bed is used to grow a large block of sunflowers. These showy plants mature in 12 or 13 weeks and the children broadcast the seed in late June so that when they return to school in September, the plants are mature and ready to flower.

Every child and adult has a handful of seeds to plant and the seeds are bought in bulk from the pet shop. The build-up of seed in the soil allows a big margin for failure that the slugs guarantee, but enough sunflowers grow and bloom to make an extraordinary statement – changes to the landscape that can be made by crop growing. It is not only

beautiful in itself, it is a constant source of interest to see the way the flower-heads incline towards the sun, to see and hear insects collecting the nectar and pollen and to see how the birds are drawn to the first seeds. Teachers cut a path through the sunflower plot so that the children can walk up close to their plants and make size comparisons between their own height and the height of individual plants.

At harvest time, we look at the sunflower paintings of Van Gogh, David Hockney, Georgia O'Keefe and Monet. At the peak of the sunflowers' blooming time, we pull out one sunflower plant for each child: we parade our sunflowers on the school field and then the children draw their flower on the playground and take it apart so that they can better understand its structure. This tradition of sunflower growing has become an enduring feature in our work. For us, it reflects the long history of planting in our school to create some understanding about the complex web of life.

Improving the soil

The cold clay soil has been improved in the vegetable beds and flower plots by having leaf compost, compost from our own composting bins and animal manure worked into it. Children plant potatoes as a main crop because they are reliably productive and need minimal care. Parents and friends prepare the ground by weeding, adding organic matter and digging it into the plots. This routine is applied to sunflower patches and vegetable production in the raised beds and for the pumpkin garden. The children use trowels to dig the holes and they plant the sprouting potatoes in them at a good depth. We find that to work through a planting scheme as part of our science programme is a great benefit. When the potato crop is ready for harvest, the children dig them up with their trowels and cook and eat them as a celebration of their success. This is literally down-to-earth education as well as a real culinary pleasure.

Hedges

Our boundary was originally marked with chain link fencing on concrete posts. A hedge was planted to mask the traffic fumes, the sounds from the road and the ugliness of the fence. This hedge could have been much more traditional with many species represented but we were so anxious for quick results that we planted common hawthorn that was also cheap. During its history, the hedge has been laid on three occasions in the time-honoured way, causing it to thicken as it re-grew.

Additional species have been planted alongside the hedge on the school-side but this is not quite as satisfactory as having the variety in the main hedge line. A good hedge is a sanctuary for wildlife providing food and shelter and impacting on the number of wild creatures sharing the environment with the children. It is a living boundary, elegant and ornamental, retaining moisture and acting as a micro-climate and habitat. The complexity of life in this habitat means that it can be a nature walk to enjoy from the start to the end of it.

Colour walks

Children collect tiny bits from the natural world during walks along the pathways and fasten them to cards covered with a strip of double-sided sticky tape to create 'colour walks' as we call them. They also tie bits into frames hung from the ceilings. The frames are made from willow sticks cut from the garden and tied with fine wire. The specimens that the children collect represent personal choices from every child as well as the season. This sort of display also works well on hazel sticks from our grounds.

Lichens and mosses

Lichens and algae mosses were some of the first forms of life on our planet. Nearly every school site has abundant examples of these simple plants and we encourage our children to locate and examine them in situ. Many mosses grow among the grasses, the lichens will occur naturally on the trees, school walls and fences. Mosses will colonize old carpets (preferably natural fibre) if the carpet pieces are pegged down on a slope. The carpet can then be lifted, used as a display base and returned to its position with very little disturbance. Moss grows in cushions so that the individual soft, water-filled cells of the plant are supported. These tactile plants can be collected from around the school gardens (and sometimes from the roof) and arranged by the children into moss gardens. The children take turns to water mist the mosses with a fine spray of pond water and to observe the effects of this under magnifying lenses. After a few days, the moss gardens are taken apart and we return the plants to their habitat pressing them back into their original locations. Mosses have no root system and because they attach themselves to their stratum with small suckers, they can refasten themselves.

Ponds and wetlands

The range of species available to the children is increased through having wetland areas and ponds. Children are fascinated by the progress of the frog, toad and newt from spawn to fully developed amphibian. We often net these pond dwellers and put them into transparent plastic tanks for close-up inspection. This 'hunting' behaviour is a great favourite with the children and the finds are described and enjoyed until it is time to return the pond-dwellers to their environment.

The teachers felt that we should have more than one pond to encourage the populations of plants and animals that we hoped to study. One pond was located near the staff room at the front of the school with a low wall and a wooden lip attached to it on which the children could lean, and on which they can rest their specimen pots and reference books and charts. A larger second pond has a board-walk running around two edges so that the children can look directly into the deeper parts of the pond. Now and again, during hot spells, we see grass snakes hunting in the water, and periodically ducks visit this pond. A third pond is located at the edge of the wooded area where we dredged out the grassland to encourage insects, birdlife and plants that need wet habitats. This is a vernal pond that usually dries out in July and refills with the rainfall in the mid to late autumn.

Naming the pond specimens, describing their diet or metamorphosis is all part of the science curriculum. Even more important is the flying start that experiences such as these around the pond produce in the children's hearts and minds. Holding a caddis fly larva in the hand and looking at the minute particles that it collected as camouflage and barrier brings an awareness of small organisms that is deeply personal and spiritual. The joy of discovery and the 'grown-upness' of being the wardens of wildlife start here. Hours of contentment are passed detecting damselflies skimming across the water, watching the ballets of the whirligig beetles and looking at the reflections mirrored in the water. All this instils a keen interest in and respect for life.

This year, we put our young ducks on one of our ponds and watched them dive underwater and break the surface, and seeing the details up close allowed the children to notice the hundreds of beads of water on the ducks' feathers, showing the watertight quality of the plumage.

Safety is an important priority. However, sensible behaviour cannot evolve in a vacuum. We risk assess, use landscape methods to separate wet areas such as open fencing or we put the pond areas where they can be visually checked by adults most of the time. The deepest pond is next to our nursery garden and separated from it with a strong open-mesh fence. It would not be reasonable to ask the nursery team to monitor this stretch of water, but it is a counterpart to working nearby and being aware.

The natural world is always in a dynamic state. Over time, a pond becomes colonized by plants, the area becomes a wetland and ultimately returns to dry ground. In rural areas, many ponds have dried out since farmers no longer need them to provide water for their livestock. This means that ponds in gardens, in parks and in schools have a greater importance in providing aquatic habitats to support certain species. Regular checks and a running list of jobs to be tackled are essential for the good of the plants and wildlife. Leaves blow into the water, silt builds up and the 'wrong' kinds of plant invade the pond.

Topology

Scooping out ponds and ditches helped to alter the topology of the school site. Surplus clay has been used to make banks and mounds such as the one dividing the amphitheatre from the busiest pathway running between the school buildings to the playing field. A mound in the field defines the labyrinth zone and makes a story-circle meeting place quite discreet. Another bank was created to border a pathway so that the adjacent woodland area with its groups of bluebells and celandines can survive intact. The strategy that helps wild flowers and animals to multiply year by year is about making sure that the children get clear messages from the landscape. As well as banks there are some low fences that give views over the surrounding small-scale spaces. The banks and small hills have pathways on them that are restricted by planting (mainly willow) on the outer limits.

Pathway planting

Pathways need to be unambiguous and some of the plants alongside them should be of the tough sort. Thistles, nettles and briars are providers of much life that can be observed from the pathway and such plants can check the tendency of the path to get steadily wider through use. Deep top dressing with sawdust and bark chipping is a convenient way of making all-weather paths for crowds of children (some of whom have rather flimsy footwear). The top layer of woody material allows moisture to pass through it and the paths can be walked a short while after a heavy rainfall. The paths get undermined by moles from time to time, but they get pressed back into shape by walking children. When the children walk the paths with their adults, they get knowledge that they can apply in other places. The walker through the woods gets insights about other woodland areas. Our deciduous wood at school has similarities to every lowland wood.

Once children have seen something like the green oak roller caterpillars in rolled up oak leaves, they are likely to recognize the signs when they come across them elsewhere. This is one example among hundreds of learning and teaching for transfer. In the spring, the teachers lead the children along the pathways in search of wild flowers. Whenever wild flowers have gained a footing they appear in similar spaces in country parks and rights of way. Primroses on some railway embankments and occasional canal-side banks are the same species as those on the school bank.

Paths link parts of the whole school site. They wander between different areas and open up new vistas at every turn. A good path system can show the children that there is plenty going on even in winter. There are changes of level, hard materials such as the huge rocks and soft tactile mosses that flourish through the winter for us all to experience. There are a handful of elegant structures for all time, such as the covered bridge, the series of willow arches on the high bank, the tree houses and the planted sculpture of our willow giant. Looking towards these from the pathways gives a trompe-l'oeil effect that suggests space way beyond the garden's actual area. The paths tempt the children around the landscape characteristics of the site. It is expected that they can feel the way the spaces change as they move through them.

Some paths have developed naturally when a surface is worn by persistent use. At this point it is often best to make an extension to the path system to include the informal route. Our observations suggest that dead-end ways are unsatisfactory because they spin the walker back to a return journey too quickly and cause confusion. If a new path needs laying, it needs to be a pleasing alternative separated by planting from the original track and then rejoining it. The only path with no exit crosses a pond. It was always intended that this would eventually be completed with an outlet to the top pathway, but the costs have proved prohibitive.

The sports pitch was on land beyond the school building and because there were no distinctive features along the route to it a pathway was simply defined by use. Within the first few weeks the grass had ceased to exist and heavy wear had reduced the surface to clay and mud. There is a good deal of pragmatic learning in situations such as these. Over the years we have created an all weather pathway to the field simply by laying down tons of bark chipping.

Walking is an enjoyable way to build up fitness and knowledge. Designing pathways that go somewhere and refresh the spirit give us a major educational tool for all levels of age and ability.

Meeting places

As part of the plan for children and adults, group locations are provided by three story circles on the main pathways. These ring-shaped constructions have been worked out so that through use of each sitting area the children get contrasting information about their environment. One retreat has bench seating under the deep shade of a group of wych elms: another is on a high bank with views across the playing field and the third is at the bottom of a slope with a woodland aspect. The last two circles have seats made of half-buried logs and all three have seating for groups of 30 children. These spaces play a key role in providing comfortable areas to examine finds made in the gardens, or to share food and reverie, to listen to stories, music and poetry or to make a composite weaving or piece of ephemeral art.

For an amphitheatre, we shaped the ground to make a concert shell, partly to connect imaginatively to the past when dance, drama, music and pageant was re-enacted outdoors and partly to encourage the children to demonstrate talent to each other or to take part in parades, improvizations and exhibitions. There are three entrances/exits to the amphitheatre and these fit into the scheme of pathways that give form to the whole site.

We see paths as lines that help elements of the grounds to fit together rather like jigsaw pieces. The vitality of the plan depends on the site being able to relay many stories about events, planting choices, history, geography and how the outdoor classroom is used. The stories are about changes over time, about scenes from the four seasons of the year and there are many personal anecdotes embedded in the connections that the children have to their outdoor spaces.

A tour of our site would include front and back gardens, visits to the ponds, rests on the seats of the story circles, the enjoyment of our collection of rocks and looking at the mossy banks. The large grass clearing of the playing field is accentuated by the wooded perimeter walks and on the northern edge we have our Bluebell Wood to enjoy. The fruit trees are scattered around the site, wildflowers are established in zoned areas and the hedge is a highway for small mammals. The paths criss-cross all these areas and join them and the children's gardens and suggest exploration and encouragement to spot and identify the wildlife.

Litter

Children work hard in keeping the grounds tidy. With such a lot of traffic on the main road and such continual usage of the site (a population of more than 500 children, a Breakfast Club, a Nursery Lunch Club and an After-School and Holiday Care club) there are inevitable litter problems. We do not have 'litter monitors'; instead we prefer to remind the whole community about personal responsibilities for clearing litter. On an ad hoc basis children volunteer to help with litter picking and in school we keep referring to litter as an individual and group responsibility.

Children and teachers replant trees to replace dead ones and help with gathering autumn leaves from the playgrounds and hard pathways. The leaves attract and support wildlife but they are something of a hazard in the playground when they start to rot. This is a downside of having a playground with a woodland edge. Fallen fruits are also messy and they attract wasps. Low branches can present a problem and the most usual way that we deal with them is to cut them off at the point at which they originate. A woodland edge has a pattern of life with a rich wildlife community. There are problems and responsibilities in supporting this scheme that first and foremost has to benefit the children. We believe that it is critical that the children understand that we share our habitats with masses of plants and a huge range of living things.

Managing the gardens

Parents, governors and staff join forces once a term to do work in the school grounds. We set dates early and split the work into different focus areas so that everyone can opt into jobs on arrival. In late winter we are employed digging and putting manure on the seedbeds, spreading bark chippings to resurface pathways, replacing wooden shingles on the tree houses, cutting back the willow and clearing coarse growth ready for the primroses and violets to flower. We clean ponds of reed mace and scum, empty the compost bins and spread compost. Some volunteers prepare a small patch for a wildlife summer meadow and put boards around it so that it does not get trampled.

New seasons bring other sorts of work but this system has proved beneficial for many reasons, not least that it brings our community together out of school hours. We get to know each other in these flexible working arrangements; we share knowledge and anecdotes, the children are also welcome and the jobs get done. The working Saturday starts at 9.00 a.m. and ends at 2.00 p.m., although some stalwarts soldier on until late in the afternoon. Volunteers drop in for as long or short a time as they can manage.

Some companies are involved in community projects by giving labour from their own workforce rather than money. One company, 3M, has given us a regular workforce twice a year: usually seven to ten volunteers, one of whom is a parent and governor. Seven workers for a whole day get the burning problems dealt with and this means that we can develop our ecological work. We always photograph the volunteers at work, and send a report for their company news bulletins.

A less regular boost comes from visiting students from Reading University studying Landscape Management or Horticulture. In exchange for a tour of the grounds and a school lunch they work for two or three hours for us. Soldiers from nearby Arborfield Garrison often help us out with people-power to work in the gardens and to help us in different projects and these are welcome volunteers. Children with parents in the armed forces get the chance to see their grown-ups working in a school context as well as the Garrison one.

Noting wear in the landscape is a way of receiving feedback. Balancing the conservation aims, the need of the children to play and explore, the involvement of the community in the project and the search for new and evolving aspects to the work, keeps us all thinking about our outdoor landscape. Wear and tear drives us to respond in a number of ways. One way is to increase the time spent teaching in the outdoor setting so that the children value the qualities of their landscape much more. Another is to broaden the approaches by teaching all subjects of the curriculum out of doors. In this way, the activities themselves support the environment by demonstrating it as a valuable resource.

4 The outdoor classroom – the hard landscape

Playground development

Originally our playground was a rectangle of asphalt that was completely open. Between the school buildings and the playground lay a wide unpromising strip of clay that was designated 'garden' on the architect's plan. Two paths connected the building to the playground at opposite ends and these paths were in line with the side entrances to two main doors. A door to the hall and a classroom door opened onto concrete steps and to serve these exits there was a narrow path running beside the building. The children were supposed to follow this path around the uncultivated area so that they would eventually arrive in the playground. Quite naturally they took the fast track option and cut straight across the clay. Playtimes were full of calls to the children to come off the muddy area and get back onto the playground. It was a landscape of anomalies that bleakly stretched over the strip of clay, across the playground and over the field to a chain link fence at the boundary.

Initially plans for the open area had a planting scheme featuring rose bushes and imported topsoil that could be sloped to overcome a change in surface levels. Work on the school building was complicated because the site was not level and grading it had upset the soil profiles. The design had been transferred from another school and applied to our school, but the cost cutting, the 'simplification' of the original plan and the contrast between the two sites meant that the building went over budget anyway and was left with a rather basic finish. Many finalizing touches were absent and the topsoil around the building had been compromised during the partial levelling of the ground.

The appearance of the site was an incentive to create a scheme where teaching by doing would shine through. Transforming the environment would eventually mean that when we stepped onto school property we would feel braced by its potential. If the place felt bursting with good play experiences, was an affirmation of all kinds of life with fruit, vegetables, flowers, animals, woodland, ponds and intriguing contrasts of light and shade, rounded and angular shapes, it would speak of the endless and changing nature of education. The doing would be about making improvements, mixing mortar, laying bricks or sometimes just watching construction. Bright colours would mark maths games and alphabet trails on the asphalt surface while children's drawings and practice writing in chalk on the concrete pavers would give a message about certain freedoms in mark making. All change would involve the children and no work would be undertaken in their absence. The environmental project would have a beginning but no ending. In that way the whole grounds could become an outdoor classroom without limits to children's and adults' involvement in the future. Rethinking the school inside and outside would enter our planning year in and year out. Our pursuit of our ideals would prevent us from growing dull and practice in the creative processes would bind us together as a team.

Paved area

The expanse between the building and the asphalt playground had first claim on our long list of changes to be made. For planning purposes, it was divided into three parts: a play area with access to the doorways, a wild section with trees that would help take up surface water and be a backdrop for the playground, and a border area of shrubs. The play/access area was paved as a contrast to the asphalt. We opted for pavers because they can become a rather exciting set of 'pages' for writing and drawing with chalks. Their surface is lightly textured, catching the chalk as it moves but making colour-blending and smudging with fingers quite easy. This very physical writing and drawing is ephemeral, social and space-changing and disappears after rain.

Mini-beast sanctuary

Our belief in the influence of the 'hidden curriculum' led us to work out a plan whereby the children would play and work among plants. In time, plants would attract wildlife so that children going outside would be in rewarding proximity to the natural world. Work on a child-friendly, eco-rich environment started in the area called the 'mini-beast sanctuary' and the thinking behind it was extended to the whole school site. Essentially it was about combining the needs of the children with a life-support system for plants and wildlife.

A broad, low brick wall defines the edges of the mini-beast sanctuary and this wall gives wide ledges for seating or working. Children climb and walk on the wall. Running is impossible because the wall is crenellated and the plants in the wild area grow over and beyond the perimeter wall. The proximity of the wild areas to the children at work and at play was planned so that we emphasized a spiritual, physical and emotional connection to plants, animals and birds. Life in the gardens would be right beside us, protected by the wall that sheltered a tiny imitation of natural woodland. Apple, silver birch and holly would constitute a canopy and other plants would develop as an understory.

We believe that our school needed to provide natural resources to increase the possibilities for observation and to collect personal memories and private anecdotes. We do not walk through any wild area that we treat as a sanctuary for such things as spiders, beetles, snails and birds. It took 2 or 3 years to get native plants established in this small woodland garden that was planned and planted as a living green solid. The dense planting breaks up this end of the playground and is one of several ways in which children can escape from each other by going around the green screen. The mass-planting acts as a contrast to the openness of the playground. The appearance we aimed for of a tangled secret garden among the trees finally came into being with the addition of ivy that colonized vertical and horizontal surfaces. Contrasts are a way of enlarging the feelings we all have about the space we inhabit and noticeable differences contribute to our aesthetic awareness. This is a core idea that permeates action and change right through our teaching inside the school and outside.

Playground features

Part of the fun of playing in the playground is that it is not a straightforward, geometric and open place. If a glance from any spot in a play space can give a child or an adult an assessment of the play potential or an instant image of playground quality, it is not consistent with human needs. We wanted to involve the children in the design of their playground and so we asked them for their ideas. Many said that they would like a castle. George Prior, our then caretaker, laughed when he heard this but he later thought that he could build something for us that had the feel of a castle. News that a large construction company was prepared to donate a lorry load of bricks, sand and cement meant that we could start work on a major project. By making the entry to the structure at the edge of the asphalt we could push back the boundary of the playground.

Children worked with George and the teachers to plan a modest fort-type building by using the donated bricks. During the practical planning with the bricks on the playground, the shape turned into a hexagon. The hexagon shape was adopted and block walls were set on a deep foundation that raised it above playground level. Two steps were needed to reach the new height and the entrance was deliberately narrow so that it would restrict circulation. The block-work walls functioned as seating and as a low rampart for walking around. The interior could accommodate a group of 20 or more children and their adult using the walls as seats. The project took several months to complete.

By revising ideas as they slowly develop, modifications can be incorporated into the design and the children have a chance to compare their hypotheses of the work with the emerging shape. The children 'helped' George by putting on mortar, taking readings from plumb lines and spirit levels and by applying their special type of energy and interest to the project. A class group was always present helping George as the hexagon took shape.

Earth banks and off-ground pathways

We raised an earth bank around the walls of the hexagon so that we could plant trees there. In time the planting would turn the hexagon into a shelter from the sun and add a feeling of mystery to its setting. It was built facing south-west and set on deep foundations that our caretaker declared would make the whole thing more permanent than the school itself and that would certainly withstand any root pressure. The result of the planting was to give the hexagon castle a calm, green feel that intensified with each year's growth.

Another idea that came from the children was off-ground pathways. We thought we could make these available by building walls around the playground boundary on which children could practice their balancing skills. Key to the success of this would be long lengths of wall that the children could walk along without needing to step down and the width of the wall that was bound to be used as informal seating. This wall also broke through the old boundary and re-defined it with shallow extensions that changed the form of the play space.

Along the boundary line there is a small covered shelter, the steps to two tree houses and another brick and block design adding to the variety of meeting places and stops on a playground journey. The brick and block model can be anything a child needs for his or her play. The width of the wall is 34 cm and the children often lie down on the top. There are two levels: one at 42 cm and 45 cm and a higher level at 54 cm. The different heights add variety to the wall, is non-uniform and much more natural. An additional benefit is that it can be acted upon to adapt to life. A Whitebeam tree and a Scots Pine are backdrops to this play space and a variety of native species has been planted around the playground edges (some partly hidden playground features among the trees). This woodland belt is also an introduction to a pathway that edges most of the playground. One half of this perimeter path is always open for play and it leads back into the playground: the other half is not used for free play because the exit for it is beside the gate that is a main thoroughfare. At this point vehicles pass the gate on the way to an additional parking area. The adults regularly walk this path with the children but the children are always accompanied.

The off-ground brick pathway in the playground is not continuous but it is a limited expression of the children's need for height and variety of levels is part of the scheme. The playground's original military square was slowly being offset by these new features and changes were evolving naturally and slowly. Observation of the children using the playground led us towards new thinking as much as what the children said about the area. Integral to the designs was our view that the children should have challenging and socializing opportunities and that we should be closing the gap between the hard and soft landscape. The playground walls were used to front banks of earth made from imported soil. Some of it arrived from the Local Authority as leaf sweepings gathered from rural areas in the vicinity and a great deal of it came from contractors working on road-widening schemes: some soil was donated by parents. When the broad expanses of earth had settled we anchored it by planting trees in it. The children were the planters and we promised them that they were going to see a school in a woodland setting grown from their efforts. The playground 30 years on now feels very different and through the year it feels protected from wind and weather. It is a natural backdrop that harbours birds and invertebrates: it provides blossom, fruit, catkins, leaves and pine cones to the children and gives them resources that they appreciate around their school.

Tunnel

At one point in the wall there is a tunnel. This is a wide-diameter concrete pipe slightly set back from the playground edge. At the front there is brick step that is part of the wall and by means of this step the children have to check their speed before diving into the tunnel. The tunnel is sloped to keep it dry and it has a friendly feel. This is an underground route to the back pathway that merges with an A-frame wooden den to give a longer, darker route. Viewed from either end the tunnel disappears into the ground. Once it had been set in position it was covered with masses of soil and turf to give it the appearance of a subterranean passageway.

We are exponents of contrasts and the tunnel is a darker area between areas of sun and long views. It was built to admit an adult so that the teachers could also experience the effects. The A-frame den has an off-ground wooden floor raised to meet the level of the concrete pipe and with an interior that is a total contrast to the concrete tunnel. We absorb views from above, but in this enclosed part of the route from the playground is the worm's eye view and another concept for the children to explore.

Ryan's bridge

We built a covered bridge as a focal point at the end of the playground area and the beginning of the playing field. The bridge was designed and built by Clive Winson, a friend of the school and an occasional worker for us: it is a beautiful miniature version of the old pioneer covered bridges of New England. The short, well-proportioned bridge carries a path across a ditch and is one of the main routes out of the playground. The pathway opens out onto a short avenue with Wych Elms on one side and a stand of hazel on the other. The covered bridge gives this space an aesthetic value and from both ends it makes a frame through which the next part of the grounds may be viewed. We named the structure 'Ryan's Bridge' to commemorate one of our staff group, Suzan Ryan, who died in 2000.

Stairs

A flight of stairs leads down from the playground to the bridge. These stairs are identical in style to those that provide access to the tree houses. Each step has a broad tread with a shallow depth and the whole stairway provides lots of space to run up and down its length. This is an area of much activity that shows us just how eager children are for changes of height in their play area. Although the function of the stairs is to link the playground to further pathways and to Ryan's Bridge, they have added value. Their position, facing the west but shaded by trees means that they make a comfortable gathering place for a story, or a briefing meeting for teachers and children, or an ideal place to hold a drumming workshop.

Large logs

A group of tree trunks on one side of the playground invites climbing and imaginative play. Initially the children asked for trees in the grounds: they associated them with being able to climb, swing and hide. To meet their immediate need we brought huge tree trunks into the play space, each massive length with its own distinctive character. The logs arrived on two vehicles, one with a crane and we were able to position them so that we got a big structure where the children could circulate around, through and across the logs. As an early development this was ideal: it met specific needs to climb and hide and balance as well as giving long stretches of different level seating at one edge of the playground. Logs have to be renewed from time to time as they decay but we would never want to be without these basic materials. Our present tree trunks are sixth in the series: not as extensive as the first set to arrive but the children's needs are now being met in a variety of other ways. Change and renewal is a theme that should impact on the children's landscape as well as on other aspects of their lives.

Boat

A boat of some kind has been a feature of the playground for many years. The first one was a large clinker built rowing boat and all the boats used have been the genuine article. A boat, by definition, must be able to float and any company manufacturing boats for children's play schemes in parks and motorway service stations is unlikely to make them so that they square with this notion. Old vessels stripped of oarlocks and other metal parts contribute to the romantic aura of a playground and they have proved their worth in the past. We have used a variety of fibreglass dinghies and wooden boats in our playground but the best boats are the cavernous punts that stand securely on their base and give a group of 10–15 children a scenario for an adventure or just a place to have fun. A boat loved and played to death has its two stories: one from its first life on the water and the second from its use as a set piece in children's play.

Seating

Our walls and tree trunks make lots of easily available seating but sometimes the children need a den to share secrets or negotiate with one or two friends in a more private space, or they may wish to sit alone and dream at times. This calls for cherishing or recovery spots in the playground and several possible solutions exist. One is a formal high-backed wooden seat under a classroom window and another is a small brick-built shelter. This is closed on three sides but the playground side is open. There is wooden seating for eight or ten children under a low-pitched roof and access is from a single step to the interior. Children call this 'the shelter' or 'the bus stop' and its cosy feel attracts those in need of some quieter moments.

A third structure designed for privacy is the A-frame den connected to the tunnel, which has already been described. It is part of a route from the playground to a back pathway but it is wider than the tunnel and the children often sit against the sides to see who will crawl through next.

Playground markings

We take for granted that quality play is essential and the play for every child's outdoor environment should be complex, open to many uses, predominantly natural and sensually stimulating and fun. We also look to the playground for pattern and markings to strengthen children's skills base. Reasoning skills, deductive thinking, alphabet and number practice, singing and rhythm work and mathematics can be enhanced if we paint outlines and patterns on the playground in order to extend and support the curriculum.

Playing strategy games such as chess or Nine Men's Morris can encourage reasoning skills. Moving along alphabet lines improves familiarity about alphabet order, and activities on a one hundred square are an integral part of mathematics. A space made up of concentric circles is ideal for singing games, dancing and rhythm work and these circles are also used as a zone for gathering together. Circles painted on the tarmac are adaptable spaces where children can be near one another for toe-tapping or spread out on another colour to skip or run around the circle.

Our music specialist, Gill, regularly uses the concentric circles to get children moving in opposite directions as they sing in parts. She also presents the children with one metre length hazel or willow sticks (harvested from our grounds) and they beat on the ground as they walk around. She has invented a variety of passing games and rhythm games using the big sticks and these are always popular with the children. The creative and thoughtful use of the circles and other patterns helps adventurous teaching and defines working space for the children. Many of the designs are board games from across the world (Pong Hau Ki, a Schlegel Diagram, Achi, Muterere). We use non-slip coloured paint for the designs, that is expensive but that should last for 5 or 6 years before being repainted.

Stepping stones

We have very few commercially produced items in the playground. They include three or four concrete stepping stones with some much better school produced ones, and a concrete hump back bridge. Dependence on the ideas of others will not fit the unique nature of every location. Buying ready made things is like making a blanket declaration that the playground is a recreational space when it needs to be so much more than this.

Tree houses and look-out

Our tree houses have been built to last using high-grade second-hand timber or timber from managed forestry. They are all places where adults and children learn together and we use them for music, story telling, having a snack together, drawing, writing, reading or RE. We talk through our discoveries and projects in them, set up displays there, prepare work by making them temporary collecting points for such things as chalks, shells, clipboards, lenses or cameras. Our idea was to contrive outdoor classrooms to diversify the routines and help children (and adults) to keep moving around the site. The use of shelters such as the tree houses keeps us in touch with the outdoors; they mean leaving the classrooms to use them, breathing the fresh air, walking and collecting incidental data about the weather, the season and each other.

Two of the shelters have been planned to that children have a place where they can climb and play. A flight of stairs up to a landing is an access for the two tree houses in the playground. In reality, they are not 'tree houses' as such (although one does have a tree growing right up through it) because both structures are supported on wooden stilts. The approach steps provide experiences of height that is a very necessary play experience. Risk of a long fall is reduced by the width of each stair; the climb to the landing is very gradual. There is a seat on the landing and right and left of this are doors to access both structures set between the tree branches. The teaching areas are not open during playtimes unless an adult is setting up in them as a place to practice skills or as a teaching base. Children constantly run up and down the steps using them as a climbing challenge during free play or to sit on the bench at the top with friends to survey the playground scene below. These two classrooms are named Aspen Lodge (with the Aspen tree growing up through it) and Pine Lodge (Pine being the tree supporting this lodge). Each varies in area and the smaller Aspen Lodge is wired for lighting and heating (as well as cooking when needed).

Our third outdoor classroom, known as the Lookout is also set on stilts to give it elevation and it is slightly bigger than the other two. This timber building is the perfect den for small group craft experiences where clay modelling, weaving and the like can be experienced without the necessity of having to do a complete clear up before the work is finished. Some materials need a 2- or 3-day exploration and while work is in progress one solution is to lock the door on it without needing to be precious about the mess.

All three wooden rooms are designed to extend the circulation between classrooms and the outdoors and they function in a variety of ways. They are a means for us to put our own stamp on the school where one of our stated objectives is to have an evolving number of outside spaces to meet both the children's and the adults' needs. This developmental process is somewhat instinctive and it is a vision that has to fit in with the changing nature of the whole landscape. Solutions to our various needs are not so much about erecting timber lodges or building shelters for the playground, but more about revising and transforming the connections between children's outside play and learning and teaching out of doors.

The height of the three structures provides good views of the outdoors from the windows. Aspen Lodge and Pine Lodge overlook the playground and from the window height it is like looking into an animated Lowry painting when the children are at play. At other times the views are of the coming and going of people and of teachers and children undertaking various activities in the playground. The Look-out window is designed for a long view of an adjacent field behind which there is a sewerage treatment plant and a long view towards woodland. This is not a zone that is ever likely to become a housing estate, and birds, sheep and horses spice up the views.

There is no ceiling in two of the tree houses. We opted for open beams that can be used for wall hangings or for drying tie-dye work or to demonstrate hoists and pulleys. This enlarges the potential of these spaces as well as showing the internal form of the buildings. We might have made these buildings bigger but we were anxious about the footprint on the land. We were also mindful about the image of a 'shed' that they might present. We wanted these structures to be eco-friendly and pleasurable to a child's eye and resonate with rest and climbing associations. Although not as high as we would really like them to be, they do nevertheless feel suspended in the trees or above the bank and all are a contrast to a standard indoor classroom.

Geology trail

A link to the most ancient history of the earth is provided by a geology trail. This was started in 1995 when two limestone rocks from the Mendip Hills in Somerset and three large granite blocks from Cornwall were installed in the school grounds. We sited the large limestone rocks in our Nursery garden so that the youngest children could enjoy these 'mini-mountains', exploring their properties and characteristics. The rocks are set with crystals of different types and are both full of colour. The children often scrub them with soap and water in order that the colours and different forms show up. When the stones are wet, some areas sparkle and catch the light and the range of colours in the rocks is better defined.

The Cornish granite blocks were installed as a set of steps on the edge of a pathway and leading onto the playing field. They are used for play, as seating and as a facility for exhibitions so that when the children are involved as artists in the environment, the blocks may be used for exhibition spaces. There is a tunnel effect underneath the top stone, and the children particularly enjoy wriggling through this to the other side.

All grounds need landmarks and large rocks in their spaces define and identify niches in our gardens. The rocks represent some major geological characteristics of mainland Britain and stimulate interest in Museum Education. It has taken us a long time to resource rocks for our geology trail because it involves visits in person to the quarries with plan drawings, photographs and descriptions of our work. The rocks are offered to the children as social places, places for games, ideas and imaginative play and they are there to strengthen the ways in which the outside comes alive for children.

Culture and history are expressed through the use of local stone and this led us to want some of the rocks to be arranged in ways that would convey a sense of pre-history and legend to the children. A donation of Yorkshire Limestone was delivered and set in a ring where two of the columns would carry a cross-beam similar to those seen at Stonehenge. The children call this particular landmark 'Coombeshenge'.

Columns that were as tall as a maypole lost much of their height when one third of their mass was buried in each post hole but this was essential for stability. As a finished stone ring it seems like a quotation from the past rather than a composition of 1998. It has a cohesion that ties it to the landscape and to the series of other stones in their distinctive spaces. The limestone glitters with crystals and the children love to go on the hunt for small patches of iron pyrites (fool's gold) that can be found on two of the rocks in the arrangement.

The development of our specialized geology trail included positioning a dolmen (burial chamber) along a woodland pathway. Gritstone from Derbyshire was donated by a quarry where there was a nearby dolmen. The quarrymen kindly searched out similar shaped stones for us from their excavations in order that we would be able to set up a facsimile of the genuine thing. A very large slab of rock sits on the shoulders of four boulders that are shaped to bear the weight without any wobble. The children go under this low rock ceiling and experience the sound quality, the gloom and the unique atmosphere there. In the children's mythology, there is a body buried underneath the dolmen (we are happy to say that this is merely myth!). This set of rocks gives us an architectural context that is designed to reflect a much earlier world in which our ancestors demonstrated considerable engineering ability.

Rocks from a quarry in the Isle of Purbeck in Dorset were put together as a great stone seat at the top of an earth bank. The children call this 'King Arthur's Seat'. A staircase framed by railway sleepers and filled with pebbles and bark chippings leads up the bank to the seat at the top where there is space for seven or eight children to sit. This assembly of rocks gives a long view across the playing field and the installation underlines the power of legend and folklore. At the opening ceremony for the structure, we asked one of our parents, a keen equestrian, to dress himself and his horse in clothing and apparel suited to the time of the mythological King Arthur. The children made pennants and tabards, and we enjoyed a day of pageant together.

One of our aims is to keep children in touch with history and folklore through their outdoor environment. The content of the environment should provide immediate access to information where the imagination has not been bypassed. This can mean rocks and fossils at our fingertips where we have a physical link with evolution, caves for a storyline to the fugitives or the primitive people who once may have sheltered there, or tumuli to evoke feelings about buried heroes or tribal sites. Any of these things can be a focus for the individual's contribution to folklore. The children are always circulating theory and gathering leads for their own stories.

In one area of the perimeter pathway great slabs of red sandstone from the Scottish borders are constructed as a cave. This installation has several purposes. It carries the pathway across its megalithic capstone and changes the character of the existing walk by presenting this alternative. The original path takes a line around the cave structure that does not involve any climbing, but most children prefer the upward scramble. The cave is a monument to King Robert the Bruce who is said to have been inspired by a spider. It has been inscribed with the words, 'If at first you don't succeed, try, try, try again.' Initially we had hoped that our cave would resemble the one in Scotland where the King is reputed to have sheltered. Such a structure was technically very demanding to build and we had rather less material than we needed. After an experimental build was compromised, we redesigned the installation so that the greatest part of the weight was moved downward and children would be able to walk over the most spectacular stone in the group. Practice in doing and constant testing are part of innovation and it is through these means that we all stay true learners.

Teachers and parents have always given strong support to the geology project. One didactic element in it has often been the carving of scripts to define a guide for living. A parent started us on these maxims by paying for one of the first. 'We Care For Each Other' was inscribed on slate slabs positioned between two pathways as part of a screening system. A dove of peace, a Celtic knot around the slabs and a beautifully inscribed alphabet for touching, completed the design that the parent had commissioned. These slabs had been the bedrocks for a snooker table and they were recycled into our environment when the table was broken up. The slate originated in central Wales and by setting each of the six sections into the ground at right angles to each other, they are mutually supported.

Basic to our appreciation of stones is to see them as part of everyday equipment in building, tool-making, road construction, recreational use and as essential commodities. Four millstones from a working mill in Wiltshire represent a traditional system to extract flour and make grain fit for consumption. The Welsh rocks from Bangor are straight from the mountain and they make a useful contrast to the dressed slate slabs from the snooker table. The same seam from which these rocks were extracted extends under the North Atlantic all the way to Canada where it is also quarried. The fine Bangor rocks stand alongside the back drive to the sports field and they were installed in height order starting with the smallest. The smaller ones are roundish and sit on the grass without being anchored but the bigger ones are fitted into the ground so that they are stable.

Three groups of Sarsen stones that have been carried enormous distances by the moving ice during the glacial periods are features at different spots in the gardens. Their texture has been scoured over time to smooth curves and dimples and they are natural pieces of art.

There are 16 sets of rock making notable features all around the school landscape. The rocks improve the relationship between the school building and the school garden and the whole landscape gets a large part of its attraction from these 16 focal points. The largest single structure is the set of rocks from Aberdeen in Scotland. The pink granite structure is set as a rough hewn dolmen with all the drilling scars on show. As a place of shade and shelter it 'feels' like part of the mountainside where it originated and it has mass, height and grandeur. A contrast to this primitive art is a red sandstone block from Penrith in Cumbria that has been carved into a gigantic head by Ewan McEwan, a sculptor in residence. The detail came from the skin deep lines on the children's hands and from its completion, this figurehead has been a school celebrity. It is flanked by two sentinel stones from the same quarry.

The spaces in the grounds where the rocks are located provide for the underlying impulses of children to play, to hide, to climb and to socialize. These activities are not separated for reasons of formal teaching or to acknowledge the artistic or aesthetic value of the rocks. Different activities overlap so that children eat their snacks on the rocks, practise climbing and balancing, view the rocks symbolically, examine texture and silhouette or use them as a powerful stimulus for poetry, music or story.

A line of Cotswold stepping stones aligned to the pathway offers children the prospect of walking into or out of school at the same height as their grown-ups. The stepping stones are on a raised bank that has paper bark birches growing out of it that combine with the rocks to make better ecological and safety sense. The entire geology trail is about improving the quality of the children's surroundings and using the outdoors to tune the school community to a sense of design and a feel for ecology. As such, it is limited by capacity, cost and maintenance but it is better than what it replaced: nothing for the children.

A set of Farringdon Sponge rocks contain the fossilized remains of billions of sponges and early sea creatures that multiplied in the salt water lagoon around Farringdon. Rocks such as these can only be found in two places in Europe: in Oxfordshire and Greece. Children can get an insight into the changes that have shaped our earth from their direct contact with these rocks.

Not all of our rocks are huge. River pebbles from Stirling in Scotland, a pair of Hornton Blue stones, a red rock from the Great Rift Valley and a rock from a road built by convicts in New South Wales, Australia add to our growing collection.

Labyrinths

We have a tradition of laying out large labyrinths using stones or paint. There is always a labyrinth on site providing a quiet space. The children walk these pathways in silence with their teachers and we all find our own moment of calm as we walk together; growth and change require reflective periods. Out on the open labyrinth a silent walk seems like a straightforward exercise. In reality it is about self-control in a limited amount of space where learners move together to reflect in silence. There are three aspects to this exercise all of which interact when children work and play together.

One aspect is about the power of contrast. Moving through a labyrinth provides a very different experience from other activities. Class groups of children and whole school groups walk in silence through a defined route that leads everyone to a centre and out again. Nothing is required of the children and the adults except a respect for the privacy of every walker. In order to recognize this private time we do not talk, touch each other or overtake once we are inside the labyrinth doing the steady walk. The urgency of daily routine is put to one side for this act of reflection that might result in solutions to problems or the chance to put a difficulty into context: it might just be a few moments to stop thinking and just 'be'.

A second consideration is to give a reflective view of the school community to itself. When following the direction of a labyrinth the walkers are turned in many ways as the design unwinds. From every viewpoint the walkers see each other going in different directions to arrive at the centre or at the end. Every person is sharing the space along the way and experiencing and enjoying the silence. It is a concrete example of movement and change, of travelling together and individually and of being in a culture that values sympathy, empathy and a respect for others. Supportive communities do not just happen, they grow from foundations gained from collective situations such as this one.

A third aspect that is fundamental to group and individual wellbeing is our connection to nature. During the labyrinth exercises we walk the ground in a concentrated way. We notice a daisy or a worm cast, smell the bruising on grass paths, feel the breeze, watch the clouds, hear a bird call or see it swoop and dive – it is time spent in the fresh air and in contact with the living world. We also note traffic noise from the distant motorway, aeroplane noise, a dog barking and other happenings but in this regard the walk is similar to a walk in a park. A benefit of silent walking is a heightened appreciation of those around us and of things natural. We hold life and death in common with other living beings, we are born, we live and we die. Meditative silent walks centre the individual and are symbolic of life's journey. They are one way of expressing our journey from birth to death and our connections to all forms of life.

September 2008 marked the beginning of our future as a primary school and we needed a new logo. Following ideas given by the children, Sue Coffey one of our governors and a professional Graphic Designer together with her husband Andrew Evans offered a labyrinth design inspired by the ideas of some of the children. They used the

Chartres Cathedral labyrinth design to encapsulate the idea of the merging of the Infant/Nursery and Junior Schools and children, staff and other adults were invited to walk into the school logo on the first day of the academic year. This was marked on the field and was walked through many times during its 4-week life. On the formal Opening Day of the new school, more than 600 children and adults were on the labyrinth together in silence and listening only to cello music being played in the centre of the labyrinth by a musician friend of the school, Gabriella Kapfer.

The tradition of returning to school in September to a large labyrinth on the grass is now 10 years old. We have used many patterns and different methods of marking. The simplest marking on grass can be made using a line marker of the type used to define running tracks. It is necessary to run over the line twice to get a 12–15-cm width to mark walking routes and to apply the paint generously. Wide lines can be seen more easily and the whole pattern tends to last longer. Lane width is also crucial especially when the route doubles back on itself and involves walkers passing each other in opposite directions.

Teachers hoping to experiment with labyrinths may like to try depriving the paths of light by laying old carpet or thick black plastic over the turf. In this way, the grass turns yellow and makes an eye-catching contrast to the surrounding green turf. If this method is used the labyrinth should be of the simple sort or only a quarter of a more complex design. The uncovered part must be approximately 45 cm wide so that the green grass stripes are in striking contrast to the light-starved path.

Other variations include scorching the grass with a horticultural appliance, laying stones or bricks, and using skewers and tape or string. A lot depends on the size of the labyrinth required and on the resources available. Some excellent labyrinths have been hand painted by parents (brushes must be the same width) using surplus emulsion paint from home. Applications of multi colours are strangely suitable and cause the labyrinth to appear undulating: an effect that surprised us. It is always good not to allow the limitations of conventional solutions to stand in the way too much. Success here depends on scale and careful measurement; smaller labyrinths can be set in pairs side by side so that walkers may move across when they complete the walk and join the next labyrinth. Virtually all pairs that we have painted used contrasting designs. For instance, we prefer to put angular (masculine) beside circular (feminine) patterns and use blue/purple colours for one and red/yellow tones for the other.

We needed a labyrinth in our environment that had a longer life than the 3–4-week life of the painted ones. This became possible when a set of paving slabs at the school was replaced. We asked the workmen to break up the old slabs for us and we used the fractured pavers as building material for our labyrinth.

Our plan was to lay this labyrinth with the children's participation and to change the design every 2 years so that the children removed the stones and reset them in a different pattern each time. Our thinking was that every time the stones were removed the convention would change to make a balance between known and unknown using the same materials. Experience showed a major flaw here. The hundreds of feet using the first pathways wore a pattern that could not be eradicated by relaying the stones. The grass was totally eroded by use and the surface worn to a deep groove. We saw our work in a new light and realized that we must deal with the erosion problem. The children removed the stones as planned and a parent with a machine redistributed tonnes of bark chippings to make a floor for the next design. The new surface improved walking conditions and it is topped up every time the labyrinth is changed. This is a

cheap, sustainable and good-looking solution to the high impact erosion problem. We usually paint the stone pattern with emulsion paint in order that the stones stand out from the bark chipping floor and make the design more easily visible.

The labyrinths are planned on paper and copies are given to all the children. We see the papers as social documents to be discussed and taken home. They are predictors of the walking experience and the labyrinth routes can be traced by finger or crayon. These plan drawings relate to maps. They indicate movement and describe the route of the traveller through the pattern. A collection of these plans tells the story of the designs we have used in previous years. Photographs also record the experiences for us and one of our governors, Robert Howe, uses his video camera to make reference material for us. Key to all of this is the social, emotional, spiritual, mathematical, geographical and aesthetical experiences that help our children and their adults at school to gain insights into the world around them.

5 Spiritual growth and development

Introduction

A strand of ceremonies through the year increases our awareness of each other and helps us to build ideas of what 'spiritual' means. In these ceremonies we are connected to each other through sharing food and focusing our attention as a group.

Carl Jung suggests that we must move away from second-hand ideas handed down to us, to religion as a first-hand experience that transforms us. In our work we use the impact of carefully constructed experiences to deepen the children's understanding of our sense of social responsibility and self-awareness.

Stories that might inspire and guide belief need to be interpreted by the individual. Our function as teachers in guiding children's spiritual development is not to impose beliefs on them but rather to help them discover meaning for themselves. In our use of stories from the Christian faith and other faiths, the stories are frequently viewed through a social experience. For instance, Jesus washing the feet of his disciples will be portrayed through the washing of every child's feet. Teachers will describe the act and the context and culture in which it took place while washing the children's feet. The Brahmin parable of the group who went to heaven but who were not able to feed themselves is re-enacted to its resolution out of doors and as part of the Key Stage 1 and Key Stage 2 assemblies. The food was eaten because people fed one another. Children skin satsumas, wash grapes, break bread and peel bananas then put the food into the mouths of others and are themselves fed by others in turn.

Joshua's spies going into the promised land are older children in role searching for proof that the ground is fruitful. They return with grapes, olives, dates, apples, grains and fresh water. When they rejoin their tribes with life-supporting evidence, it is shared and eaten in an inclusive way. Life in the promised land is suggested as an exercise in trust through this activity. The state of the natural world is fundamental to survival and the group left behind want evidence about the intended homeland.

Each individual is different from every other individual and his or her value in the community is centred on the unique contribution of each member. In a balanced and carefully proportioned way, the person and the community are meant to enhance and complement each other. We try to focus on self in the natural world and on community in leading children through stories, enactments and experiences.

Sometimes, the feeling of joy comes from solitary moments when there is no action other than observing nature around us. This can happen in an RE lesson when we walk with the children and one by one at a signal they detach themselves from the group to sit alone under the trees, besides the ponds, on the rocks, the steps, the grass, next to a path or on the edge of a bank. The children carry a carpet square for this experience so they are not needled by dead holly leaves and such things as fallen pine cones or thistle heads. After four or five minutes in this silent state the children are gathered up by the teacher in the order in which they left the group and silence is always maintained. These ritual walks are talked about before the experience and sometimes at the conclusion. The silence and the trust helps children to feel a multi-dimensional world of meaning. Nothing demonstrates the value of this activity more than the children's evaluation of it that is revealed in the way they often see day-to-day things anew and adjust their appreciation of them. This activity is based on Steve Van Matre's[1] work with young people in the United States.

The inner world where emotions reside and experiences are stored is where we can feel God inside us. Experiences shared as a group can extend the individual consciousness and align the feelings of the whole group towards values and concepts in its community culture. Our ceremonies and activities are a participatory calendar with ideas for self-identity and group identity.

At the start of the academic year in September, we all walk round our large-scale labyrinth.[2]

It is a whole school assembly where staff and children are in motion together. A smaller labyrinth is available all year for individual class use. At the end of the summer holiday, we mark out and paint a large labyrinth of about 28 m in diameter on the school field and we walk the pathway, having been given a thought to carry with us about the importance of being an individual with the group (such as 'I am a leader and I am a follower'). This is to foster a sense of interdependence and security about the new school year.

During this walk the entire school population follow the path in mixed age groups in order to get the feeling of our community working together. There is no talking but one or two teachers will sit within the central rose and play reflective music. A labyrinth painted on the field with marker paint lasts 3 or 4 weeks, but its life is rather dependent on the weather. Generally it lasts long enough to be walked or danced five or six times by every child and adult in school.

Some ceremonies are rites of passage. The dancing-in of the Chinese New Year is always the responsibility of our Year 2 children, as is the series of Passion Play presentations by the Key Stage 2 children just before Easter. They are markers of responsibilities for Key Stage 1 and Key Stage 2 children who will be moving through the phases of their development and during which the children will live through varying degrees of loss, home sickness and pleasure as well as a period of accelerated emotional and physical growth.

Physical contact

Reassurance and comfort comes from holding and touching each other. Adults in distress will reach for friendly hands and make a physical contact in order to feel a sense of safety and protection. Children are in greater need of these instinctive gestures, both giving and receiving, and we need to introduce appropriate touch techniques that are non-invasive and so help the children to recognize benevolent and appropriate touching. Primitive survival mechanisms are often about touch, and the impact is similar to the unconditional love that good parents lavish on their children. We often celebrate the power of working together by starting the day with a group hug: foot-by-foot touching so that a circle is joined, or resting a forearm on the arm of the adjacent person and passing this touch around the circle so that everyone will receive it.

A sense of physical connection arises from dance. We touch one another in the traditional ceremonial dance that marks the end and beginning of each term. Through our turning, coming together in large and then small circles and in our random greeting and touching each other on the shoulder, we prepare for both closings and openings.

Such times are full of contradictions since we are regretful and grateful about the coming holiday or the start of the next term. Our dancing marks the break with the past as well as the shift into new routines. Symbolically we move with the music and into new times carrying our memories. The ritual described is an element of our religious education and spiritual growth programme, although other forms of dance such as country dancing and interpretative dance also spread the culture of gentle, appropriate touch and community ethic.

Massage

Attention to each other's needs can be given through simple massage routines. Massage of the head, neck, shoulder, arms and upper back can relieve anxiety and be a comfort to children who are feeling temporarily alienated or isolated. As a staff group we were given a course on how to follow massage conventions for children by one of our parent group, Susie Bastow. Teachers lead their classes regularly each term in massage sessions. The framework for the exercise is first to ask for permission of the partner to massage him or her, and then to do the massage procedure in a particular order and sometimes accompanied by quiet, reflective music. There is no talking except by the leader of the session. We then say thank you to each other and change places so that each partner experiences both the giving and receiving of touch. The teacher acts as the leader of the activity and the whole routine takes about 15 min. Our intention is to get in touch with our common human needs and to add to each other's sense of well-being.

Circle games

We use a variety of circle games as part of our social and cooperative learning programme.[3] Working in the concentric ring pattern painted in our playground, we throw balloons or pillows to each other or roll body balls around so that every individual gets a turn: at the same time the children are calling to each other by name and are aware of the whole group. From exercises such as these we learn to put energy into remembering individuals getting to know them through directed involvement. Circle games in the school hall or the classrooms have similar aims and use singing, stick passing, passing a cushion with a hug and other ideas in the context of teaching about individual expression and group responsibility. As a staff group we feel that God's care and protection can best be understood through the concerns and responsibilities we have for each other. We become what we repeatedly do.

Social and cooperative exercises

Social and cooperative exercises can be as simple as holding a silent minute together while walking a labyrinth. Sometimes the exercises are demonstrations about what we can do together. For instance, we can raise a washing-up bowl full of water to head height on a sheet of fabric without a spill by lifting at the same time and keeping the sheet level and taut. Concentration and cooperation are required for this challenge and mistakes make the learning true. When a group can manage this degree of collaboration, it is ready to lift a person off the ground (preferably the adult leader of the group). Blowing a collection of feathers into a pile in the centre of the room takes a lot of teamwork and similar exercises demonstrate the benefits of group solutions.

Drama and role play

Drama and role-play make situations live in a new way. Teaching with this method is empathy extending and can promote a change in thinking. Role-play can help children say things that they may be reluctant to say in more standard situations, and it can help everyone find a voice. Working in pairs as guide to a blindfolded person for instance and then exchanging roles, can prompt ideas about our need to give and receive. To control the safety of someone and then to experience the handicapped role promotes a depth of understanding in the children without the need for words. Intuitive understanding is one of the basics for a good life and exercises such as this help us to improve our instinctive knowledge.

Yoga-style exercises and breathing exercises

Three or four minutes of simple yoga style exercises and breathing practices as part of a lesson can promote feelings of well-being, self- and group awareness. Learning gentle, stretching movements that are practised slowly and smoothly can build up flexibility, while holding positions for a short count and then relaxing contributes to strength and control of the body. These skills can help children to be more aware of their inner self as they follow these steps. This activity can precede or be part of assembly time.

Exchanging treasures

Exchanging treasures, lovingly holding animals, old photographs, bubbles, flowers, money, eggs and the like and gently passing them to each other is a trust activity. The manner of holding, examining and passing artefacts needs a protocol that allows close contact and order. The habit of holding on too long for instance or the pulling at the frayed edges of a piece of fabric can limit the possibilities for everyone. We have to teach so that we recognize that each person depends upon all others for fair shares and looking after the precious things that are being passed around. The more often a satisfactory procedure is modelled, the more the etiquettes become established. The risk taking that accompanies these expressions of trust leads to trustworthiness. Our Christingle Service is a good example of this: from Year 2 onwards, the children stand in large circles and each child holds an unlit candle with its base in foil. One candle is lit by a teacher, and the children in turn carefully light the candle of the person next to them until there is a completed circle of light.

Listening to live music

Listening to live music together is a regular social activity. The teachers sing together for the children, and parents, friends of the school or professional groups play a range of instruments for us; this carries a strong message of community. Our music coordinator, Gill, often plays the piano, the harp or the piano accordion as part of our religious education programme, and Neil and Mark, two of our teachers, regularly play duets as backing for the children coming into the hall. Music can accentuate our spiritual awareness and it also sets the mood.

Music can lead us to a greater understanding about ourselves: members of staff offer different music to the whole group. For instance, Shirley is a very able drummer and she regularly leads drumming workshops; Sally our school secretary often plays her clarinet for the children. These musicians and many others support our cultural identity.

Puppets

Relationships between people are of especial importance to all communities. Trust and personal growth within the communities is difficult to sustain when some members are perceived as 'insiders' with rights and others are seen as 'outsiders' without rights. When this happens, it is fertile ground for sexism, divisions about faith, racism, age-ism and other harmful prejudices.

Protective regulations need to be framed with care in order not to harm those they are meant to protect. Overweight individuals, for example, can become a bag of nerves if we insensitively scold those who use exaggerated language to describe them. Issues around name calling and prejudice are raised in our school assemblies because we need to recognize these as denials of human feelings. All name calling is a form of hypocrisy and is frowned upon. Sometimes we bypass direct teaching about prejudice, preferring an oblique focus played out between puppets. In preparation for the presentation we ask children to use the silences between the puppet exchanges so that they can work out what they are seeing and hearing. A typical few minutes might be heard in the persistent heckling of the giraffe in respect of his coat:

- 'How do you get up and go out in that ugly coat?'
- 'Pay an artist to finish you off!'
- 'Why are you dressed up as a map of the London Underground?'
- 'You are a walking jigsaw puzzle!'
- 'You wear my eyes out!'

and a wide range of 'funny' and offensive remarks at the giraffe's expense. Hearing the abuse, the giraffe says simply, 'These are racist comments' and 'I will not stay to listen to this personal abuse.' Silence follows for the exchanges to be inwardly processed by the audience.

This interplay is adapted from Marshall Rosenburg's workshops.[4] His work has influenced us because he advocates helping people to understand their own behaviour as part of conflict resolution. One of his resources for learning how to listen is a pair of animal puppets, giraffe and jackal. The giraffe uses language free of judgements and he is in touch with himself. Essentially he is living by the golden rule. The jackal's language is aggressive because he transfers his egocentric needs into day-by-day living. Jackal gets attention but not in a way that is fulfilling. His grudges multiply and he is unable to recognize the cause. The giraffe–jackal relationship helps us to examine other sorts of prejudice and conflict. For instance, the two of them house-share and jackal gets a paid job. The nature of the tasks each has agreed is questioned by jackal: 'I thought my supper would be on the table when I finish work . . . it's not fair that I'm supporting you when you have your friends around while I'm slaving away to earn money . . . you didn't make my bed yesterday'. When giraffe has heard lots of criticisms in this vein she appeals to the children, 'I'm hearing some prejudice. We need to change something here. Is there a way we can help jackal?' There is a minute's silence, and then giraffe helps jackal to give his honest views. He is unhappy at work, bored by the routines and he wants to swap roles. Giraffe says, 'Now I understand. Of course we can swap roles.' Naturally there are further outcomes. There is no best way for teaching about conflict resolution or how to deal with prejudice, but giraffe–jackal conduct draws a lot of attention to common problems.

Experiences

We believe that human beings are programmed to need spiritual and mystical experiences. The benefits of such special moments provided by picking flowers, sharing food, arranging shells, studying bones, lying on the floor and listening to a musician playing a harp can give mind and spirit the foundation on which to grow. We make displays of natural things in seasonal contexts, in the style of Andy Goldsworthy.[5] It can be more rewarding for an individual to work on his or her own or with a partner to make these displays because the search and choice of the natural material can give the experience greater meaning. There are also times when the learning objectives need the class group effort to accomplish a piece of ephemeral art. This is because the small amounts brought to the display by the group quickly make a whole that is more than its parts: it can be dramatic in scale.

Ray and her class of 5 year olds made many of these compositions in the Autumn term teaching the children to combine their contributions for maximum effect. The result is a way of sharing group achievement that is recorded stage by stage with a camera. The essentials for learning are very much in the process – the confusion and muddle, the tendency of the work to spread, the rivalry between individuals to get the biggest pine cone or toadstool or to get moss from the steepest part of the bank, to put their pieces right in the middle and in doing so step on other's set ups. These behaviours reflect the real learning taking place and are the tension around emerging social, responsible thinking. Finally the work is taken apart and the components restored to their rightful place in the environment. The message here is about sustainability.

Sustainability

Teaching for sustainability is multi-layered and the theory is easy to accept passively. We think the three key features of sustainability are about caring for one another, looking after oneself and caring for the environment. Environmental concern means active engagement in planting for a short- and long-term future, composting, rain water retention, recycling and walking our pathways and helping to maintain them. The global dimension of sustainability means circulating news about good practice in other communities and meeting professionals who manage recycling plants and sewage works. It could involve reading the packaging on food and goods, buying Fair Trade examples, shopping locally, insulating homes and schools, awareness of landfill issues, water use and democracy.

Animals are another element in helping to make contact with the spiritual dimension of the curriculum – the birth of lambs to our school sheep, the hatching of chickens, bantams and ducks in the classroom, or the caring for a class guinea pig helps to link children to the natural world as well as the rhythms of birth, life and death. Animals at school help us to connect with other living creatures.

We use rituals and traditions to create loving and positive surroundings. Through blending what we know with the need for self-knowledge and the search for meaning in life, we are attempting to hold a mirror to ourselves and our group.

Religious education, interpersonal skills and assemblies

Everyone's response to the notion of God is unique and depends upon personal experience. Discovery and re-discovery of answers to this and other profound questions are a part of our inner journey towards spiritual awareness. At school, we offer moments throughout the curriculum in order to help the children to discover their capacity for kindness and intuitive wisdom, honesty and generosity. Our religious education (RE) sessions, interpersonal skills teaching and hall-time assemblies are a basis for recognizing some of the difficult challenges we all face. We seek to be thought provoking in order to explore different spiritual points of view and to respect faith and beliefs different from our own without necessarily sharing them. Exactly the same attitudes apply to those of no faith whatsoever.

Another of our purposes is to extend meaning beyond ideas by using events that are lived through and that can become part of each child's biography. Recognizing these events, even in retrospect can offer support for the challenges of life on a daily basis and it colours the children's view of their school or indeed of any community. We think that the children can engage more fully with life and incidentally with the 'big questions' if they are put in situations where they are physically, emotionally and intellectually involved.

Good stories explore the realities of living and interpersonal relationships but many children are cut off from them because listening requires a high level of skill that they are still building up. Hearing a story during a school assembly in the presence of two hundred plus other children is quite a test. The children are very conscious of each other and they have to suppress a desire to move about. Perhaps they are learning more about submissive behaviour than about the message of the story. This could be true of much of school life where children are stuck in listening and viewing postures and their perception of learning at school is about long periods of being passive.

We want children to feel the relevance of what we are doing at school. It seems to us that because human and planetary survival will increasingly become an important concern in the future, the children should know many survival legends and tales. Focusing on creativity, talking about feelings and getting authentic glimpses of human nature can shape our hopes for a fairer society and help us to think more flexibly.

Childhood is a vulnerable time. Activities where the world is perceived through the five senses is critical for real discovery. Getting on with one another must be an ever-present condition and daily contact with the natural world must be a right of every child at school. Competent, empathetic teachers working with children and developing a school community with these ideals are better able to give moral guidance because their capacity to do it has reasonable foundations.

We believe that every child has a spiritual need and potential. This is outside and beyond the narrow confines of religious faith. Many have no faith but are sustained spiritually by other means such as membership of groups, close friendships and the natural world. The result of combining the two schools has been to give us Church of England status.

A number of our teachers are fervent in their belief in the power of prayer and their membership of a church. There are also Christians in the group who are equally fervent in their belief in the power of prayer who are non-attenders of church. Others are persuaded by the idea that Jesus was a great leader born in the conventional way. All of us see the claims of other major faiths as relevant to our culture. Our position on religion is that we must teach so that children can make up their own minds as they become older and that they should have the knowledge and experience to choose a particular faith or not. We point out the golden rule: 'do unto others as you would they do unto you'. There is an equivalent in all the major faiths of the world.

Some of our prayer is spoken. Much of it however is silent prayer and unspoken hope. This allows children to pray in their own way or simply to have a moment to dream. We trust that this silent withdrawal during a school assembly or an RE session can be a moment of pleasure and peace for each individual.

Our assemblies are illustrated with examples from different cultures and different historical periods. When the children come into assemblies they are large groups of different ages (usually the 5–7 year olds together and the 8–11 year olds together) and we think it is justifiable to treat them as an audience. This audience is being required to focus on the meaning of the assembly and to place the meaning of it in the context of their own lives. Themes such as 'what goes round comes round', 'the gifts of the spirit', or 'we care for each other' colour each assembly or series of assemblies.

The settings for the school assemblies are changing and experimental. They are led from different positions in the hall and not just from the front. An effective setting is to sit in the middle of the group with the children sitting right around us. At other times, we ask the children to sit in a large circle or square and the presenters move around the edge. Sometimes two presenters sit at opposite ends of the hall with a path defined by masking tape between them and at other times there are empty benches down the centre with the children sitting on either side of the hall. The benches are ready to be covered and a display compiled on them. The display being built up is concurrent with the story: two things are going on simultaneously.

Children have lots of intellectual energy and they infer that at the end of the assembly they will leave the hall by walking down the line of objects on display. The children's interest in actual things helps their recall later on. For instance, when Sir Isaac Newton's life was being described, several children had banknotes to pin on a line, two children brought Newton's Cradles to the display and set them in motion, some children brought a basket of apples, a maths dictionary and copies of Newton's Laws of Motion and Laws of Gravity. At a January assembly, where the focus of the theme was on power, ten crowns of different styles were positioned one by one on the display as the assembly unfolded. Children like interaction. They hunger to share it themselves, they like to see adults modelling it and they work alongside the adults co-leading the sessions.

It could be that when the children are presenting, it is in a class circle to the whole school, or it could be several classes taking the stage from one another and presenting from each class's circle. Re-ordering the setting for each assembly adds an element of novelty that 'grabs' the children's attention when they come into the hall. They do not know what to expect, and consequently they give more focussed attention and hopefully, more thought to the content.

Getting the audience of children to think with us is achieved through interaction between two or more teachers and often with children to help them. Role-play is close to drama and theatre and more likely to take the audience along with the presenters' intentions. Narration on its own requires exceptional storytelling skills and a lot of concentration from the listeners. Both types of presentation with and without music are used every week but our preferred style is to reconstruct a story or situation for role-play opportunities. Involved adults and children add to the power of the moment and deepen children's levels of concentration by being part of the scene. Serious issues are brought into the open in this way. Everyone benefits by seeing and feeling a situation where we all react to make changes for the better or struggle to find solutions. Sometimes we just have to live with the problem and this is one of the messages.

The children watch as one of their teachers struggles with his or her feelings after ageist, sexist or racist or aggressive remarks are addressed to them by another adult. They see the teachers present in the assembly form a support group for the distressed individual and consult with each other. It could be that one of the assembly leaders will call the other one 'fat' or make offensive remarks about other aspects of appearance or clothing. The children in the audience register shock and empathize with the 'victim'. They listen carefully as other adults register shock or offer support.

The UN Charter for Human Rights and Individual Liberties is mentioned and talk will move to the school where success is reckoned in terms of kind, non-judgemental approaches. Throughout our lives we are often in the presence of bullies and among people with limited social conscience. At times this is every one of us. Sometimes we have to make up solutions as we go along but the children need to learn the skills that will help them meet the negative impact of bullying, loss, misunderstandings and a host of other hurtful scenarios. Equally it is important to recognize yourself as the culprit and not only as the victim.

In the need to consider the difficulties of living alongside each other, there cannot be facile conclusions about interpersonal harmony. Cultivating attitudes will always be a work in progress. Our emphasis on these skills gives us a limited but powerful vision for a world harmony in which we might have hopes of living in peace, justice and fairness.

Another vital consideration is that we need to educate the children about the needs of our planet and respect for it. This has been slow to reach our schools. Father Thomas Berry[6] calls this period 'a moment of grace' where peoples of the earth can prepare themselves to live differently. Our attempts at ecological education with a focus on the importance of growing food, planting trees and caring for all plant and animal life is a way of involving and preparing children for planetary and community responsibilities.

A common factor for all schools is the interaction between the landscape and the built environment. Our deeply held belief as a staff group is that effective survival, growth and learning for our children depends on exploring the meaning and message in the dynamic natural world. Much of our syllabus for teaching about spirituality and RE is followed out of doors. The natural world is used to support many aspects of the curriculum, and the notion that human beings are just one species among many is emphasized. 'It is only with the heart that one can see rightly: what is essential is invisible to the eye.'[7]

Being part of the story

It seems to us that some frequently told stories need open frameworks so that the children can be included in the telling. One approach is to give the children models of characters from the most often met stories so that they could put them into a scene at the right moment. Over time, we have planned and made sets of wooden figures which are hand painted by friends of the school, such as Mac Collingwood, an artistic grandparent, and a gifted book illustrator, Eva Koltai. The wooden figures relate to six particular stories: the Nativity (with 26 human figures and 60 animal figures) and the story of Saint Francis; the story of David and Goliath, David, Jonathan and King Saul; the Good Samaritan and the Small Miracle, a story by Peter Collington.[8] Since children are in charge of the figures, the storyline can be an interactive element while the narrator (usually the teacher) brings the storyline together. All animals and human figures are in ratio with each other and the clothing style is as accurate to the period as we could research it. The smallest lamb is 4 cm tall and the whole flock is a mixture of lambs, sheep, kids and goats so that it resembles a Biblical flock. The sheep represents all the known breeds that are documented and David the shepherd boy grows through his story by means of several figures, from a baby in swaddling clothes to his late adolescence.

For many of our RE sessions, we sit in a circle and so the central area can be a natural display space. Some everyday objects such as rocks, stones or driftwood can be put down to form a background. The base is a piece of hardboard on which we put gravel, sand or sawdust and sometimes turf or leaves. As well as being able to present six important stories more vividly, teachers working with the models can deal with a mixture of abstract and concrete. The models are a description in themselves: the wise men in their painted robes with the camels in their harnesses; David practising with his sling shot; the Good Samaritan with his pack animal; Joseph with his bag of carpenter's tools. All the figures are small, unique and there is quality in the artwork. Children like to handle the figures from the youngest children in our Nursery Unit to the 10 and 11 year olds. The story presentations vary according to age and the appreciation of the folk art is keenest among the older children.

Water – making a splash

The theme of water recurs very often in our science work, social studies and in association with dance, drama and festivals. In the summer of 2009, the theme of 'water' was a large-scale project with an ambitious form of development. We decided to build three dams and a canal system in half of the playground. One of our teachers, Patrick, led the project that had several aims, and he talked us through the details so that we reached an agreement about it. He thought that the model would be a pleasure for all the children because it would produce running water (the playground is on a slope) complete with sound. Informally and directly it would give information about flow, reservoirs, evaporation, environmental impact including troubling failures such as leaks and the implications of risk for the children in getting around the structure. There were opportunities to describe or demonstrate irrigation, dam building, hydro-electric generation, filtration and the reshaping of half the playground region. Our water source was a tap and we planned to think about the responsible use of water. A bucket with holes drilled in the bottom and filled with water was symbolic of a rain cloud. The idea of the water cycle was demonstrated when the children suggested that a pump could be put into the bottom reservoir area and the water there could be sent back to the first reservoir via a pipe and the bucket. In its own way, this project gave us all a new appreciation of our site and we were intrigued with the scheme. However, where this sort of engineering happens for real in tribal lands and among poor farmers the upheaval is often acute and the human and environmental cost plays out for years when rivers are diverted or stopped. We used the interest in building our water system to talk to the children about the Narmada River and the Sarada Sarovar project.[9] In an assembly we described the 75,000 kilometres of canals and the sorrow of the displaced people as a vast region of India is being reshaped.

We also talked about the huge impact of the harnessing of the Yangtze River at the Three Gorges Dam; its massive scale and the centuries of regional culture destroyed by these improvements. The key idea of this examination is the recognition that there are no ideal systems nor ideal solutions. We strive to be the best kind of human being we can be. The children were encouraged to think about the responsible use of water and the avoidance of wasting this precious resource. All the considerations have a bearing on our approach to appreciating water as an essential for life.

We educate to strengthen the individual and help each person to believe in him or herself. Our intention is to work from an authentic focus that always touches on real life and actual experience.

We planned for the water focus to finish with an inter-faith story that we could dramatize. We chose the story of Noah and the flood so that we could add a survival story to the science, geography and technology work that had driven the project. Two parents Ben and Amy Sandiford, with one of their friends, Kim-lin volunteered to adapt the story for maximum dramatic involvement and a plan was made which would include every child and every teacher in role. Another parent saw the opportunity to move beyond the drama so that children could experience installing a sculpture trail. This parent worked with Jo, our art coordinator to help all the classes of children to make a life-sized model of the animal they chose to protect with a place in the ark. The models were installed along the paths and among the trees and with a shark in the school swimming pool. The efforts from our creative parent, Susie Stallard, the children and the teachers resulted in non-traditional modelling materials being used – hedge trimmings, logs, orthopaedic appliances, rocks, bicycle wheels and other random junk.

Patrick and our chair of governors, Chris put up a telegraph pole as a mast to hold a giant sail and outlined the shape of the ark with metal posts in the ground and rope outlines. A hosepipe was attached to the mast with a rotating spigot at the top.

The concept was to bring animals from their hiding places in the school gardens so that they could board the ark as Noah called them. When they were all assembled in the ark Noah directed them to build the roof. The children in animal role did this by unfolding umbrellas that were put up edge to edge. Chris turned the power hose on and 'rain' fell on everyone.

There were several elements that took the children by surprise and helped the whole group move beyond simply enjoying the coordinated story. We had not told them that a parent (Ben, who is a professional actor) would be Noah on the day. His idea was that the traditional story would come together without rehearsal, ad hoc and linguistically rich. He sang, had conversations with God and improvized with the children. Children and teachers kept in role and reacted naturally so that the experience was richer for being spontaneous. The rain was forecast by Noah when he got his cast of animals on board, but despite bringing their umbrellas most children were surprised by the reality.

Once the rain stopped, two children dressed as doves flew to the olive tree in the school garden to collect proof of life on the land. The animals were released and bread, olives and olive oil were shared by everyone as a thanksgiving. All of this is a view of the way in which we teach. There were many parts to this theme starting with the movement and characteristics of water. In our view, a good educational system is marked by innovation and expanding ideas with children, teachers and parents working for the benefit of all. Susie Stallard formally opened the sculpture trail following the drama and it was visited and revisited many times. The trail was a combination of art and nature creating images to fuel the whole project.

Feelings about the water project were the basis for a writers' workshop led by Ben and Kim Lin with help from the teachers. The writing was drawn from a variety of water experiences and extended with some visualization exercises. It was presented to the rest of the school as two radio productions using a talented approach. Ben put together the broadcast in the manner of a radio programmes featuring high-quality entertainment. Children write well and a gifted presenter can move into the realm of the child's imagination to recognize this. Synthesizing the writing to represent every author is a tough process too, but all the children were able recognize their individual contributions to the writers' workshops.

Remembrance Sunday

Our act of remembrance for school assembly is held on the day before the 11 November weekend of National Remembrance. Our purpose is to help the children understand and be interested in the commemorative events held during that weekend locally and nationally, much of which is shown on TV and heard on radio. We use resources similar to those used at the televised remembrance services.

Our ceremony is held around a white cross that is laid almost the length and breadth of the floor in the school hall. A 50-cm path is marked with masking tape around the cross. Every child and adult in school brings a handful of Royal British Legion poppies from the classroom to put on the cross before the start of the service. The white cross is eventually covered in poppies. A church candle is lit and put on the centre of the cross and household candles go down the length of the cross and across the arms. We tell the story of the First World War briefly and dwell on the Armistice and the intention that followed to live in peace. This is our main message. At this service, there is always a cornet player or a bugler to play the Last Post (for many years this was Dave Edwards). Two minute's silence is observed and then the Reveille is sounded and class by class, the children walk the pathway around the cross and leave the hall in silence. The last group of children blow out the candles before leaving.

We aim to be a responsibly minded group that is always exploring peace studies. During the week leading up to Remembrance Sunday our large collection of poppies is used in the religious education sessions to describe the countryside in which the brutal massacres of Ypres came to stand for all the deaths suffered by those called to arms by their countries at that time and since. Our thick-piled library carpet is used by each class of children to anchor hundreds of poppies so that they appear to be growing out of the floor. Against this stunning background, we think about the daily Last Post that is sounded at the Menin Gate for those service men and women who died in the many military campaigns of the First World War.

Part of the work is concentrated on the International Red Cross and its origins. We tell the story of the Battle of Solferino that gave rise to Henri Dunant's humanitarian work that established the Red Cross organization, and much later the founding of allied associations such as the Red Crescent and the Jewish Red Cross.

Seasonal celebrations

On 6 December, or as close to that date as possible, we celebrate St Nicholas's Day. In the period before Christmas our children, their families and our whole society is in danger of an overdose of consumerism. We need to question and examine the impact of this and help children to look at their expectations regarding Christmas, partly to protect them from the voices of advertising.

Santa Claus and Father Christmas are the supercharged version of an historical figure who is believed to have visited poor children in winter with gifts of food. His friends are said to have helped in delivery of vitally important gifts and in mystical tradition, the good deeds were done at night and in secret. There was no benefit to the givers other than in the satisfaction of the sharing. We resolved to introduce Christmas every year with this story and take a critical look at the general direction in which our culture has taken us. The leading teacher tells the story and the children are asked to go into role as the children wasting away for want of food. They pretend to go to sleep on the hard floor under their coats and leave their shoes next to them. The lights are turned out and two or three candles are lit. Bells are heard and following this, Gill our music specialist plays the auto harp to represent the prosperous families' celebrations.

Nicholas and his helpers, dressed in cloaks and hoods come into the darkened hall and deliver a small bag of gifts into every empty shoe. The storyteller lets the silence last for a minute longer than it takes to visit each child and bless each of them with a loving touch on their heads. Then the dawn comes (the lights are turned on) and the children wake up to realize that St Nicholas has remembered them and delivered gifts to everyone.

The bags contain fruit to symbolize the harvest of the earth, a new penny to represent the power to buy essentials, a biscuit to depict generosity and a badge to illustrate the caring community. The badges are small wooden shapes, hand painted and ribboned, individualized with each person's name, and pinned so that they can be worn or pinned up in the bedroom at home. Children first bring their badges to the Christmas tree where adults with ladders are waiting to dress the tree. As decorations the badges can be appreciated at two levels: as unique individual tokens and symbolically as representing the entire school family. Except for the white lights no other tree trimming is used. Souvenirs such as these badges[10] support the learning and in a limited way continue the school's value system.

The festival of Hanukkah is an opportunity to learn more about the Jewish faith. In this festival of light, our Israeli parents together with their children dramatize the story of the Maccabees' revolt against Antiochus. They dress up, use artefacts and then they encourage us all to think by candlelight before we share the fried food (doughnuts) that we eat together as a second breakfast. The year is rich in Jewish festivals that are usually presented to the children by our Jewish parents. This tradition dates back 20 years and has been inherited by several groups of families.

The festival of Sukkot – the Feast of Tabernacles – is marked by the building of sukkah – shelters made from natural materials. Our Jewish parents built a sukkah in our library and the children contributed written prayers to decorate the walls and roof of the sukkah inside and out. The Jewish parent group also built a sukkah out of doors in the school grounds to resemble the outdoor sukkah in which Jewish people would lodge during the festival.

At this point in the year when Christmas is drawing attention it is good to help children sense the closeness of other beliefs. We talk about the connections across the faiths that can be felt in the autumn/winter festivals. Father Thomas Berry,[11] theologian and philosopher remarks that 'nothing is completely itself without everything else'.

In the Key Stage 1 and Foundation Stage 1 and 2 groups, the story of the Nativity is acted out by each class group. The children do this four or five times, playing different characters in turn so that each child changes role, from choice, every time the story is told. This has a bearing upon children's rights to the broadest possible range of parts and the rotating roles help them to experience the action in another context. Children should be able to learn about fairness and taking turns through every aspect of school life. The school hall is used for these sessions and the stories are shared in the round. Each group of characters (Roman soldiers, Caesar's palace in Rome, shepherds, three kings, inn keepers, star, messengers, citizens of Nazareth, Roman Army barracks in Jerusalem, Herod's palace in Jerusalem) sits on carpets of Middle Eastern origin set around the edge of the hall. The adult narrator tells the bones of the story and the children are free to say what they like in role; there is no formal script and each time the story is re-enacted, it changes slightly depending on how the characters react. The resources include dressing up clothes (tunics, cloaks, soldier's outfits, Caesar's purple robes, shawls, animal skins to represent the stable which is situated in the middle of the hall, hats and crowns, torches to represent the star, gifts of gold, frankincense and myrrh).

Dressing up is an important lure and the children can choose what they want to wear. Setting the scene before each re-enactment of the story is important. In the stable area in the centre of the hall, candles are lit for each day of the advent period and incense is burned to remind the children that 'God is everywhere'. The teachers scent the children's wrists with frankincense and myrrh oils so that they can sniff them during pauses in their acting. The preparation for the story ends with the blessing, sharing and eating of bread together and at the final re-enactment, the parents and friends share bread with us. The children also present an outdoor, evening Nativity for the parents. The playground is the setting with the backdrop of the tree houses that we flood-light. Each class takes on the role of one set of characters (Roman soldiers, inn keepers, Mary, Joseph and their friends, stars, shepherds, wise men) and each group parades around the playground introduced by a fanfare of trumpets.

For the older children in Key Stage 2, each year group presents a part of the Nativity story in Mummer's or Mystery plays. These interpretations are shared with the rest of the school at assembly times, the parts are chosen by the children themselves and the tradition, history and meaning behind each part of the play is taught in the classrooms.

The Feast of the Epiphany usually coincides with the start of the Spring term and at this point we involve all the children in school with gift-giving originating from them. Donations of money go to a charitable cause. If the children are seeing and hearing distressing news about natural disasters or more local needs we can turn their concern into practical help.

Epiphany is the focus for two weeks of work which concentrates on eight related interests: a journey to be role played, food of the Middle Eastern region, the Babushka story, the spices and herbs of the Levant, folk music to entertain travellers, Roman soldiers, light to represent the coming of Jesus and an inn displaying copies of works of art focused on the Magi's journey. These interests are a means to study geography, history, spirituality, astronomy, music, story and legend. The different inns are set up around the school and in the gardens. The indoor inns are tented with swathes of material and the children and teachers journey around each inn during the course of 2 days. We also set up a crown walk of 12 crowns to be found in the outdoor landscape. At each inn, there is an adult role-playing the part of the inn keeper who explains his or her particular role and the sensory resources he or she will be using.

Sometimes one of our parents, Howard, sets up his Yurt in the school hall in which we put Turkish carpets and cushions and a range of precious resources. In this inn, the children get to experience an overnight stop. The school library is transformed with carpets and hangings that change its ambience. The innkeeper invites his or her visitors to rub herbs between their fingers and to smell a variety of teas, coffees and spices common to the southern and eastern Mediterranean regions. She explains the mysteries of curries and tagines and talks about medicines based on such ingredients as ginger, peppermint or juniper. There are bouquet garnish, nosegays, hops, garlic and culinary smells to explore and the innkeeper gives each child as they leave her inn a small sprig of fragrant rosemary or bay.

The Inn of Food is a setting for tasting. Food which is typical of the Middle Eastern countries is served to the children in small quantities: chopped dates, pita bread, hummus, olives, curd cheese, onions, yoghurt, honey and grapes are offered by the innkeeper. The children think about seasonality and the differences and similarities between European and Middle Eastern food. At the Story Inn, the storyteller will describe his function in society as an historian, his repertoire, his worth as a news gatherer, information giver and entertainer. He tells the story of Babushka and asks questions of the children about their journey and its purpose.

At the Inn of Light, the children help to light candles and oil lamps, they enjoy the darkness and the tonal quality of light and they pass lighted candles from one to another. They think of goodness and virtue and how we all turn to the light. They create images from watching the flame and the flickering shadows, and they reflect on how these small lights shaped the lives of people who relied on them. The innkeeper leads the thinking and listens and responds to the children's ideas and questions.

The southern and eastern Mediterranean lands were part of the Roman Empire at the time the Magi are said to have made their journey. Having 'Romans' set up a camp validates the children's interpretations, so we make a point of bringing in 'Roman Soldiers' to be on site for 2 days. Often we have a fire beside the encampment, and for the last eight years, we have been fortunate enough to have a Roman Soldier and his wife[12] (members of a re-enactment society) who describe scenes of Roman everyday life and traditions.

The 2 days of the Epiphany Journey are carefully timetabled so that each class of children has a 30-min slot at each inn, followed by a period of reflection or prediction of the next stopping point. We also set up scenes outside for the children and their teachers to visit when they have a free period. Some parents, grandparents or governors act out the role of the Magi, bringing their horses complete with saddlebags and blankets. Every third year or so, we organize a visit from camels from a camel Sanctuary in Norfolk: these impressive animals are beautiful and have a 'wow' factor, but they do not respond reliably to being walked along the pathways!

A parent who is a farrier sets up his trade on one of the pathways and every group of children stops off in the journey to watch a horse being shoed. The farrier makes the shoes on site and the ringing anvil is one of the most wonderful parts of the larger action. He gives every child a horseshoe to take home as a lasting reminder of the 2 days and of his own technical skill.

The Inn of Art is usually in the school hall: some of the walls are decorated with copies of famous works of art depicting the Epiphany Journey, and a resting area is made up with benches and tables covered in middle Eastern rugs. Precious objects (silverware, camel blankets and stools) are displayed for the children to touch. Across the hall of the floor, individual pictures forming Peter Collingtons's picture book story of the Small Miracle are set alongside a pathway marked out in masking tape and surrounded by the small wooden figures that retell the story of the Nativity and Epiphany Journey. The innkeeper discusses the works of art and invites the children to study each picture, as well as to walk the 'Small Miracle' pathway, examining each image in turn and concentrating on the story depicted by the wooden figures.

The inns are a virtual adventure that entail real action by the children. We are experiencing this journey together. The demonstration and practical work described has a similar set-up to an open-air museum. It is planned as a circuit for the sake of the all-important journey component of the 2 days. Preparation for the journey comes from the children's suggestions that are articulated by the teacher in colourful and emotive language:

Climbing exhausting heights	Fording icy and swollen rivers
Threatened by the possibility of outlaws or wolves	Sharing cramped spaces at the inns
Sleeping on the floor	Meeting blinding sandstorms

The realities in the setting are steep banks to climb or are realized by walking through flooded bits of the playground, sheltering around the cave, getting 'lost' and finding the correct location on a map, hearing 'wolves' howl from a distance. A dramatic form of teaching appeals to individuals to find their own voices as scenes in the story are relived. In all of this there will be two kinds of treasures exchanged. At the end of the journey the travellers find a baby and give their donations as gifts. In the second there will be an intrinsic reward of knowledge: the knowledge that is rooted in gathered experiences. At intervals during the 2 days celebration of the Epiphany, the children return to their classrooms. In and out of role they draw, write and look at images taken in previous years: they confirm and rearrange their impressions and anticipate the scenes still to come.

The description of the Epiphany work is about translation of aims into practice. It is cross-curricular and multi-sensory, it presents an account of the many people involved and the participative culture that affects the children. It is an attempt to make a chronicle in which children find a sense of meaning and pleasure. There should always be times when teachers consider new approaches: consultation with the children in particular can be a lasting help to write the next chapter.

Looking at the solar system and studying the night sky

One of the most widely recognized symbols of Christmas is the star. It is also generally used as a sign for leadership, quality and charisma and as an emblem on flags. Star gazing and enjoying the night sky is a real pleasure for those who can see it clearly. There is one sloping area on our school field where the moon and stars can be enjoyed relatively well so we use this space around the time of the Epiphany celebrations. We invite children and their parents to come back to school in the early evening in the second or third week of January to do some observations of the night sky. Jenny, one of our teachers, gives a short talk inside followed by practical help on the field. The aim is to find and identify some of the constellations and to look at the lunar phase. Everyone shares binoculars, telescopes and information about where to find blue stars, white stars, red stars, the Milky Way, the Pole Star and all the well-known features of the night sky at this time of year. Sometimes a shooting star or a satellite is spotted, but generally the movement is in the flight paths to and from Heathrow Airport.

A mobile planetarium usually visits the school at this time and an expert demonstrates the earth's rotation and the phases of the moon. The astronomer pinpoints the constellations and talks about wandering stars, Halley's Comet, solar flares and what may have been the star over Bethlehem more than two thousand years ago.

Cross-curricular elements

Our religious education and assembly programme is cross-curricular: we believe that spiritual growth, ethics, social responsibility and morality flow constantly through every part of our living. When we teach directly about these things, we consider them in a concentrated way. Like Dewey[13] we believe that all education is bound up with politics, democracy, ethics and new experiences.

Each year we explore the symbols of Christianity and the other major world faiths. We all need help in understanding and dealing with the challenges of living in a multi-faith society. The children engage in freehand cut paper work: they cut out examples of sacred geometry that they are already aware of (the cross, the crescent, the Maltese cross, the fish, the star, the Jewish Star of David etc.) and they make a floor display of their work. Each group of children walks slowly and reflectively around the finished display.

Guidance from the children

At the end of the academic year we have group sessions to review our teaching and to assess the value to the children of the different experiences they have had in the RE and hall-time assembly programme. In 2008–2009 we listened to 12 groups of mixed ability children talk to us about the lessons of the previous 12 months. This was time-consuming but the individuals who took part very much enjoyed hearing the case notes read back and after each session they could have gone on talking for another hour. The feedback was sincere and showed us how often we were presenting ideas in a smokescreen of detail. It was often these details that were remembered rather than the explicit message. In light of this we have tried to maintain the essentials without so much detail and get a better balance. This work benefited our teaching during the following year.

In 2009–2010, we reviewed our teaching again in the light of the range of experiences given to the children in the RE/Spiritual Growth programme. The reviewing process went to a deeper level and had three parts. The first raised awareness through group discussions with every class. By asking the children which of the lessons or assemblies they could call to mind we made a skein of memories which summoned up the best bits for each child and each group. When we set group memories side by side we can use the result as data to study preferences in teaching styles and content. A key role of the class teacher is to scribe the ideas as they are spoken and the group leader tries to draw views from everyone. These get total acceptance in a neutral way. We do not prompt the children's recall because this makes the exercise value-laden and skews the results towards what the teacher hopes to hear. These free-style reminiscences may not identify bits in the curriculum that teachers have spent a long time preparing, but they do constitute a sort of map about what the children remember and see as useful.

The second and for us the more crucial part was through individually recording the children's memories. A week after the group memory exercise was finished, we gave a paper to every child. There was a diagrammatic head, heart and carrying case on each A4 sheet for individuals present at school on the day to enter the RE lessons or assemblies that appealed to them. The head space implied challenge and achievement, the heart space was for heart and soul-stirring moments and the carrying case was for ideas to store. In fact the relationship between the categories was so strong that we decided to give every recorded memory an equal rating of one point.

Memories were elicited in this simple diagram because it was one way of stimulating recall and making the exercise engaging. Many more than three lessons and topics could be called to mind by almost every child. We needed to limit our model and assume that the three recorded memories were well judged for personal reasons. Many children wrote more than five memories on their paper but we counted only the first three recorded. Children's opinions about the content and learning activities need to be drawn from them impartially, otherwise this kind of exercise serves nobody's interests.

For the third part, we asked each child to cast his or her mind back to the beginning of the academic year and think through the RE and school assembly timetable. Crucially for us it was a way of putting our teaching methods to the vote and we told the children this. We explained that the poll would help us by consulting them about how good we were as teachers. Each activity confidently remembered was given one point and those activities that were remembered muddled or confused were discounted.[14]

The list of memories that teachers noted and the children's individual sheets with the three contributions were used as pointers to help us to determine our effectiveness. An analysis would not always mean that we jettison unmentioned sessions. Some unmentioned parts of the programme such as the life of the Prophet Mohammed (Peace Be On Him) may simply not have been taught vividly enough. This could also apply to the life and teaching of Buddha, the Enlightened One; we always reflect on the lack of mention and determine to use a different approach in our future RE and assembly programme. The way that ideas are produced drags down or drives up their appeal: enactments, pageants, badge-giving, food sharing, music, exhibitions and working in the open air can all help the children to get a grip on the themes, as much is taught off the topic and in tandem with it. The total of knowledge acquired in this active way is bound to be much greater because the ideas are interlaced with each other. Our experience is that a broad and imaginative approach appeals to children and keeps them open-hearted and open-eyed. It is about boosting and supporting intellect when we all pick up more than what is being specifically pinpointed in the lesson. In all our teaching, we are aiming to give over and above the story and the facts. We are encouraging children to go beyond the surface and become aware of what is waiting to be discovered.

Probably the most direct way to transform practice is to get in touch with children's thinking and their memories. Our premise is that if the children can recall lessons given through a year those lessons had value to them. It seems safe to assume that a child's recall of a lesson will be based on emotional engagement, or the first-hand experience offered or because the lesson had personal meaning for them. This probably operates at every age level. The teacher, the methods and the setting are critical to learning as every school child knows. In teaching cooperatively, giving each other candid feedback and by constant attention to the heart of what we are doing we aim to be more effective teachers. Consulting the children is part of our teaching style.

In 2009–2010, we undertook additional research to determine the children's feelings about the setting in which our spiritual and RE teaching takes place. We asked 30 children of varying abilities across the primary age range for their opinions on our use of our school library as a setting for our programme of teaching. The same group of children were also asked what they thought about following lessons for our programme out of doors. The 30 children were a small sample, and we talked to them in the playground while they were at play. Each child was asked if they would like to help with our research. The children's responses showed that our teaching in the school library and out of doors was appreciated as a benefit to all lessons. Children believed that leaving their classroom for the sessions had a revitalizing effect on their learning. They thought of the library as 'cosy', 'friendly', 'relaxing', 'quiet', 'comfortable' and the children said they 'liked being surrounded by books and pictures'. They also said 'it helps you feel different', 'you can't move around much', 'it smells of wood', 'we sit tight in there' – all were positive comments about being taught in a different workspace.

The children's views about teaching and learning outdoors were given forthrightly and spontaneously. They said that it was 'the most fun', 'cool', 'where you can use all your senses', 'it's about the real world', 'learning about actual things', 'getting exercise while you learn', 'breathing fresh air', 'getting creative', 'it's more chances to learn and see things', 'you get to think more', 'it's God's whole creation' and 'you are more independent'. These views were typical of the group's perceptions. Children have a talent for appreciating details and they value non-standard approaches without being confused by them. There was a consensus among children who contributed to the action research that the library venue and use of the outdoor environment was positively beneficial to learning.

When the children thought back on a year's work they were able to recapture experiences in detail. The scope of memories ran through the whole year without the greater weight of memories coming from the most recent work. Judgement about the preferred topics seemed to be based on involvement and multi-sensory opportunities (Epiphany, sunflower planting and harvesting). Every topic had cross-curricular aspects: the sunflower topic included watching insects at work in the flower heads, dance and the emotional dimension of individual picking and ownership. Silent walks were effective in terms of trust and for the older children they were associated with risk. The walk was high on emotional energy and the independent dimension.

Children like to be the source for data collecting and we give them the reasons for seeking evidence. We are checking our effectiveness as teachers. We depend upon the children's attention and cooperation as their memories will reflect these as well as the appeal of the lesson. The best souvenirs any of us can have are the memories we carry.

Notes

1. Steve Van Matre: An American environmental activist, author and educator. He is the founder of the Earth Education movement and chair of the Institute for Earth Education.

2. See Chapter 4: The Hard Landscape.

3. S. Rowe and S. Humphries. *Playing Around: Activities and Exercises for Social and Cooperative Learning.* Forbes Publications: London, 1994.

4. M. Rosenburg. *Nonviolent Communication: A Language for Life*. Puddledancer Press: California, 2003.

5. Andy Goldsworthy, British artist and sculptor.

6. Father Thomas Berry, 1914–2009. Cultural Historian and Ecotheologian (Geologian). Founder of The Thomas Berry Foundation, 1998.

7. Antoine de Saint-Exupery in *The Little Prince*. Galimard. France, 1943.

8. P. Collington. *A Small Miracle*. A Knopf: New York, 1997 (also available in paperback).

9. Examples of large-scale environmental changes in India.

10. See Chapter 9, School Traditions.

11. Thomas Berry. *The Dream of the Earth*. Sierra Club Books: San Francisco, 1988.

12. Roman Soldier – Peter and Angela Pooke, Woking, Surrey.

13. John Dewey. *Experience and Nature*. Dover Publications: New York, 1958.

14. See Appendix 1 for an analysis of this research.

6 Science – at the heart of our school

Science in the nursery

Our science curriculum starts with the 3-year old children in our Nursery. They get a broad education and this is especially true in the field of science. The children cook and eat cakes, blend and drink their own smoothies, extract juices to make ice lollies, vote on pizza toppings and bake to order, barbecue sweet corn and literally swallow a lot of learning.

Anne and Donna, our Nursery teachers, are very concerned that the children can identify ingredients and know about healthy eating so the whole group plant, nurture and pick food from our own gardens and prepare it in different ways. The late potato crop will become warm potato salad or potato bread, but before this the children will dig up the crop with trowels and sort the tubers so that the tiniest potatoes can be boiled with plenty of mint cut from the nursery garden. These will be eaten at snack time. Blackberries, plums and apples available to all of us in the Autumn term contribute to a range of dishes that will be served simply but imaginatively, sometimes on washed leaves or with plain yoghurt to illustrate seasonal food grown on ground they know. At other times, the nursery children will combine oats, sultanas and raisins to make their own muesli or granola and then serve it with plums or blackberries with local honey. The portions are small but they illustrate many scientific processes and a fundamental concept: that life comes from the soil and all life depends on soil.

Learning science outside means that children can get wet and messy; they can spill water in the working space without restrictions (we write this in July as the nursery children have been using lengths of tangled hose in their own pond). At this time, a small pond constructed with pond liner on a wooden frame links the learning experiences in the nursery to those of the older children. In the older children's playground, water is collected in reservoirs made in the same way and the nursery children have daily visits. These visits enhance the experimental play when the children return to their own garden. This to and fro movement is frequent and vital for everyone whatever the projects and the time of year. We have the chance to learn from each other.

The nursery children make many learning journeys along the pathways criss-crossing the school's woodland and gardens. Sometimes these are journeys to search for molehills, spiders' webs or to gather snowdrops or cherries. At other times they set out to come face to face with the giant stone head and to scramble over all the rocks on the geology trail. We introduce variation by having bear walks – 20 or so bears half hidden in the trees. Sometimes the children go on shape walks or colour walks where the teacher carries a tray to collect their findings. Story walks feature characters at the pathway junctions or words that can be built into a rhyme. A walk becomes a special event when there is a sharp frost and the children go out to make body prints on the frozen grass or leave tracks on fresh snow. Observational skills are part of the scientific operation and the work in the nursery is a flying start to a keen interest in science later on.

Our scheme for science is described in the context of the cross-curriculum work described in Chapters 5, 7, 8 and 9. The philosophical justification for this is based on Johann Comenius's[1] notion of an authentic curriculum where deeper learning is about participation and active engagement. A key element in all our work is community involvement and above all, this is teaching the children about common goals and cooperation. Not all our science is planned ahead. In due season, toadstools, fruit blossom at its peak, autumn mists, winter fogs, frosts, rainbows, bouncing raindrops, an ant invasion or a dead fox are turned to good account to support scientific discovery. Small gadgets come in from home on the understanding that they will be stripped down by the children and the parts recycled.

Ice sculptures

During the epiphany celebrations this year, the temperature was below freezing for five consecutive days. Carol and Jane seized the chance offered by the stability of low temperatures to make ice sculptures with all the children in their class. Troughs, trays and lengths of guttering, fancy Christmas shapes of strong plastic, polythene sandwich bags and aluminium foil were used to create different shapes. These were filled with water and sometimes ink was added without agitating the water. A cord and a weight were offered to the children. When each child had fixed the weight (a pebble, a metal button or a shell) on the end of the cord, they chose a collection to tie to the cord using florists' wire. Leaves, seeds, fruits and bits of bone went on some lines; forks, spoons, keys and paper clips were popular; hair clips, ribbons, unifix cubes and such like were lowered into the containers. These were then left outside overnight and collected by the children first thing in the morning. The cord that ran right through the ice shape was a reliable way to secure them in the branches of the trees when the casing had been removed. There were pillars, towers and pyramids of ice hanging in the branches with ink-staining patterns in some of them. In others there were beads, cubes, spoons and sundry objects captured in sheets or cylinders of ice. The results of this inventiveness and enterprise were beautiful shapes to decorate the epiphany trail. This was using elementary physics to transform the ordinary into the spectacular. It lays the foundations for teaching about light travelling in a straight line and as it passes through another medium (in this case, ice) it refracts. The surface of the ice was bumpy and its irregularities caused some optical distortion and some odd magnifications. The ice was a sort of lens adjusting our views. Children enjoy this type of experience all through school and these ideas will be revisited at different levels as Jerome Bruner[2] strongly advocated.

Deconstruction of machines

Valuable scientific discussions take place when parents bring mechanical things into school to be taken apart. This happens regularly and because large appliances take up a lot of space, they are deconstructed fairly immediately. There are always surprises: for instance, the large cabinet of a washing machine is the housing for weighty concrete bricks. The plumbing, the drum and the programme board take much less of the overall space than expected. There is much debate about the purpose of the apparently functionless space fillers that are vital for stability. Working at a very intuitive level, the children arrive at their own conclusions:

'These are to hold it down'
'The bricks stop it moving around'
'When it spins it would wobble without the bricks'
'It would shake across the room'
'It would be dangerous'

For our purposes the deconstructed vacuum cleaners, cameras, floor polishers, toasters and the like are about aspects of mechanics and design. Taking them apart deepens understanding about essential components and stimulates questions involving function and design. There are also desired end results for the way the material is systematized in its parts. We recycle everything after we have made a tally of the parts and purpose. Screws, rivets, springs and other fragmentary parts are collected in separate containers. The tools for the dismantling are specific and the children are taught how to use them appropriately and safely.

Plants

Sometimes bringing things to life means destroying them in order to understand them better. The children can recall planting bulbs to produce daffodils so that they can later pick them and take them home. It is equally wonderful to dig up daffodils in bloom and be reminded of their origin. Opening the bulb, chopping up the stalk and slicing through the flower head generates a lot of concentration and the children begin to see science as a study of life. Only a few daffodils get this treatment and the children are spellbound because this examination is counter to expectations. We talk to them about plant dissection and how the investigation of plants requires this skill as well as the skills of analysis. It is vital to use protective gloves and soap and water to wash hands in order to remove all traces of the dissection as the sap is an irritant. Sunflowers and honeysuckle blossoms are also cut and probed for study and some of the plant parts are named. Smell, taste and touch make it possible for the intellectual curiosity to develop and the results should be an appreciation of beauty and purpose. Dissecting a sunflower head to show the arrangement of seeds is authentic rather than merely talking about it or looking at a diagram.

Life rhythms

We need to help our children glimpse the fragile nature of our planet and link the human to rhythms beyond the single life. When parents or children come across an animal killed on the road and if it is not in too bad a state, we encourage them to bring it into school. This is a contribution towards experiencing life and death. It is sad that the animal died but its burial in the garden gives us a chance to value it in death. We can see that the animal is without pain or needs and that death itself is perfect still-ness. This fact needs to be met truthfully in all aspects of the curriculum but in terms of science the teacher watched by the children can exhume a buried carcass after 12 months (or more or less depending on its size) and after treating the bones in the way that zoologists recommend, we have an interesting skeleton for study. Even without the exhumation, profound questions have been raised by the children that otherwise might never have been voiced.

During the autumn term we bring huge quantities of fallen leaves into the library. A large groundsheet is laid on the floor and the leaves are spread on this to dry out. The children stand around the pile of leaves and together they gather up a double handful. On a signal from the teacher, the children throw the leaves up into the air and watch them fall back to the ground. This generates a lot of excitement and we repeat the exercise two or three times. Following this indoor event, we take the leaves out of doors on the groundsheet and toss the leaves into the air again to watch them fall.

We then talk to the children about decomposition, death and renewal. Autumn leaves provide shelter and warmth for many animals during the winter, and we explain why many of them will hibernate for the winter months. Back in the library all the children are invited to 'hibernate' in the pile of leaves: they stay quite still as the teacher explains what is happening to the 'hibernating' creatures.

The heart

The heart of a pig is nearly the size of a human heart. During our celebrations for Valentine's Day, we put pigs' hearts in our science work. The children are being involved with ideas about hearts and so we integrate the facts about the heart as a major organ. A parent who is a butcher delivers fresh hearts for dissection. One of our teachers, Gail, has unrivalled access to laboratory apparatus and the children wear masks, goggles, lab coats and gloves to handle the animal tissue. The children dissect the hearts with sharp scissors examining the ventricles, feeling inside the chambers with their fingers and cutting through muscle tissue.

Learning is on many levels depending on the age of the children. This teaching breaks down the traditional boundaries between primary, secondary and tertiary education. It is about coherence between subjects and current interests and demonstrates an integrated approach. The hands-on experience with the hearts advances understanding in the same way as the hands-on deconstruction of machinery or plants: it is holistic and relevant to children's needs.

Food analysis and testing

The fruit gathered in late September and October is picked, eaten fresh, cooked or pickled by the children at school. Different curriculum specialities are involved and they are all connected to the practical realities of gathering the harvest, processing it and eating it. We use the apples in an exercise to demonstrate the value of fair testing. Children rotate around tables each of which displays one of six apple varieties. The children's first task is to compare the appearance and the smell of the fruit. They cast votes for their preference using maths cubes after a timed five minutes of study.

During a plenary session the results are recorded by an adult. In the second experience, the apples are rated for flavour. The fruit is divided into small equal size sections and the children move around to eat one portion of each type of apple. The children again cast their votes for their preference and during the next plenary session, the results are noted. Following this, bowls of peeled and sectioned apples are put on the tables for a blind tasting. The children repeat their voting for flavour and texture and at the third plenary session we compare the results. We discover how influential appearance is in our decision-making and how difficult it is to make a judgement against appearance even when we agree that flavour and texture has the greater value. The more knowledge we have about testing, the easier it is to stay open-minded and live with a degree of uncertainty.

One of our teachers, Chris, was eager to help his children look beyond appearances. The children provided him with an idea when he realized that sausages were the preferred food for most of them. The group walked to the local farm shop to look at the sausages and hear how they are made. The butcher showed the children a pig carcass, he named the parts allocated for the sausages. He divided the carcass, minced the meat, added the crumbs and seasoning and put the mixture into natural casings. With help, the children selected cuts of pork on their own to set up a sausage making experiment at school. The children minced the meat, made breadcrumbs from brown bread, chopped onion and prepared the seasonings, combined the ingredients and packed the casings. The sausages were cooked and the children ate them that day.

Creative exploration is a basis for informed decisions and working with skilled professionals from other fields is learning in a broader context. This piece of work tested the children's assumptions about what went into a sausage – seeing them made and then making your own gives greater insights into what we might be eating. It is all about the beginnings of analysis of ingredients.

Animals

We feed the wild birds and study them as part of learning out of doors. To discover more and deepen our understanding we raise chickens, bantams and ducks from

fertile eggs to birds. Another of our teachers, Mim, established this yearly practice from the science base making sure that the children opened eggs and that every child examined sterile and fertile eggs under magnification. Children made a diary for the expected hatching and put the fertile eggs into the incubator in the classroom. These could be viewed at any time but the children appreciated that they must keep an eye on the humidity and temperature levels. Nine ducklings hatched and nine eggs failed. Mim recorded the point of failure by opening the eggs with the children and using the diary to mark the days when the embryos ceased to grow. There was a spread of deaths from day 2 to day 20. It is hard to understand death and we think that experiences such as this are vitally necessary for the spiral curriculum that is life itself.

The ducklings lived in the classroom under a brooding lamp. They were handled all day, had their first swim in a paint tray on the floor and gave endless everyday fun and learning. Gradually they were introduced to the fresh air in a small wire run. They continued with their daily swim under observation and finally they were settled in the grass verge adjacent to the classroom and with a temporary pond.

Another teacher, Sarah, raised a pair of fancy bantams with the Foundation Stage 2 children. Their plan is to keep these birds as pets and they hope to get eggs. Bantams are similar to game birds and if we are lucky, they will learn to roost in the trees.

Mim and Patrick organized a focus for the science curriculum: they thought that the children would benefit from a repeat experience of seeing ducklings mature to fully grown birds. Patrick started the next brood with the children who broadly traced the same learning pattern described earlier. Second experiences consolidate and develop the powers of prediction and worthwhile knowledge: life and death cycles talked about in situations organized for that purpose connect to profound knowledge and understanding. Some children have very little contact with animals and birds and it seems important to us that schools should do what they can to meet this need.

We keep a few sheep to provide opportunities for learning about life cycles, textile production and our dependency on animals. The responsibilities of caring for them are obvious and we focus the children on these. Once a term Mim brings horses to study by using her own horse as well as ponies and horses owned by friends. Recognizing parts of the animal's body, and discussing different behaviours and characteristics between species is a step towards valuing biodiversity. Hands-on opportunities are part of the planning with the grooming, harnessing, feeding and foot inspections to discuss.

Water

As a background for understanding that water is a vital part of life we regularly experiment with it formally and in play situations. We turn it into bubble mountains when we blow air through straws into plastic beakers causing cascades of bubbles to fall over the rim and build on each one until we get peaks a metre high. Children reshape wire coat hangers and bandage them with wool or fabric strips so that the solutions of liquid soap and water cling to the frame. These frames can produce jumbo size bubbles that can catch the breeze and float over the school roof. We invent flavours for water and also drink it plain. We force it from pressure hoses to make rainbows in the summer sun or we stand under the hose showers to test waterproofing and our umbrella designs. We make reflecting pools by flooding the depressions in the playground and study the overhead trees mirrored in the pools. Sometimes we add a small amount of cooking oil to make a shimmering surface and to display the colours of the spectrum.

The younger children have active phonics sessions using water; they 'wash windows on Wednesday with warm water' or they 'wait and watch wonderful water wandering to a way out' (this while pouring water down the bank and seeing it percolate through the soil and disappear). More complex notions such as the water cycle and sustainability are taught in the big practical sessions such as the river and canal experience detailed elsewhere. We enjoy studying life in our ponds and this gives us the opportunity to talk about what we can to do to keep safe near bodies of water.

The children are attracted to water in all its forms. Running water has sound, bubbles and force and its volume can be altered by building dams. We link lengths of roof guttering with guttering clips to make a channel for moving water. The necessary gradient is managed by a line of chairs set in descending size order. The guttering is run across the backs of chairs so that the slope keeps the water moving. The dams are made with clay, play dough or pebbles. When the children put the pebbles into the flow of water they notice that the water flows around them and it is necessary to caulk the edges. They experiment with buoyancy using whole corks and then corks cut into sections so that they float rather than roll down the guttering. Small pieces of polystyrene packing material can also be used for demonstration. When the flow of water is turned off, the perimeter of the puddle at the end of the guttering is marked in charcoal. The greater the volume of water, the greater the area of the puddle. At the end of the session we let the children splash and play in the puddle and have fun.

Air

Investigating the properties of air always starts from the obvious aspect of breathing. We pump air into inner tubes, hold air in our lungs to a count of 12 and check chest measurements between inhaling and exhaling. We blow into balloons and bags and do many social and cooperative exercises with parachutes and sheets to see how trapped air changes the shape of its container. Lighting a camp stove to warm air in a bin liner helps us to demonstrate the lifting power of heated air. The bin liner is semi-stabilized with a hoop of cane or wire set in a hem that is taped to the opening. Some rigidity at the opening makes it easier to hold the bag over a heat source. Whenever we can during this project, we try to arrange for a hot air balloon to take off from our school field. These make a magnificent spectacle as they inflate and take off.

Flight

There is a source of fun and learning in working regularly with homing pigeons. We can get unique insights from these birds and from having the chance to come eye to eye with them and to stroke them while they are being handled by their owners or the teachers. Two or three teachers have been taught how to do this and the birds are not fazed by the children as long as the sound levels are low. Homing pigeons

are semi-tame and because of their innate instinct to return to their roosting place they often make long journeys to get home.

When the birds are released they gather in the sky and orientate themselves before departure. The experienced birds support the less experienced in this essential flocking behaviour. All birds can fly tremendous distances and for some this means journeys to and fro across continents. The stiffest feathers on their bodies are in the wings and to look at wings in detail and get first-hand evidence about feathers and flight is vital. This knowledge is absorbed by the children through repeated experience with the birds.

The children experiment with the wings of partridge, grouse and pigeons, cooling each other by moving them, creating updrafts to raise bits of paper from the floor or fanning currents of air to drive grains of rice from side to side across the room. Pulling feathers out of the wing shows how the feathers are graduated, diminishing in size from the leading edge feather and curving to reduce the drag from air moving past: this curvature of a feather is replicated in the wings of aircraft. We sterilize all the wings and feathers before the children work with them. Wing feathers cut laterally and longitudinally reveal their structure and the bracing inside the quills can be examined. Details such as these give birds the capacity and strength to fly – they have evolved for this purpose. The fringe of fine strands on a feather are hooked together by tiny barbs. Children unhook these barbs and zip them together by running their fingers up and down the length of filaments. Individual feathers are asymmetrical and in falling from a height they spiral downwards. The children can discover this by standing on kitchen steps for additional height and letting quill feathers fall: the feathers need a long drop in order to rotate.

When tiny down feathers are thrown outdoors into a breeze, they respond to air currents in a flighty way by changing direction and swirling like snowflakes in the power of the wind. To see this effect, the children go outside with handfuls of down feathers taken from old pillows. They turn their backs to the wind and on a given signal they toss the down into the air. Generally the lightest, fluffiest down travels the furthest and often out of sight. The curly feathers corkscrew downwards and sometimes a mass of falling feathers can loop again and be carried off on a sudden gust of wind.

The symmetry on a bird is illustrated by its matching halves. When a damaged feather is shed, the bird casts an exactly similar feather from its opposite side. With the combination of explanation and experience we are trying to show the children that every feather interacts with air; either to insulate or waterproof the body or in the fundamentals of flight or nest building where the birds plucks itself for a final layer of down to line its nest.

Carole used goose wing pen feathers (an early writing implement) and the children drew up and recorded a word collection of pen-related words (pen-pusher, pencil, penner, pen-name, put pen to paper, pen feather, penmanship, penknife, pen wiper etc.) and they wrote these in ink with quills.

Some of our understanding about what makes things fly comes from making paper aeroplanes and testing the designs for them. In other experiments we up-end chairs and by using two of the legs as prongs we stretch thick elastic bands between them. These simple catapults or trebuchets fire small dried clay balls or paper balls saturated in water and squeezed. When these are launched we check the distances they travel. The children notice that weight as well as shape determines how the missiles fly, and we introduce them to notions of trajectory.

The simplest way to illustrate how to check the speed of falling objects is by attaching a parachute to the object before launching it. The children select fabric to make a canopy and fold it to mark the centre of it with a permanent marker pen. They select the object they want to experiment with (a model car, a small plastic figure, a stone with a hole in it). The children know that the object should be suspended under the centre mark and tied to the edges of the fabric. At this point, they generally discard any awkward-shaped objects but sometimes modifications are made with paper clips and rubber bands.

Further adjustments are made in the light of trials; this generally involves changes in the lengths of string. Success depends on the height from which the parachute is dropped. We think the only feasible way for us to do this is from a flat roof. An adult launches every parachute one by one and repeats this three times. These tests confirm the best designs. Lengths of string, balance, weight and shape of the object and the type of fabric used will all have a bearing on the results. While carrying out this task, the teachers talk about fair testing. They give further confirmation of this when discussing results.

Ideally the learning from this project continues when the children take home their models and with their parents or carers they can launch them from their own bedroom windows. At some point during this topic, we organize a helicopter landing on the school field. We stand on the perimeter of the field until the helicopter puts down on a clearly marked base, the engine is switched off, the rotor blades stop turning and the pilot gets out. Visits are worked out in great detail and depend on weather conditions and other factors. We do not assemble until the pilot has confirmed that he has left base and our viewing of the landing and take off is strictly controlled and based on approved guidelines. Classes of children go round the helicopter and talk to the pilot in rotation. At this point the co-pilot might talk to individual classes waiting their turn.

Kite making with young children is complicated but achievable with lots of adult help. The rule is that the kites the children make have to be able to fly at the end of the day. We do not make them to be a display of decorative pennants for the classroom. The children take their kites home to work on and play with them there. When we plan to build kites, we usually link the activity with one of our termly grandparent /family days. In this way, we can angle the day towards cross-generational learning and teaching and meet an important social target.

Fire

Fire is studied in the Autumn term when there are changes in the daylight length and falling temperatures. We see how different things burn: there are noises and smells, the shapes and colours of the fire change and finally there are ashes to examine when cold. We prepare fires for each pair of classes – the children collect combustible material from our woodland areas and families contribute fuel as well. We ask for paired items from the children to put on the fire – damaged luggage, cracked walking boots, old shoes, broken roller skates or umbrellas, empty tin cans, glass containers are all ideal. We are hoping for things that are composite in construction so that when the cinders of the fires are sifted, there will be collectable remains. The pairs of items are displayed in the classrooms and the children make their predictions about what will burn and what will not burn and what other changes may be observed when one of the items is put into the fire and subjected to heat.

Even the youngest children are surprisingly accurate. Each fire is divided into two: one half for each class, and the children place their objects into the fire before it is lit. Old or broken wire baskets from supermarkets make ideal containers for the smaller objects. One of the paired objects remains in the classroom for comparison with the one that has gone into the fire. Before the fires are lit, the children make a simple oven with a biscuit tin into which they place halved potato pieces wrapped in foil. These tins need to be close to the edge of the fire because they will need raking out while the fire is still burning. The children eat the cooked and cooled potatoes with a little butter and sea salt. When the fires have died down and cooled, we sprinkle the ashes with water in order to stabilize them. The children help the teacher to sift the ashes, taking great care if glass objects were put into the fire. The remains are taken back into the classroom and compared with the control group. The children look for the effects of heat on their objects and check their findings with their earlier predictions. Sometimes this is easy: the umbrella's metal spokes and the metal centre in the roller skates are immediately recognizable. Other evidence is harder to identify, or indeed there may well be no remains. The children really enjoy this encounter with forensic science and it confirms our motives for teaching in this way. Heat is a force that wreaks irreversible change and the experiment is about safety as well as physics.

Earth: Working with clay – a case study

In describing our clay work we have tried to give the essential flavours of a big science project.

Typically we would work through two of these large-scale projects a year. Hatching eggs and learning about birds fairly well represents a medium-scale unit of work and other topics are typical of the year's planning for science. The common shared experience is basic to the programme and although meticulous planning makes for rewarding experiences, there must also be time for morale-boosting spontaneous science.

Last year, we decided that we could use clay in an extensive and collaborate science project that would also be cross-curricular in its scope. Jo, our art coordinator and Patrick, one of our science coordinators, led a staff meeting to discuss the range of opportunities that exploring clay could give to the children. It was agreed that we should resource the clay from our own grounds, that we have done many times before. This was the context for teaching about the melting rivers at the end of the Ice Age laying down the great clay beds. Over time, the silt deposits increased to great depths and in our area the dependability of the clay beds brought about a brick-making industry thousands of years later. The brick-making clay is rather coarse and models made with it cannot have workable details on them. For our purposes it is ideal because our focus is on process and on turning local geography to our advantage. We intended to fire some clay in our kiln but clay for the kiln needed to be in a purer form. We bought sufficient high-grade clay for every child to make a disc that they could fire, thread on a leather lace and take home. The properties of clay can vary and this gave the children a chance to experience contrasts in consistency and malleability.

The clay theme was divided into two parts. In the first part clay would be experienced as an art medium. On the first day, every class would have their own builders' bag (kindly given by a local business) to collect their clay. Steve, a parent who owned a digger, welcomed each group in turn, fired up his machine and cut through the strata of topsoil. Our chair of governors, Chris, pointed out the soil profile to the children in its thin layers and then the bucket of the digger was changed and the clay was gouged out and dropped into a builders' bag. With much effort the children in their class groups dragged their clay across the field to the art studio. Each bag was labelled so that when the clay was used, the children could work with the mass that they had seen extracted. These sessions were repeated until every class had observed the mechanical operation, stepped into the hole made by the clay extraction and towed their clay off site.

We needed a large art studio for the experimental stages that would surprise and inspire. A parent, Andy, offered us a marquee that he had made and a grandparent helped him to erect it. This took most of a morning and children visited and watched while a very large space was enclosed. In the first phase, geology, physics and topology were aspects of the work: the erection of the marquee was concerned with measurement, geometry, physics and area. In both cases there was a demonstration of skills – a slice of life on view involving adults other than teachers. The nature of the learning process is about the excitement of seeing things happen, making things happen and being part of the changes.

A marquee is a very outdoor facility and in keeping with the project. The extraction holes were not too far away, the builders' bags of clay were put around the tent and we were always conscious of the elements. Four days of continuous rain followed this start but it did not interrupt the project. During every session there were 60 children at work in the marquee: 30 from Key Stage 1 and Foundation stages and 30 from Key Stage 2. Occasionally there were 90 children but always in mixed age groups and with the working companionship of their teachers and 5 or 6 parent volunteers.

Jo's plan was to guarantee all children a total of four hours working with clay through handling it, squeezing it, rolling and squashing it and investigating its properties. Trestle tables were set out for maximum interaction. Children retrieved clay from their own bag and water was freely available. Part of the first hour was spent refining the clay by removing grit and vegetable matter. Water was worked into it to restore its plasticity and the mess at the end of each first session was shocking and overwhelming. This very wet first hour with each group was well worth the doing and the mess because we were able to learn about the collapse of clay into particles when it is flooded with water. It was a small-scale demonstration of how the clay travelled by water aeons ago and then settled at the location from where we had recovered it. At this stage, when slip was everywhere, the children wrote in it, made patterns, signed their names and went around to see other people's mark making. Paint scrapers were invaluable for abrading the clay-laden surfaces and restoring the status quo for the next group. As clay was scraped off the surfaces it was squashed into big balls and returned to the group's bag. The children used pieces of industrial-sized rolls of paper towels to clean themselves before leaving the marquee and in doing this, another process was observed. As the paper took up the moisture from their warm hands the clay pilled into the towel and minutes later the dried residue would come off as dust when the children clapped their hands together. After this, thinking and doing centred on the first contact with the clay and it was brought to a state of readiness for modelling. It was very wet and slack but evenly soft and satisfying so we covered it with plastic sheets and left it until next time.

When children returned for their second hour-long session and then their third session, they were supported through stages of creative modelling. They worked individually and cooperatively to make pots, dishes, skyscrapers, animals, space stations, dragons, dinosaurs, lighthouses, rocks, zoos, ships and 3D maps. One last development of football pitches and teams was the least satisfactory but with guidance this group (after heated discussions) ended up by cutting the football pitch with kitchen knives and making slab pots.

We all blocked clay, banging it together to make the texture consistent and sprayed our work with water to make slip to secure joins. To get textural effects involved pressing feathers into the surface, brush stroking with forks or combs and applying hessian strips, elbows or carpet scraps. Things such as cord, rope, links of chain and keys can develop the work a little further but the greatest joy comes from the material itself, with its tactile nature.

All the children made thumb pots from balls of clay. When they had drawn up the sides and smoothed them the adults went round with jugs of water and half filled the pots. We then challenged the children and adults to rest the pots on their heads to check the watertight quality of the pot. Following this, the sides of the pots were pinched together and collapsed so that as much water as possible was incorporated into the clay.

Scientific knowledge is built up through this personal hands-on research. It is scientific, artistic and social with partnerships across the age ranges and dialogue that focuses on the material and what is achievable with it. None of this could have worked without the unstinting help of parents and friends.

The climax for part one of the project was an Antony Gormley[3] style installation. Jo showed pictures to the children of Gormley's mass groupings and talked about how he had influenced a lot of our art work. We agreed to use this inspiration again, so we planned that everyone would contribute a figure; the children chose sheep. Exhibitions of this kind are democratic and inclusive for all levels of ability, and this makes them perfect statements of philosophy. The sheep would be installed as a mass grouping along our line of Cotswold stones and the outdoor gallery would open to the public for 2 days.

Clay is a fundamental resource invisibly present all around us. It is vital in industries such as ceramics, building, drugs and paper manufacture. It clarifies water and wine, purifies sewage and is part of plastic and rubber making. Roughly speaking, clays are grouped according to the rocks from which they originated and the distances they have travelled. Our clay bed is secondary clay and in its long journey it collected a number of impurities. This is the stuff of bricks, pipes, cement and tiles so when we are inside our building we are surrounded by it. When the children made their individual discs the clay contrasts were felt through the fingertips. The particle size of primary clay is smaller and its plasticity makes it suitable for pottery work and detailed modelling. Back in their classroom, Carol and Jane introduced their class to reverse print making. Clay slip was spread on table-tops and the children wrote their names and drew patterns and pictures in the slip. Large sheets of paper were then laid on top of the patterned slip and reverse images were seen when the paper was lifted off.

Clay museums

We needed to display examples of work that were the result of using different types of clay. Four or five times a year we open a school museum that depends on contributions from our community. These museums are organized so that they are significant contributors to any project we are exploring. Museums can integrate cultural values with facts and can be a springboard for visits to real museums later on. Borrowed objects from parents and friends were assembled and Carol and Hannah put the museum together. They used a variety of traditional hand-thrown pots, some of which were signed. The Leach family[4] were all represented and there were named stoneware items. We had Devon poetry pots and reminders of early style Coalport, Meissen and Staffordshire china. Everyday objects were included with dinner and tea plates, jugs, bone china cups and saucers and mixing bowls. Museum collections can highlight ordinary things and give them clarity and educational value.

We were given masses of pottery pieces and fractured tiles when we took a group to the site of the Roman town at Silchester. Children tried to fit together the fragments of Roman tiles and they looked at the blackened edges from the firing. This was detail from almost 2000 years ago and on one pottery shard there was a perfect thumbprint from the maker. The hands-on component was made up from historical evidence and such things as glazed tiles, quarry tiles, chimney pots, pipes and bricks of different kinds. Many were examples of bricks made in Arborfield at the ancient brick works when they were still in production. There was also an original brick mould from the same site. The museum was open for 2 days. The children had free access to objects from the building materials section and the remainder was an eyes only experience.

On the ninth and tenth working days of part one of the project, the sheep exhibition was opened. Most of the rocks had been dressed with moss by the children to represent grass and the scale of the background rock gave resonance. The children wandered about viewing the flocks of sheep that they had made in the marquee. After 2 days, the sheep exhibition was dismantled. Seeing the marquee come down, the rocks cleared of moss and the field restored was part of the whole experience.

A high consideration at this point in the project was to illustrate sustainability and recycling. Children could take home a plastic bag of school clay to make something for their own gardens if we could reconstitute their models. This would satisfy both individual needs and organizational goals because we wanted their sheep to be a constituent of the building marl for the next part of the work.

Part two of the project was intended to develop the work in a similar vein with children of different ages involved in the tasks and the workload shared between teachers and parents. Expectations about the nature of clay and how we would handle it had been partly set by the first art experience. We all gain understanding by relating what we are learning to what we already know. This time our work with clay would evolve from individually made things to one shared structure.

Ray and Patrick talked to all of us about the food and cooking traditions of indigenous peoples in Africa and South America. They described the shared bread ovens in the villages where the technology of building is learned by the less experienced as they work alongside the more experienced. We thought about the cultures that do not accept private property and would think of an oven as a community resource. We moved on to consider the sort of grains that were milled for bread, the baking method and the fuel for the oven. We made a list of the things that we would need to build an earth oven. Ray said that she would research grains and breads of different types so that oven-building groups and bread-tasting groups could see the relationship between the two interests. It was also practical to teach the groups outside where they could see each other working and move between situations. Our objective was to experience earth and clay as a building material by using it to set up a large bread oven. This needed to have sufficient capacity to bake bread for big numbers so that it was a genuine example of a shared resource. Oven building, grain studies and bread tasting would progress together until everything was ready for communal bread baking in the completed oven.

The sheep models and all the clay from the original dig were reclaimed, apart from the 500 gm per child that went home. Old bricks were donated by parents and brought to school; ballast and sharp sand were donated by a local firm of builders' merchants. We used bark chippings from the quantities regularly donated for landscaping and composting and we collected empty wine bottles for insulation purposes.

Five kilograms each of wheat, barley, oats, rye and maize seed were gifted by a local seed merchant. Parents helped us to build up a collection of pestles and mortars, hammers, chopping boards and round pebbles for grinding and crushing the seeds. We bought bread of different types: naan, challah, bagels, crisp bread, zwieback, pitta, bannocks, pumpernickel and locally baked loaves. Contrasting sorts of bread would be used each day to represent the customs and choices of a multi-cultural world.

When teaching outdoors the most irritating situations are the ones where plastic groundcovers, papers and lightweight cloths get lift-off in the breeze. Good presentation makes the work visually attractive, speeds up its delivery and clearly identifies the focal points. We used a large and heavy groundsheet as a group base and a thick linen tablecloth for the bread baskets, loaves and breadboards.

Mindful about everyone having equal chances to contribute to the plan, a timetable was drawn up. Plans of earth ovens had been referred to and adapted until we felt we had a pattern we could follow. During planning meetings we had all agreed that we were working a trial and error approach and that if we mastered oven construction and bread making and baking, then the project had served us well. Setting the expectations for the children was at the heart of the work.

We needed to get children experiencing some of every kind of work and to make casual but regular visits to see the rest of the workforce in action. This would be the means of adjusting their view about the plan in progress and the techniques being used. There is value to the imagination in seeing a task you have undertaken also being carried on by others: watching people at work is a way of organizing our thinking. As teachers we tend to be suspicious of children watching the action. We tell them to get on and do something or to remind them that they will get another turn later. The truth is that they need to watch but without drawing attention away from the core activities. Shared access has to be controlled but flexible with a clearly marked boundary for viewers that can be moved to suit the work. In this vital observing and hypothesizing situation the position of the supervising adults needs clarification. They are responsible to the teachers managing the action, for seeing that the job gets done and that the observers play their part. The disruptive influence of too much sound in the background and from the non-supportive adult or child is very difficult to sort out; effective communication at the start of each project helps.

In every circumstance we try to recognize the negative sides of our schemes and styles of work. This helps us to agree our actions within the scope of our philosophy, for instance when we meet the consequences of the disruptive behaviour just described. The options might be to exercise power to prevent free access to the work site; to require groups to visit with clipboards and govern their responses; to timetable access in order to limit the size of visiting groups; to allow access when the site is inactive; and to revise the terms of reference with staff about the range of behaviour that raises concerns but agree that we do not skate past the problems. Clearly this is all about agreed organizational structure.

We also recognize the positive sides to our style of work and it is clear to all that the most successfully participating groups are those that have benefited from a comprehensive briefing prior to arriving on site to work. Teachers might take 5 min to remind the children of the significance of the project and discuss their personal contributions. They might speculate on the progress since their last visit and reaffirm the importance of commitment to the project. In this way, the appetites of the children are whetted and the expectations of the teachers are made clear. Groups of children prepared in this way tend to approach the work eagerly, positively and focused.

When groups are working with trial and error approaches and using the actual work as a scientific investigation, creative energies are high. Talk about the value to children of innovative and creative thinking has been slowly creeping back into our educational system, possibly a result of reaction to test-driven routines with very narrow measurable objectives. The science work described draws on ordinary abilities creatively charged. It is in working with non-standard approaches, persevering when things get tough, cooperating, remembering, talking and listening, noticing, thinking imaginatively and being open to change – all these traits are more likely to evolve in the context of this type of work. The traits are familiar ones but in conjunction with opportunity they can stimulate a person towards fresh thinking and unconventional solutions. Everybody is creative in some degree.

Time is valuable and limited so every project is planned to make the best use of it. With parent help and help from governors, we anticipated completing the work and firing up the oven for a batch bake in six working days. The timetable ensured that every child had three working visits of 80 min each. There would be 60 children at work outside: 20 would work on the bread and grain study, 20 would work on the production of mortar and 20 would work on the construction of the oven. The children would rotate through these activities. There was open access and high visibility with everything on show throughout the workshops. The working area was defined by a bark chip zone and the viewing areas were outside this. Every time a new group of children came to work, Patrick and Ray would orientate the group. The children sat on ground sheets, listened to descriptions of the work and were given assurances about being able to try every skill.

On the first day the children gathered for the orientation briefing. Two different types of building mortar were required and we were going to pound this adobe with our feet until we got the required consistency. The insulating mortar was to be a mix of earth, clay, bark chip and water and the building mortar was to be a mix of earth, sand, clay and water. The large builders' merchants bags were our mixing vessels and the children measured the constituents for the mortar with buckets. There were four bags for each mortar type. Two children and an adult or three children got into each bag and mashed the contents with their feet. This method of mixing adobe has been used for centuries because it maximizes pressure needed to blend the ingredients. We told the children how indigenous people scoop a bowl out of the ground to make these adobe mixtures. We explained to them that the moving weight delivered force through the feet that their hands could not manage. The children stored the produced mortar in plastic bins for later use.

The children were also given the task of cleaning approximately 300 high-quality second-hand bricks. Wearing goggles and gloves, the children scoured the bricks with wire brushes to restore them.

The need to build a foundation for the oven was explained and tools were laid out for the job. Patrick described the difference between sand and ballast, safety codes to be observed in handling materials and rods, and a rotational pattern of tasks to ensure the sharing of experiences. He read a list of specialist terms in relation to materials and techniques and these were displayed in prominent positions. Running over the teaching points and summarising the progress expected got everyone thinking about what they would be doing and how they should be doing it. To save time this briefing was given to both class groups and then one group immediately started on the earth/clay oven activities.

Attention in the third group was focused on a bunch of mixed grasses with seed heads. We described seeds found in the graves of early peoples. The children were given scissors to cut their own bunches of seeded grasses from the margins of the school field. They returned with the grasses to the area that we had prepared for the bread and grain study. Ray and Sarah stripped seed heads and showed the gluten in the centre of each seed by milling the seeds between two round stones. The children did the same and the crushed seed heads were put in a saucepan with a little water. The water was heated over a camping gas stove and stirred constantly. While this porridge thickened we plaited grass stalks to see if we could make containers for seeds. When the porridge was ready it was tasted. Ray explained that a Neolithic tribe might have mixed the softened grain with other foods to make it tastier. Early people relied on grains just as we do and many of the grains our ancestors ate were the smaller wild versions of the ones grown as farm crops today.

Sarah took the children in groups to find wild oats. We compared wild oats and the oats from a cultivated crop, barley from the verges and from the farm and we examined the rye grass and rye bread. We learned that the grains come from grasses when they seed and that the plant family of grasses provide us with cereals. Flour for the bread comes from the centre of grains and we had all been able to identify it. We ate the rye bread and shared some wholegrain granola.

This experience of seed gathering and what followed was given to each group before or after they helped to lay the foundations for the clay oven. In this way, 60 children experienced the technical building side of the work as well as the practical botanical element. There were constant adaptations to suit different age groups. Meanwhile, the clay oven was inching forward and the briefing Patrick and Ray held with the groups changed slightly every hour.

When the next 60 children arrived, the measuring and the chore of digging, removing soil and barrowing it away was complete. The talk was about a clean, clear site that had to be maintained for safety and efficiency. Explanations about the dimensions of the footings in relation to the top structure were given and there were descriptions of the next work stages. Children stood in the foundations and thought about methods of bringing loads of ballast to the hole and tamping it flat, checking horizontal quality with spirit levels and collecting and stacking bricks in preparation for laying them as a flat course for the next part of the base. Before the groups dispersed to work, more technical terms were displayed.

Our experience so far was helping us to be more effective and the children were enjoying the variety of learning. At the briefing session the children were asked about the ballast foundation. Several children pointed out that the sand between the stones was soft and that it might move. Others considered the piles of bricks and said that we ought to spread them around the ballast to hold the weight of the oven. The children themselves had identified the problem and the solution. We would set the bricks horizontally across the ballast and make a floor for the structure. The level was crucial: spirit levels were needed for every brick and more importantly, for the whole floor. The children were shown how to use lengths of wood to balance the spirit levels and how to set the bricks in place.

While one group started the grasses examination the rest devoted themselves to mortar production and construction. This was one of those times when we heard Jerome Bruner's[5] words in our head: 'An educator's task is to stir things up'. Progress in building the floor could not have been achieved without competent adults working alongside the children. When the groups changed over there was still a lot to do. The value of this work is that it is not contrived to fit specific curriculum objectives. Practical physical work in a learning group of mixed ages resonates with the philosophy of John Dewey[6] and with the theory and practice of Reggio Emilia.[7]

The welcome and the introduction to the site followed the same principles with every group. On the second day, everyone arrived wearing boots and prepared for more strenuous work. At the end of this day the clay oven was starting to have physical presence on its base and all the children in the school had worked on both parts of the project. After school, the teachers met to discuss levels of participation and to think about progress so far. There were very few mistakes and only one erratic time when enthusiasm became competitive and the two mortar producing groups stopped communicating effectively. We paused for a few moments to consider the issue and when we restarted, progress continued without further antagonism. Generally we were pleased with the enthusiasm and pace of the work.

The following day we changed the grains workshop to provoke more and different thoughts about cereals. We used cornflakes, corn on the cob and cornbread for tasting and we hammered individual kernels from the cobs and compared them with the breakfast cereal flakes. We rolled and pounded oats, tasted oat bread and oat biscuits and everyone helped themselves to a spoonful of rolled oats and ate them dry. We analysed two brands of muesli for the oat content and finally scattered some of the various cereals we had used around the school grounds. Ray suggested that these grain deposits should be checked early the next day.

In the other part of the study the expanding vocabulary continued to be clearly displayed and the children read the technical terms before moving off to their tasks. Children squashed and squeezed mortar with their feet until it had the consistency of putty from which bricks were then shaped.

The foundations and a circular brick base one metre high with a diameter of one metre were finished and the children back filled the empty cylinder with sand and stone. The materials were continually compacted and the children reminded that this structure would have to bear the weight of the clay oven and the mass of mortar they had prepared in readiness for this. Attention then turned to the top layer on which we would position the hearth. Following guidance from Denzer[8] the children had cleaned 30 bricks reclaimed from a Victorian fireplace in readiness for the laying of the bread-baking surface. The children took a great deal of care with this process. They appreciated that they were laying the floors on which fires would burn and transmit heat to the bricks. The principles of thermal conservation and loss were discussed and a layer of bottles was set below the hearth to improve insulation in the oven.

In turn, every boy and girl brought sand to the dome, pressing it into the contours until the profile grew bell-shaped and very firm. The building mortar that had been shaped into bricks was laid around the edges of the sand dome. Children painstakingly began to raise the level of the oven using the sand dome as a proforma for setting their bricks. On the fourth day, the combination of tasks on the clay oven had been working well. The children continued to mix two kinds of mortar and use it for building. Having built the base and hearth the functioning centre part had to be put in. At this critical point during the building, Patrick gathered 60 of us round the adobe construction. He explained that we would need to visualize our heat source: a fierce fire burning in the oven. He gave us time to get a picture of this in our mind's eye. During the briefing sessions we were frequently reminded that our oven was going to be similar to a wood-burning kiln. The children were asked what a fire needed and there were many responses: 'air', 'fuel', 'time to get going', 'flammable material', 'nothing that makes heavy smoke', 'it shouldn't be explosive things', 'it's got to be fiery and make lots of heat', 'we can't use starter fuel: it's got to be clean', 'a floor for a burning fire'. The children were then asked to think about the internal shape of the oven. During the planning stages, the children found out that it needed to be round, with no cold spots, constant temperature front and back, easy to stoke, safe to get the bread out and built to keep heat in.

We were going to represent the volume inside the oven with a sphere of sand and use it as a pattern. The children collected sharp sand and then shaped and compacted it until it became a very large orb at the top of the structure. The measuring, consulting the diagram, standing away from the work to study the coming together of the shape, the scraping of distortions and the adding of sand needed a high degree of perseverance. It also needed a degree of imagination to visualize this reverse space, as the sand would act as a former for the oven walls and would be excavated once a satisfactory form was achieved.

Having checked that the children remembered the general principle, Patrick and some helpers inserted a large arch into the structure. A substantial pipe was used for this and children laid conventional bricks around this form. These bricks were used to define the arch and to provide a framework for the oven door. They were fixed in place with the clay mortar. Work accomplished during each day relates to the activities of 120 children following procedures outlined earlier. By this time, every child had been part of the project for two and a half hours with one session to come.

On the morning of the fifth day, the adults met early on the site. The bread and grains workshops had been reorganized for the final 2 days of the project. There remained many types of bread in the freezer that had not been tasted so there was work to do there. Ray and Sarah had always been hopeful that we would find time to do a breadcrumb trail for the youngest children in school. They were also considering how we could offer toast: they felt that the children needed to do a taste comparison between the toasted bread and ordinary bread but time did not allow this. We agreed that the crumb trail was possible because we could get free stale bread from a local supermarket.

An adapted plan was made for the younger children to have their experience of trail laying and then experience it again as trail finders. Breads that had not been introduced would be the focus of the last 2 days. Every child would be given a plate on which there were seven varieties in equal portions. Small groups of six children with an adult would talk about what they saw in the bread, what their noses told them about each sample and finally, after they had eaten each square, what their mouths told them about the bread. Articulating a view is important developmentally and as a member of a group of six there would be greater opportunities for this.

Building the operational part of the oven was an act of faith. We pointed out that the ability to research theoretically was one sort of skill the children would develop but practical knowledge was flexible and allowed changes to plan. Since we had no experience we would need to follow the design plan to the letter even if we were unable to complete the work on time. Although we were following a design, it was still a research project.

When the children met for the briefing session, we referred to our roles as researchers and explained that we could not be 'wrong' in our building work but that work only became skilled after much practice. We needed to continue to build with the same amount of care because there were no margins of error for us as beginners.

It was now time for the children to build the oven walls. They had built the base, hearth and oven space and had produced the mortar to enclose the space in a mass of earth that had the potential to hold heat. The children first shaped the insulating mortar containing organic matter and air into ten centimetre sausages and pressed them edge to edge over the sand dome. This was a crucial point in the construction, as the placing of each earth sausage was accompanied by discussion about the strength of the combined materials, their ability to adhere to each other and speculation about the capacity to insulate and contain heat. When the 10-cm-thick insulating layer was completed, other groups of children repeated the operation with a 10-cm layer of plain mortar, containing only sand, clay and water.

On the final day, the briefing session was about reaching through the oven door and clearing the sand from the interior. It was necessary to remove all of this by hand while imagining the space to be cleared and picturing the dome of clay as like an eggshell. We were excavating a rotunda. It had partly dried but it would be delicate and could collapse. The children scooped out all the sand they could and adults finished the job.

Our project had caused some environmental deterioration. Rakes, spades, wheelbarrows and bins were available and we asked the children to look critically at the whole site and to restore it to order.

We used all the remaining mortar to reinforce the base of our construction. This was then decorated by the Nursery children with older children providing approval and support. Shells and beads were pressed into the clay and finally the whole thing was declared ready to bake bread.

On bread-baking day the children decided to make small white and brown loaves and they prepared their own dough. Chris's group made their dough out of doors and improvised a proving oven by using the sun's rays to heat air in a raised polythene garden frame. All the children collected kindling and a fire was set inside the oven. As soon as the kindling got blisteringly hot (and this took quite a time) the fire was stoked with oak off-cuts. Bellows were used to increase the airflow to the fire and children came to watch the progress through the morning. At a safe distance, the children watched as the burning wood was raked from the fire: this fell on a sheet of iron placed there to hold it while it was turned to charcoal. Clouds of smoke and steam were raised when the burning pile was watered and moments later, the charcoal was shovelled into a wheelbarrow lined with sand. The remnants of the fire were smothered with more sand and wheeled away to a barricaded area.

Only a limited number of children get a really good view of the dramatic bits unless the teachers moved their groups to new positions at a signal and the children rotated around the action. Equal opportunities require good organization – it fosters harmony and encourages safety.

The children brought their batches of dough to the oven. Using a spade as a peel, Patrick slid the loaf tins across the brick floor until the oven was full. An oven door had been made to measure, and this was then tapped into the aperture.

We estimated that the bread would take one and a half hours to cook and that it would be ready to share and eat towards the end of the school day. The bread was tested at 2.15 p.m., 2.30 p.m. and 2.45 p.m. Finally, with everyone gathered around, the loaves were removed from the oven. The teachers carried the loaf tins to the field, the children sat in class circles, the loaves were broken and shared. The bread tasted good because we had made it and we were determined to enjoy it. Objectively, it was still slightly spongy and the crusts had a reddish tint suggesting under-proved dough. Eaten in small quantities it proved the point. We had made a working oven and we had cooked bread in it. Other bread was cooked and enjoyed at later dates and we found that smaller amounts of dough gave better results although this would mean a reduced portion size.

We did not envisage a long life for the oven. Our focus was on working together as a whole school in a multifaceted and multi-sensory approach to learning. We felt that the entire operation was satisfying and enjoyable, judging by the attitudes of children who were taking part.

Notes

1. J. A. Comenius. *The School of Infancy* (edited with an introduction by E.M. Eller). University of North Carolina Press: Chapel Hill, 1998.
2. Jerome Bruner, 1915: American psychologist who has made a profound contribution to our understanding the process of education and the development of curriculum theory.
3. Antony Gormley, 1950: English sculptor specializing in large-scale installations and most famous for his *Angel of the North* sculpture outside Gateshead UK (1998) www.antonygormley.com
4. Leach family: Leach Family Ceramics. Lowerdown Pottery. www.ceramike.com
5. Jerome Bruner. See Note 2. Also noted for social studies programme Man – A Course of Study (MACOS) 1970 that emphasizes the benefits of a spiral curriculum.
6. See Chapter 5, Note 13.
7. Reggio Emilia. Educational philosophy focused on preschool and primary education. Started by Loris Malaguzzi and parents in the Reggio Emilia area of Italy after the Second World War.
8. K. Denzer. *Build Your Own Earth Oven,* 3rd edition. Handprint Press: Oregon, 2007. www.handprintpress.com

7 Curriculum I

Planning and organization

Our curriculum responds to the time of year and to the cycle of festivals and celebrations in the Christian, Hindu, Sikh, Buddhist, Jewish and Islamic faiths as well as to secular events (planting, harvest, winter as a time of decay, death and waiting for new life to begin again) that are calendar related. In addition to this, we are influenced in our curriculum planning by what is happening in the school's outdoor environment and whatever current topic we are following is also central to the idea of making learning visible. As a state sector school we follow the guidelines of the National Curriculum involving different starting points.

Planning is a group exercise in which everyone is involved and ideas are brainstormed at our staff meetings (whole school and in team meetings for the different Key Stages). During the course of the week, the children will have a daily literacy and mathematics session: at Key Stage 1 (Infant), these are not usually discreet sessions: four mornings a week will see elements of literacy and numeracy being taught alongside other curriculum areas (e.g. art and craft, drama, history, geography). For instance, when our potato crop is ready, the children will go out with their teachers to harvest the tubers. Food technology and science will involve the making of soup, bread and cakes while a maths strand will involve the grading of the crop into different sets based on size and the weighing of the potatoes. The literacy element will involve the writing and following of recipes to use at school and then take home, as well as rhyme ('One potato, two potato . . .') and story. The re-enactment of the Irish Potato Famines of the mid-nineteenth century will take us into history while the story of the discovery of the potato in Americas and its arrival in our country in the sixteenth century will involve us in both history and geography. Our art work may involve the making of potato figures or potato prints on fabric and paper.

Also at Key Stage 1, four afternoons a week are given over to subject teaching and the children will have sessions for science, information and communication technology, reading and appreciation of text, music, drama and physical education. The children are grouped into mixed ability age bands for these sessions, so that there is an automatic differentiation in the teaching style and level of language being used. Children who can deal with accelerated learning are well catered for in a thematic approach: much of the knowledge acquired comes from action taken in relation to the situation. This tends to strengthen thinking and improve levels of language.

There are specialized terms needed to describe materials and actions taken with them and there are better possibilities for more able children to think laterally. It is also a way to understanding complexity because the topics examined are never finished. Children begin to understand that we learn from shifting focuses where we do as much work around them as we can and then develop a new theme. The problem-solving, creating and practice of skills changes in relationship to the stimulus, just like life. Practical exploration presents a problem that is in large part solvable and the children see the visual evidence of this. Special needs provision for children who may need additional support is given within the sessions by extra adults working with individuals or small groups. The children are not usually removed from the sessions for support work. One teacher will take responsibility for a specific subject, and for PE and music there is a curriculum specialist

At Key Stage 2 (Junior) level, literacy and numeracy are most often taught in one hour blocks during the mornings, along with a daily morning session of phonics, spelling and grammar. There is a different organizational style at Key Stage 2 – one teacher takes responsibility for the teaching of all subjects to an age-banded class, although this system is beginning to change since the amalgamation of the two schools. We are currently exploring different curriculum delivery and organizational approaches at Key Stage 2 and it could be that there will be more similarity between these two key stages in the future.

The National Curriculum requirements form our baseline of what the children should be taught, although the impact of the Rose Report[1] and the Primary National Strategy[2] will perhaps make the taught curriculum more fluid and less content driven in the future and lead to a more cross-curricular and skills approach. The huge content of the Key Stage 2 National Curriculum requirements tends to put many teachers off adopting a less subject-driven style of work, and means less flexibility, innovation or creativity. The pressures of the end of Key Stage 2 Standardized Assessment Tests (SATs) has led in many instances to teaching becoming results-oriented and based on 'teaching for test'. There has been much less room for teacher or child initiative and a much more mechanistic approach. Bringing about change, and freeing up the curriculum and teachers so that it and they are more child-centred and less subject and content driven, will be a longer term process. We are convinced that happy children learn better and that happy teachers teach better.

Pulling two schools together to make one can and does bring about anxiety and uncertainty for all. People tend to be apprehensive of change, questioning of the motives for it and reluctant to leave behind the familiar. As the two parts of the school grow together and become more similar to each other we find that it is the big 'learning adventures' that make change possible and even desirable.[3] Our overall themes aim to be dramatic and exciting. They tend to make the children more active and independent in their learning and they are based on an 'authentic' curriculum which has meaning and relevance for the children, augmenting the fixed National Curriculum of knowledge to be learned. The themes are not less academic for being enjoyable and motivating and each will have been very carefully planned to ensure curriculum balance and coverage.

Mathematics

Approaches

Our way of teaching mathematics at both Foundation Stages and at Key Stage 1 is based very much on games and active tasks where there is some fun in learning. We aim to make maths exciting both in a cerebral way and through physical activity. Jean Melrose, a former Mathematics Lecturer[4] at Reading University once remarked to us that for young children, the teaching of mathematics tended to mean that the teacher was 'driving fast and having a foot on the accelerator'. Many children failed to grasp the next level as it was introduced because there was little or no time for consolidation. As a result children either get stuck at the lower levels or absorb the drills and remain unenlightened. Many of our colleagues remarked that they had moved away from maths after completing the necessary GCSE course saying, 'Thank God I've done with that!!'

The assimilation of and the ability to use mathematical concepts need to be more dependent on practice, concrete experience, consolidation and real enjoyment. Maths calls for lots of good teaching to turn it into a popular and fascinating subject. Currently bright and able children often channel their studies to avoid being transfixed by a fear of it. Fear of maths is commonplace and suggests that teachers need to try new and different approaches to the subject and focus particularly on tasks where the outcomes are jointly discovered and talked through.

Symbols on paper can represent the mathematical conclusions that the children have made and these are easy to mark. In moving too quickly to the system of mathematical symbols we put up barriers to mathematical understanding. Speaking aloud the reasons for setting out mathematical arrays is a rehearsal and preparation for clearer thinking. Sometimes we need to hear ourselves stumble towards meaning in order to get clarity of thought. Logical thinking and precise language are needed for steady mathematical progress. It seems to us that in acquiring the skills described, children must vocalize their thinking. Teachers can then identify the next teaching steps from the way that the children represent their ideas.

Calculating Competence

Many years ago, we moved away from using Maths Scheme books at Key Stage 1 and into a well thought out problem-solving approach. Games and logic work would be devised to support the plan to give children more confidence in dealing with maths. We felt that we needed our children to be able to calculate mentally, recall number facts within a few seconds and apply their knowledge of number. Our evaluations of the number programmes of commercial mathematics schemes appeared to concentrate unduly on the teaching of written methods of calculation and that children's use of creative mental strategies was part of an unrecognized ability.

We were attracted to Ian Sugarman's[5] programme 'Calculating Competence' that gave the children ample opportunities to become confident mathematicians with high levels of understanding of the subject through a games approach. Sugarman says that the emphasis upon mental calculation means that there should be a greater concentration on developing 'a feeling for number' than with written computational exercises. Because this feeling for number implies an instinctive understanding of mathematical abilities it tends to be accompanied by a facility for operating on numbers in a range of problem-solving contexts.

Many children do not progress beyond purely counting-based strategies for solving arithmetical problems. It is necessary therefore to focus their attention regularly on the wide range of ways to reach solutions. Sometimes these strategies are invented by pupils from their own creative instincts and sometimes they are borrowed from others. They rarely arise from what is commonly regarded as direct teaching but rather, adapted because they make sense to the individual concerned. Calculating Competence tactics are designed to make efficient strategies of mental models inherent in the brain.

Kriss Turner,[6] then a lecturer at Bulmershe College (now part of Reading University) inspired us to focus on intelligent guesswork and the need for teachers to respect individual children's approaches to problem solving. She emphasized the importance of understanding how children arrived at their judgments and the need to get them to talk about how they reached their answers or guesses. In this approach the teacher jumps straight to asking the children for their schemes rather than remarking the 'right' answer. The nearly correct answer is not a wrong answer; it is a route to the correct answer. The National Numeracy Strategy[7] also encouraged much more of a games and analytical approach to the teaching and learning of mathematics, with less emphasis on the abstract and a focus on the children's frameworks for calculating mentally so that their thinking becomes apparent.

Our mathematics curriculum at Key Stage 1 and increasingly at Key Stage 2 is influenced by the current theme as well as by our outdoor environment. All of our themes and whole school learning adventures and topic work will have a mathematics element for the teachers to draw on in their planning. Underpinning all this are the guidelines of the National Curriculum for Mathematics and the National Numeracy Strategy.

Playground designs

It was Jean Melrose[8] who many years ago inspired us to paint maths games from around the world on the playground, among them Nine Man's Morris, pong hau ki, fox and geese, the Schlegel diagram, muterere, achi and a range of simple grids. These games were used for formal lessons outside and then informally by the children at playtime. We noticed that the children were making up their own games and sets of often complex rules, as well as playing the games they had learned during their maths sessions.

All the games encouraged logical thinking and planning ahead strategies. Our counters were tins of vegetables that could not be easily knocked over or blown by the wind and these were stored in wheel-along trolleys donated by a local supermarket. Jean then went on to paint smaller versions of the games onto vinyl mats using acrylic paints. This meant that the games could also be played indoors in the classrooms or spread out en masse in the school hall. Even smaller versions were photocopied onto A4 sheets so that the children could take the games to play at home with the family.

The Key Stage 1 playground is painted with a variety of mathematical designs and games from across the world, and the children use these in formal teaching sessions as well as in their free play. Number trails are often set up in the school grounds and it is standard practice to see children engaged in specific mathematical learning out of doors. The one hundred square which is painted in the playground is big enough to accommodate a whole class of children at a time, and we use the children themselves as counters to reveal number patterns (e.g. stand on the even numbers: what do you notice?) and multiplication patterns (e.g. what pattern emerges from multiplying by 5?). For this work, we divide the children into two groups: one group will act as the counters on the hundred square and the other group of children will be observing and checking for emerging mathematical patterns. We often use carpet tiles that fit inside each square, as markers in order for the children to see patterns: these can be removed to reveal the hidden numbers and this can develop into Pelman based games.[9]

The counterpart to the permanent one hundred squares in the playground is our set of 0–100 separately numbered squares. These are rubber backed carpet tiles, 25 cm squares of identical colour on which the numbers are painted. They are very good teaching aids if the detail is accurate. Each number symbol must be of equal height and thickness and positioned with precision in the square. The predictable patterns of number can be recognized when the alignment of painted numbers has proportional spacing and every tile can form part of a whole number sequence. These sets of tiles can be used as number lines set down in ascending or descending order and that when placed in a 0–100 line can be walked as a pathway in say odd or even numbers: the children break their step with a jump over each odd or even number.

The children can also lay out the tiles in rows of, say, four, placing each row of tiles directly under the corresponding row above. In this way the children get a very clear idea of the four times table and can visualize it as a pattern of continuous addition. The number line can also zig-zag in lines of ten, change course in lines of twenty or in whatever way the teacher plans. The manoeuvrability of the carpet tiles means that the tiles offer child directed opportunities for exploring mathematics. The tiles have potential to lay the foundations for a reliable understanding of the way in which numbers have constancy and can be reorganized for day-to-day exploration.

Carpet tiles or rubber-backed felt squares marked with numbers are available commercially but in our experience these are less satisfactory than our home-made versions. We make sure that all our tiles are the same colour, but in commercial sets the tiles are randomly coloured: this detracts from the children's understanding of number patterns. We have also found that the commercial brands tend to be lighter weight and shift easily as the children walk on them and they deteriorate more quickly.

Using natural resources

Autumn harvest time brings us a wealth of resources for exploring mathematics: crab apples can be gathered and strung on wire in groups of ten; conkers can be collected in singles, set of ten, sets of a hundred, and sets of a thousand; leaves can be arranged in size order or shape order; cooking apples can be weighed for a range of recipes. All will involve the children in mathematical thinking and exploration.

Pip counting and working out the average number of pips in an apple always intrigues the children. We collect windfall apples or pick from one of our trees and then cut the fruits in two horizontally. The children are given toothpicks to scrape out the pips from their apples and count them. The children then place sets of pips from each apple in groups of ten (for ease of counting) on clear sticky back plastic. The display can then be read as a maths statement. The children are next helped to count up the total number of seeds and the total number of apples. Following this the teacher helps the children to calculate the average number of pips in the apples collected by the group. The total number of pips is divided by the number of apples. Results are collected from each class and by using a calculator a whole school result of the average number of pips in each apple is reached. Every year we confirm that the average is 7 pips.

In September, the children are encouraged to bring conkers into school. In the classroom, the children and their teachers share the wonder of seeing the nuts in the unopened case being revealed for the first time. This is the start of a huge collection project in which everyone is involved. As the collections of conkers arrive in the classroom they are tipped into a large basket labelled 'singles'. Some children are possessive of their horde and immediately start counting their own finds but they are usually persuaded to add their collection to that of the group. Another container is placed beside the singles basket and this is marked 'tens'. Carefully checked and sealed bags of ten conkers go into this. There is always someone who announces that there are ten bags of ten and at this point, a third container is added marked 'hundreds'. We usually reach the thousands, and by this stage all the children have been involved in some way with the progression of the place order of quantity and easily remember the left to right arrangement of the receptacles. The horse chestnut is not an indigenous tree and we eventually get rid of the dry conkers by putting them in our November fires and the ash is spread on the gardens.

In the Spring term, children go outside to estimate the number of daffodils in bud and to work out approximately how many flowers may be collected by each child for a Mothers' Day bouquet so that everyone has a fair share. Everything has its uses; over the years we have scattered small rounded pebbles in different parts of our school grounds. We can then get the children to collect these, knowing that they will reliably find some. We use typing corrector fluid to paint on numbers or mathematical operation symbols (e.g. +, −, ×, =). The children are attracted to these natural materials: they enjoy the physical activity involved in collecting them and they like working with them. There is something satisfying for the children (and adults) about holding a pebble in the hand, or counting out bundles of small sticks cut from our willows or estimating the number of recently gathered pinecones in a basket. We believe that it is vital to manage the environment for these types of resource and it is important to ensure that the supply is constantly available.

Understanding our number system

Children initially use base ten on trust because it is familiar. They absorb some of the knowledge of this from the environment as well as from the teaching. Everyone can learn by rote without needing to acquire an understanding of the system. Hurrying children through their learning without the pleasure of practising, consolidating and being creative can rob the children of real understanding of our number system. Sparked by the children's practical work with Dienes base ten materials, June challenged a class to invent a new numbering system. The class was made up of 5 and 6 year olds of mixed ability. The stimulus came from a crop of peas that the children picked from their garden. They thought that a numbering system could be worked around the number of peas in a pod. A single pea was seen as more of a unit than say a cabbage or a parsnip and at the time was available as a school crop. Each child was given a pod of peas to open and eat, but the average was calculated first. This was found to be six and that number was named 'pod'. A single was 'pea', next came 'ped' followed by 'pen', after that 'pep' then 'pet' and then of course, 'pod'.

Discovering from a parent that the plant on which the peas grew was in some areas of the country known as the 'rice' at the stage it was removed from the fields, this was the word the children chose to represent the number pod multiplied by pod. The number following pet pod pet became known as 'rice'. Pod multiplied by pod became 'rice', rice multiplied by rice became 'sack', and sack multiplied by sack became 'load'. The children stopped there and at various times in the day they challenged each other with questions based on the system they had invented. One boy who had some difficulty playing word games and decoding text discovered that he could manage this number system better than the rest of the class. This was a great boost to his self-esteem. We did not use our system seriously or for very long, but its invention went some way towards helping children's understanding of our conventional base ten number structure.

Sorting and setting

The materials we use in school carry ideas beyond what is aimed at in the teaching. Among our school's mathematics resources there are boxes of buttons, collections of patches and badges such as chevrons wings and logos from uniforms, different types of spoon, shells, keys and textiles cut into a range of shapes of the same size. We give the children time to explore and play with the collections before they use skills more formally as tools for understanding mathematical concepts. Contextually rich manipulatives from everyday life are prime assets in teaching sorting and setting, size ordering, equivalence, matching, one-to-one correspondence, classifying and place value.

The quality of the teacher guided talk and the way in which the teacher listens to the children for evidence of where they are in their understanding, is fundamental to the abstractions and understanding that should arise from the children's use of any mathematical models. This is equally the case when commercial apparatus is the focus for particular work. It is the teacher dialogue with the child that moves each child on in his or her thinking.

Children's discussions about their reasons for grouping or sub-setting tends to be clarified at a deeper level when dealing with the variations in everyday things. Children naturally use a mathematical framework to describe size, shape and number but they can give sensory or personal grounds for determining parts of their arrangement – 'it's nice to hold', 'smells new', 'is shiny', 'makes a nice sound when you tap it', 'feels precious'. These types of classification made against these evaluations are idiosyncratic and valid. Having a voice and a point of view in your own learning is vital because involved children feel better about themselves and dream bigger dreams of themselves. Vygotsky[10] talks about the importance of this type of imaginative thinking and describes fantasy as the means by which children can develop abstract thoughts.

Subsequent ordering objects by personal preference can lead into data handling and market research methods. Grouping keys or buttons into sets of the same number provides a foundation for continuous addition and an understanding of multiplication. Some of these objects photocopy really well and when their size is reduced, a set of ten lots of three keys or buttons for instance, can easily fit on an A4 sheet that can go home at the end of the day for more practice. Sharing learning connects school and home and vice versa. The opportunity for the children to 'read out' what they have done is crucial. The mathematical talk concerning the attributes is the basis for the children's development and the teacher or parent being able to sequence the ongoing activities.

The organizing, interpreting and presenting information about sorting and setting in any subject area is personal. The children put into words their reasons for the combinations they have made. The listening teacher gets a clear briefing about the child's point of view and sees the direction the teaching will take. The materials used by the children may have nostalgic links to home or the everyday. At another level the materials may be structured to bring about a searching examination of shape, colour, size and thickness to determine the mathematical relationships between the pieces. This relational study is the basis for Diene's Logic Blocks design. An introductory exercise might involve a whole group of children coming to a circle where they sit down beside two logic blocks. The teacher starts a pattern from her supply, thinking aloud as she puts the shapes into a sequence: 'This sequence needs a small, thin red triangle. Her strategy draws on the children's tendency to hold their two pieces and play with them as they listen.'

Big Trak

Big Trak was one of the first programmable toys and it appealed to us because at the time these toys were outside the children's usual experience. Big Trak responded to a series of instructions programmed in through a large keypad and it required systematic and logical thinking to operate it successfully. The children could send it simply forwards or backwards by pressing the arrow keys and could make it travel further by programming in the number of the machine's body lengths they wanted it to move: one length of Big Trak equated to the number 1 being pressed.

We set the children challenges down corridors, in the classrooms and in the school hall. From a given starting point, the children needed to estimate the distance between a treasure set at an opposite end of the room and programme in the number of lengths forward they felt were needed for Big Trak to 'collect' the treasure and then return to them. Sometimes we would add interest by dressing Big Trak up; for instance, the machine could be dressed as Little Bo Peep with a bonnet and stick taped to it and Bo Peep would have to go and rescue a toy sheep set at the other end of the room. The children often worked together in pairs or small groups and helped each other: there was good calibre talk between them and a lot of cooperation.

With practice, the children learned how to programme the machine to turn right and left as well as forwards and backwards and could get it to pass through a grid laid out on the floor with masking tape making right and left turns and moving forwards and backwards. The older children later wrote down the programme they had keyed into the machine.

Big Trak is still widely available along with a range of other programmable toys suitable for use in schools and they remain very popular with the children.

Logic track

Wyn proposed a logic track in the playground. A series of pathways were marked and were wide enough for comfortable walking from one path to another. A set of junctions was planned that allowed children time to make their decisions without trapping the people following into a long wait. Distances between junctions were trialled on chalk drawn plans set on the playground. This was walked by the children and then analysed, broken up and drawn many times before its course was agreed and painted. Traffic cones at each junction held laminated cards that displayed the decisions and the cards were threaded with elastic for speedy changes. Negative and positive directions were used. For instance, the first decision junction would be marked 'girl' and 'not girl'. At the second junction it would be 'sandals' and 'not sandals'. At the third junction it would be 'T shirt' and 'not 'T shirt'. We had a wide range of cards to allow for plenty of different decision options.

Ordering the decision-making cards needs care; the children have to name the set they eventually reach. Our set boundaries are shapes: circles, triangles, rectangles and squares painted at the end of the paths and they should be large enough for four or five children to meet there. Formulating questions and making decisions are important elements in everyone's life and children should experience situations where they can practice decision-making alongside each other and in non-threatening situations. On the logic track model a boy beside a junction with the decision 'not girl' would take a different spur of the track from the girl at that decisions junction. If the next decision for them was 'black shoes/not black shoes', on a simple two decision track the resulting sets would be 'boy with black shoes' and this would be reported as 'I'm in the 'not girl and black shoe set'. By having a choice of only two options, positive and negative we are entering the realm of the binary system that is the foundation of computer operations.

Chess

Chess for beginners starts with the pawn game in which eight whites oppose eight blacks moving forward or backwards one square at a time. When capturing a piece the move was diagonal and an opposing pawn could be removed. Every chess piece was introduced and practised in this manner until the full set was built in. This enabled children to be players at different levels and see the game as a fascinating progress leading to the mastery of chess. Chess emphasizes tactical thinking and helps reasoning as well as encouraging concentration. It is an absorbing game with ancient origins and has the advantage of being cheap.

Peter Guile, a parent and Wyn embarked on a project to bring chess to the playground. Enlarged versions of the chess pieces having weight and good balance were forged in steel. Peter based the shape on a cone of metal for stability and the traditional characteristics were defined on each piece. The finish was a durable polymer coating. Peter assured us that the chess pieces would have a long life and 30 years later they are nearly as good as in the year they were produced.

A chess board to match the dimensions of the pieces was painted in a quiet part of the playground and a key to setting pieces in position was mounted on the adjacent wall.

Elections

Our ewes lamb each year and this is always an exciting time for the children. When the lambs are 3 or 4 days old and well bonded with their mothers we bring them into school for a short time. The children sit in class circles to form a human fence and everyone gets the chance to cuddle a lamb. Following this, the whole school decides on names for the new lambs. We hold an election day on which everyone votes for the favourite names. After discussion, each class submits a name for each lamb and these are circulated to the other classes. We set up the school hall with a table with an adult helper to act as an Electoral Officer distributing voting papers for each lamb name. Classes in turn come to the hall and the children cast a vote for their favourite name for each lamb. The adults give help to those children who cannot yet read fluently. Polling closes when every person in the school has had a chance to vote. An adult returning officer helped by child stewards counts the votes for each lamb's name and announces the results to the whole school. We try to make the experience as similar as we can to that which the children will see on the television whenever there is a local or national election.

The children are also challenged to chart the weight, length and height of each lamb. They have to decide on the method of measuring, weighing and recording the results and this always results in lively discussion. There is a link to the charts kept on the progress of human babies as described in Chapter 6.

Literacy and the language arts

We acknowledge that the keystone to learning is the acquisition and appreciation of the language arts, and at its heart is speaking and listening. We use every opportunity to talk with the children, to listen attentively to them and to give them a voice and something to write about. We believe that our classrooms, both indoors and outdoors, should be places of involved conversation and we are suspicious of classrooms and schools that are silent.

Setting up scenarios for conversation is very important; we often put the children in mixed sex pairs to talk, listen and give feedback. The children are given protocols for the activity. There should be eye-to-eye contact and effective listening without interruption. One child in turn will have a minute to tell the story of their day so far: the paired child will then have to tell back the story in his or her own words. Older children might write a short story first and then in pairs: the children take turns to read their story to their partner. The paired child will give feedback. Older children also write stories that they read to younger children and there are opportunities to develop the conventions of audience behaviour and participative listening. Examples of other types of this work may be found in Shirley Clarke's[11] book.

There is a maxim that states 'How do I know what I think unless I hear myself say it?' The frequently used starting point is shared talk that produces more ideas around the experience or focus. Note-making is another shared activity when post-it notes with children's impressions are stuck on the windows. The cornerstone of our practice is relationships so the manner of speaking and the way we collect comments is a continuation of this idea. Swapping ideas in pairs and working in changing partnerships helps the views of everybody to come across and is instructive for citizenship.

Like the educationalist, Jerome Bruner[12] we are of the opinion that education is a 'dialogue between the more experienced and the less experienced' and it is for this reason that we encourage as many adults into school as possible. Parents, other family members, visiting craftspeople, experts in a wide range of fields, teachers and all our support staff have a role to play in talking to and listening to children, in encouraging dialogue and eliciting the views of the children and in creating a better setting for learning. Being able to explain, to hypothesize, to predict and to experience, we build a greater understanding of ourselves and the world around us. We aim for our classrooms to buzz with purposeful conversation, with the airing of opinions and with the lively involvement of everyone there.

The National Literacy Strategy[13] has had the effect of raising our awareness of grammar but has brought with it a tendency for teachers to concentrate on the mechanics of language. The ability to construe a paragraph of writing, to recognize the phonemes, the graphemes, the nouns, pronouns, adjectives and adverbs has value but does not switch young children onto reading or writing. We wonder whether George Eliot needed a knowledge of phonemes when she wrote Middlemarch, or whether Thomas Hardy construed every paragraph he wrote. The concentration on grammar and the structure of language has, we believe, led in some cases to tortured learning and tortured text. Above all it has resulted in a loss of story and narrative flow. Analysis of text should take second place to reading for enjoyment. 'Analysis destroys wholes. Some things, magic things, are meant to stay whole. If you look at their pieces, they go away'.[14]

Experiences as motivators

We believe that it is the experience that we give to the children on a daily basis that will have the profoundest impact on their abilities as language users. We use experiences as motivators. The children love having animals at school. We keep our own small flock of sheep and have also raised a couple of pigs. Porky and Brian came to us as 3-day-old piglets and we adapted a space for their pen for their first 2 weeks with us. We wanted the children to be able to watch them and appreciate their idiosyncrasies. At the same time, we invited Mary Rayner, the author and illustrator to come to work with us for the day: her Garth pig[15] stories were very popular with the children. Mary worked with each class and together they made up their own pig stories based on Porky and Brian. The workshops involved collaboration with Mary and cooperation and resulted in a large original book for each class.

On another occasion, a parent brought goats to school. The children stroked and brushed them and compared the goat's hair with their own and with that of our sheep. They watched as the goats were milked and then tasted the milk before going on to make goats' milk yoghurt and goats' curd cheese. A local farmer brought one of his Dexter cows to school for the day. The children made butter by agitating the creamy milk in small plastic jars. They added a tiny amount of salt to their butter and spread it on pieces of crusty bread for an end of day feast. Other children made ice cream using a hand-cranked ice cream maker. On all these occasions, there is an accompanying buzz of dialogue: the children are eager to talk about what has been happening and to recount the experience to their family at home.

Our Autumn term theme of 'fire' is rich in opportunities. We re-enact the Hilaire Belloc poem 'Matilda'[16] in the school hall and follow this with burning a large model of Matilda's house outside.

We read Heinrich Hoffman's 'Dreadful Story of Harriet and the Matches' and drama-tize this for the children. We re-enact the story of the Phoenix[17] and the children construct a bird from wire and brightly coloured fruit and vegetable nets. We thread a long rope through the body of the bird, so that with an adult holding each end, it can be made to 'fly'. The Phoenix swoops over the heads of the children as they sit together in the hall and then we go outside to re-tell the story. We light a small fire and cover this with a piece of old carpet to slow down the rate of burn. When flames are just starting to lick at the carpet, it is a cue for the Phoenix to fly over the fire, land on its nest and then fly up into the air again. The Phoenix story is all about rebirth and regeneration, new beginnings and hope for the future.

Fire and smoke have been used over many years for communication. We tell the children about the use of beacons of fire as the English watched for the coming Spanish Armada in 1588 and then light fires in sequence at each corner of our school field. Groups of children stand around each fire and watch out for the signal before lighting their own fire. In other experiments carpet is used to make smoke signals by lifting the carpet on and off a smoky fire. Once the fire is burning well we cover it with green wood and damp leaves, and it is adults only who lift the carpet to release the trapped smoke. In turn groups of children stand at a distance and watch for the smoke signals.

These sensory approaches have a powerful effect: the children are motivated to talk to each other before, during and after the activity and the teacher can skilfully draw out the children's comments. Each activity becomes a sensory feast that can transfix the children and each is different while carrying a tonal quality that can be applied from one to the other.

Presenting the children's work

We believe it is important that children's writing is given a voice: the adults use an element of novelty to feed the children's writing back to them. Sometimes, we present the children's work to the whole school in the form of radio programmes after we have rehearsed them. An announcer and a group of adults read out the writing with accom-panying music and sound effects. Having a number of readers gives variety and the presentation holds the children's interest. Each child is acknowledged as the author of his or her piece of writing. The children are always very pleased to be mentioned by name as authors and to have their words broadcast.

For many years, we held an annual Eisteddfod, a celebration of language and the performing arts. Each class prepared an item to be enjoyed by the rest of the school: it could be dance, mime, song or poetry written by the children. Jude, one of our teach-ers until 2003, is Welsh and she always acted as the Bard. Dressed in a long white robe she takes a sword from a scabbard and lifts it as she asks the children 'A oes Heddwych ?' (Is there peace?). The children reply 'Heddwych!' ('Peace'). She repeats this to all four compass points in the hall, so that all the children can see her face-on in turn. Each group then presents its contribution and the Bard formally closes the Eisteddfod. In a similar vein to the radio programmes described, cohesion is given by music, 'guest' appearances and jokes contributed by the staff.

Language permeates the whole of life, it cannot be taught in isolation. The children are acknowledged as readers and writers from day one in school. Each of our annual themes contributes towards the children's acquisition of the language arts: the children's involvement in our series of 'learning adventures' means that they work in an ideas and language-rich environment. The staff group are meticulous in their planning, and work hard to put together comprehensive curriculum maps for all our regular themes. Every theme is explored across all subject areas in order to contrive a balanced curriculum. Not every idea will be used: more are discarded than are adopted.

Visiting authors and illustrators

We try to use quality literature and poetry: even if this is at a higher cognitive level than the children's, it is important that our children hear and experience the words of our greatest authors and poets past and present. Over the years we have invited many authors and illustrators to school – Quentin Blake, Joan Aiken, John Richardson, Jan Pienkowski and most memorably, Roald Dahl. He stayed for a day of chocolate factory activities and joined the staff at the after-school workshop and evaluation session. Anthony Browne has also visited the school several times. on one occasion he formally opened our new school library, and reflecting his fascination with gorillas and chimpanzees, the children enjoyed some monkey business, each of them climbing in through the library windows and receiving a banana from the author.

Handwriting practice

Letters and number shapes written with chalk or charcoal in the playground can give children a new slant on handwriting. It takes more energy to write on a grainy surface and the individuality of each symbol can be clearly compared in the larger space. Writing in a bigger scale can give letters a sculptural form, and because it happens outside, it is much more fun. The next shower of rain will wash everything clean. We also get the children to use their fingers to practice handwriting on table tops using chocolate sauce, talcum powder, shaving foam, Instant Whip or clay. As well as these tactile expressions the children also practice with the more orthodox tools.

Alphabet skills

Letter order in the alphabet is not deducible: the pattern has to be remembered. Walking in a line, carrying a heavy rope in their right hands, a class of children sings the alphabet as they all move. Without breaking stride everyone swings the rope above their head to hold it with two hands to sing the letters 'm' and 'n' and the rope is then carried on the left. By emphasizing these middle letters of the alphabet the children start to realize that letters coming before 'm' will be found in the first half of a dictionary and that letters coming after 'n' will be found in the second half.

On other occasions, we get the children to march in the playground or hall, tapping out the alphabet letters with their feet or holding large sticks. We have an assortment of small wooden bears, identical in size but individualized for character. Letters of the alphabet are wired onto the bears and the bears are dispersed around the pathways in alphabetical order. The children go alphabet hunting with their teachers and mark the letters as they find them on a photocopied sheet of bears holding the letters.

A set of round pebbles of roughly equal size has been painted with the lower case alphabet and a second set of slightly larger stones is marked with the upper case letters. Activities with the stones are mainly about laying out the alphabet. The stones are set around the playground and the children find them and put them in the right space on a line marked in chalk. Learning about alphabetical order comes from doing, and the doing involves moving stones and other things with plenty of physical activity. Scope for word making and spelling out names is increased by having some extra lower case letters. There are rules for handling the stones and because they are heavy we store them in strong baskets that we can pull outside.

Information and communications technology
Photographic images

Through our Information and Communications Technology (ICT) work we bring images of the outdoor environment into school and use modern technology to map details and add another dimension to our outdoor learning programme. This extends our appreciation of experiences both in and out of the school. From the very early days, we recognized the importance of photographic images: photographs and colour slides have enabled us to track the development of our school and its landscape and gave us plenty of opportunities to use them as discussion points with the children or as predictors of future experiences. We have been helped by a number of photographers and were also fortunate to know a professional photographer, Bob Bray, who often worked at school with us and captured images of the children at work both inside the classrooms and in the natural setting. It was Bob who helped us to see the potential of putting a story together that included the children in action.

Over the years we accrued a large collection of photographs[18] and colour slides and many of them were used to make large-scale books of photographs, to record visitors or to describe an event or a change in the landscape. Making the books was time consuming and required meticulous work. Each photograph was mounted and each page bound with glued paper to strengthen the edges and the corners. Captions were usually hand-written using calligraphic nibs and Indian ink. This ink is dense and does not fade. The books have worn well over time and are now historical source material for the children as they study the school's history.

Seeing ourselves in meaningful situations has come a lot further with the introduction of digital cameras to all the classrooms. These and the interactive whiteboards bring the stimulus of yesterday into perspective the next day, making a time for contemplation and a starting point for evaluation and discussion. When the whole school were working an integrated Olympics theme its coalescence largely came through ICT.

The Olympics celebrations and the different events were recorded in digital images and film and downloaded onto the school computer network so that it was accessible by all of us. Children were looking at images of the nation by nation parade, the carrying of the Olympic torch and the lighting of the eternal flame in small groups on the morning after the inaugural day. Seeing the story on the classroom interactive whiteboards and finding out what the whole parade looked like, getting the close-up of the leading sportsman or woman taking the Olympic oath and looking at the printed words of the oath on screen is a unifying strategy carrying emotional tone. Of course, we could have taken excerpts from other websites showing historical footage, but we should lose the function that promotes the authentic learning and teaching relationship. The experiential method is about each child being his or her own textbook in the authentic way of learning as expounded by Johan Comenius in the seventeenth century.

Development of school website and intranet

Carol has developed a tremendous grasp of ICT over the years, and now works as an advanced skills teacher with the local authority as well as at school. It was she who inspired us to develop a school website and one of the parents in her class, Sian Gates put hundreds of hours into developing our school intranet which was largely image based, offering both a pictorial record of the children at work and play and the transformation of our school's outdoor environment. Sian recognized the potential of digital imagery that would allow teachers to capture experiences in photographs and video and relive them with the children back in the classroom. The password-protected website was then made available to the children's families and to other professionals. Over the years our intranet has proved to be an extremely popular resource for our staff group, our children and their families as well as for an interested international audience.

Development of learning platform

Three years ago, we started to develop a school learning platform: a national initiative called for all schools to have a Virtual Learning Environment, Connective Learning Environment or E-Learning Platform. Our system is provided by a company, Uniservity, and members of our school community can take ownership and authorship of our learning platform.[19] The biggest difference between our school intranet and our developing learning platform is that the latter is a two-way process: children and their parents can add to it and access all school events and experiences at home. There is of course an e-safety requirement, and our learning platform is a secure environment and is password protected for many sections of it.

All the children's experiences in our outdoor environment and in the classrooms are recorded in photographs and video clips that are annotated by the children or their teachers and added to the learning platform to form a diary of teaching and learning. Even more importantly, the children can record their learning and activities in many forms: desktop publishing, graphics, sound recordings, voice recordings and video.

Bears in the nursery

A tangible resource such as teddy bears is a good starting point for the development of international links for young children and is largely image rather than text based so is relevant for even our youngest children. The bears join children on their holidays and the children use a digital camera (borrowed from the school if necessary) to record images of the bears in different venues. The various journeys are plotted on a world map. In the nursery there are also two bears who accompany the children home with the digital camera. The children record the bears on their journey and at home and then Donna helps the children to upload the images onto the nursery computer the following day.

ICT links

Visitors to the school access our learning platform and use it to have direct contact with us. We send photographs, video clips and text electronically and this means that children in both schools can compare and contrast images and share information about their lives and experiences. Similarly, British Army schools in Germany use Uniservity to provide their learning platforms. This means that our school can maintain direct links with a number of British schools in Germany and there is scope for the sharing of information, images and video. One school in Germany has started to develop its outdoor environment and is using the learning platform link with our school to help them in their work. Three other schools across the world keep in touch through the learning platform and we all learn from each other.

Resources

We ensure that the children and staff have access to digital cameras, video, sound recorders, microphones and digital microscopes. Hand-held digital microscopes make it possible for the children to capture images of invertebrates such as life in our ponds or the parts of a flower in our gardens. Our older children are able to record invertebrates themselves and then use Global Positioning System (GPS) to upload information onto a map of the school – the results are used for teaching and learning both in and out of the classroom. Data Handling software also enables the children to analyse their results. For instance, recently children were able to collect data about invertebrates in our gardens and then to analyse the data and find out which invertebrate was predominant in our different micro-habitats.

We have been fortunate to have won prizes in the Rolls Royce Science awards that have provided us with a gooseneck Digiflex camera that allows us to capture time-lapse images of seeds germinating or caterpillars feeding and pupating or butterflies emerging from the pupae. We have also bought a bird box camera and have been able to get close-up shots. We were able to capture images of a pair of robins who built a nest in our science shed and the children were delighted to be able to monitor the robins' eggs and hatching young. We also trial equipment for commercial companies. Recently the TTS Group asked us test their latest digital handheld microscope with a memory card that may be used out of doors without direct access to a computer. The resulting feedback of children and teachers about the microscope and the ways in which we have used it to enhance our teaching and learning are sent to TTS. We are now planning to get an underwater digital camera that will help us to record life beneath the surface of our ponds.

The use of time-lapse motion-sensitive cameras is something we aspire to. We should love our children to be able to see the life that visits our site when we have gone home. At the moment, they can check the ground for animal spoor and on frosty mornings or on those occasions when snow has fallen they are also able to follow the animal tracks. The South East Grid For Learning has provided us with some funding to develop our use of motion-sensitive cameras and we are anxious to keep abreast of every development.

Recently, Ofsted[20] noted that many schools needed to develop Data Logging as an aid to the children's learning and that we are developing particularly with our older children. The potential is huge: the children can input data about temperature, bird life using the school grounds, daylight length before and after solstice and use data logging software to analyse results and predict trends. Other software enables us to use satellite images that are useful in our geography work. Microsoft Multimap or Google Earth used in conjunction with our interactive whiteboards offer views of the world for the children.

Whenever the children go on a field trip, images of the day's activities are downloaded each evening onto the learning platform and parents can access them and get an idea of what the children have been doing.

Ours is now a digitally complex environment and we have the tools to record and engage children in their learning. However, we believe that it is vital that the children first use their eyes, ears and hands before and as well as using digital tools. First-hand, direct participatory experience is the starting point in whatever we undertake.

Notes

1. Rose Report 2008, final report of the Independent Review of the Primary Curriculum by Sir Jim Rose et al.

2. Primary National Strategy 2006.

3. See Chapter 6 description of our clay project.

4. Jean Melrose. At the time, Lecturer in Mathematics, Bulmershe College of Higher Education, Reading.

5. Ian Sugarman. Shropshire Maths Centre. Details can be obtained from Shropshire Education Services Publications Unit, Shirehall, Abbey Foregate, Shrewsbury, Shropshire. Telephone number 0743 254321.

6. Kriss Turner – currently Director of Teacher Education, University of Winchester.

7. National Numeracy Strategy 1999.

8. see Note 5.

9. Pelmanism: a memory-training and personal development system begun in the 1890s by W.J. Ennever of the Pelman Institute in London. Related games are known as Concentration, Pelmanism, Pexeso or simply Pairs.

10. L.S. Vygotsky. *Play and its Role in the Mental Development of the Child.* Penguin Books: London, 2002. Originally published in 1933.

11. S. Clarke. *Active Learning Through Formative Assessment.* Hodder Education: London, 2008.

12. Jerome Bruner. *The Culture of Education.* Harvard University Press: Cambridge MA. 1996.

13. National Literacy Strategy 1998.

14. Robert James Waller. *The Bridges of Madison County.* Mandarin paperbacks: London, 1993, p. 39.

15. Mary Rayner: author and illustrator of the Garth Pig series of stories in the 1980s.

16. H. Belloc. Illustrated by P. Simmonds. *Matilda Who Told Lies and was Burned to Death. . . .* Jonathan Cape: London, 1991. We prefer the version illustrated by Posy Simmonds.

17. Phoenix story – an ancient tale from many cultures. It tells of a sacred mythological bird who dies in its nest of fire and is reborn.

18. For further discussion see Chapter 9.

19. Available on www.school-portal.co.uk and then scroll down to The Coombes CE Primary

20. Office for Standards in Education.

8　Curriculum II

History

Our school: The starting point

Our school is the starting point for much of the work in our history curriculum area but of course the study of history is an integral part of most subject areas. The original Victorian building of 1873 at Key Stage 2 is still standing, and we are fortunate to have many artefacts which trace the development of this part of the school including maps, old documents, class registers, photographs, the punishment books, old invoices and the like. The children have access to all these authentic resources and they learn to interpret the past from use of these. We teach the children how to handle these old treasures respectfully and carefully. Original documents and artefacts are irreplaceable and it is worthwhile discussing this before the children have hands-on experience. The shape, style and size of the original building contain many historical clues for the children to find and research – the village of Arborfield was well known for its thriving brick and tile industry (the village being situated on a band of heavy clay) and local bricks and tiles were used in the construction of the original school.

Many schools were built after the Forster Education Act of 1870.[1] Children who have studied the oldest part of our school can begin to recognize this publicly funded architecture in its recurring pattern through villages and towns. Teaching for transference gives children wider possibilities to interpret their environment. Similarly, searching for and noting old milestones, checking the position of pill boxes, mobile phone masts and churches will go a step further to helping the children read and remember a locality. The Foundation and Key Stage 1 building is much younger, being built in 1971 and we can trace its history through our huge bank of photographic and colour slide images and through the improvements made to the outside environment. For very young children, their understanding of a historical perspective starts with personal histories – birthdays, photographs of themselves through the years, starting nursery, playgroup or starting school and being a part of a changing school community and setting, photographs of grandparents and parents when they were younger. We set up opportunities for the children to investigate their own history, getting them to bring in photographs from home and using these to note changes in clothing styles, hair styles and the like.

Our local community also gives us many opportunities to study history on the doorstep. We take the children on history-focused field trips around our village and surrounding area, and the children can note the changes in building styles over the centuries, from the seventeenth century pubs to Victorian cottages and more modern houses and businesses.

Using the local Church

Last year, as part of our Religious Education programme, every child in the school visited one of our local Anglican churches, St James's in the village of Barkham. This gave them the chance to be within the building just for the purpose of enjoying it. They look closely at the historical evidence to be found in the church building, the church furniture, the many memorials on the walls and on the floor, the bell tower and in the churchyard. The children were enthralled by the story of the church silverware that was hidden in a pond during the time of Oliver Cromwell and this added to the experience of holding that same silverware and tracing the patterns and words inscribed on it.

They learned about the significance of the sanctuary and how this part of a church building directly in front of the altar was, and still is, a place of safety and protection for people who were in danger of arrest. They had the opportunity to work with Judith, one of our governors who is also a campanologist, and she taught them how to pull the bell ropes correctly to get the bells ringing. They found out about local families from details on memorials and gravestones and they visited the graves of a former pupil, one of our support staff and our former caretaker, George Prior and his wife Myrtle. They researched and sketched the cross-shaped building, a traditional design for churches; they drew the stained glass window patterns and they studied the parish records and registers of births, marriages and deaths.

We got the children to lie prone together to trace the great ceiling beams that brace the walls and support the roof. This is a hearts and mind moment that we do in silence. The children are free to wonder about the great architecture above or just to absorb the atmosphere. Children need to think without adult direction. Such concentration may or may not be about the 40-feet space above them. They also have the quiet moment in which to sift through their impressions. The children spent at least two hours at the church, and returned to school to continue the project in the classroom.

We wanted the children to have direct experience of some of the important Church traditions and planned weddings and baptisms. Children who already knew the details about these Church services used their ideas to help us to run these celebrations, and members of our local Church community offered their help. Routinely we used a doll for a baptismal service but on one occasion a parent asked for her two children to be baptised and in the following year, a baby was baptised. A boy and girl from each class were the bride and groom and the rest of the children made up the wedding party. There were plenty of opportunities for dressing up. Cakes and sandwiches for the wedding reception and the baptism reception were made at school, classrooms were given a makeover and the learning developed through the need for timetables, guest lists, invitations, photographic opportunities, planning the order of service and press reporting. We always make reference to other faith celebrations and to secular marriages in order to ensure inclusivity. Principal actors also delivered short speeches at the 'reception' and there was a toastmaster.

Detailed preparations for these types of study trip help to ensure that the children's experiences will be worthwhile and memorable. Many teachers gave their classes of children a questionnaire to fill in as they worked inside and outside the church. We also got members of the Church community to join the children in their study visit and they were able to give further details about the building and its history, about previous Rectors and other snippets of information or personal reminiscence. They also steered the children to the most detailed gravestones with interesting epitaphs and to family monuments with elaborate angels and crosses.

Archaeology

Whenever we can, we bring in experts in their field to work with the children. This year, two archaeology undergraduates from Reading University offered to lead a 3-week archaeological project on the school site. Craig and Andy planned for their residency in great detail and worked beforehand on several occasions with one of our Key Stage 2 staff, Hannah Dennis, who has a particular interest in history. Craig and Andy were joined for a few days by Rachel Farmer, a former pupil who is studying Archaeology. Their plan was to create an archaeological dig on a part of the school field. They sectioned off an area of land and fenced it with tape so that it had only one entrance and exit point (as is the case in a real dig). They removed the topsoil, and then seeded the area with a range of artefacts: animal bones, pieces of broken pottery, fragments of terracotta tiles and other bits and pieces. They created layers of artefacts for the children to discover at different levels. All the topsoil was replaced, and a diagrammatic grid system was drawn and photocopied for the children to use.

The children had several opportunities to visit the dig. At any one time, one group of children were observers around the edge of the site, and another group were given trowels and brushes to use on the dig site. The children's levels of concentration were high and interest was keen. Craig and Andy were the site overseers and resident experts. They taught the children how to reveal the artefacts without damaging them, how to use their trowels and brushes as an archaeologist would, how to sieve the soil that they removed in order to find any small fragments and how to use a spoil heap for the sieved soil. Any archaeological dig requires methodical and meticulous care from those who are working on it, and we had high expectations of our children. The children had to map their finds on the grid and label them. They were filmed at work, and they also recorded their finds in digital images. The whole project was a great success and the children learned a lot from it.

Experiences like this can be preceded or followed up by study visits to local dig sites. We are fortunate to live fairly close to the old Roman town of Silchester where there is a longstanding dig going on. We take the children to watch experts at work and to have the opportunity to talk to the dig leader. Our local museum in Reading has a fine collection of many Roman artefacts and we take the children there to consolidate their learning. Projects like our archaeological dig add richness to the children's learning. They involve direct participation and interested engagement and they reflect our commitment to museum education and exciting learning adventures. We set up our own archaeology museum in the hall showing Roman tiles, old glass and stone bottles, fossils, churchwarden's clay pipes from a stream and some old coins to round off our archaeology project.

Laundry museum

Recently, while we were studying water in our science work, we set up a 2-day laundry museum. Our staff group, friends of the school and the children and their families collected equipment that would reflect methods of laundry over the ages. From garages and attics came items such as dolly pegs once used to plunge and agitate clothes in the washing tub, charcoal-fuelled irons and irons which were heated on a fire before use, the earliest of spin dryers, mangles, washboards and twin-tub washing machines.

The exhibits were set up in our school hall, and labelled by the donors. The children visited the museum in class groups and were encouraged to touch the exhibits. The mangle was operated by an adult, and the children helped to turn the handle of the mangle to squeeze water from wet towels. Other adults were using ironing boards and our range of irons and the children worked with them under close supervision. Outside we set up a Chinese laundry; galvanized buckets were filled with water and the children had to grate up hard soap and froth it up in the buckets of water. They used their hands and washboards to wash linen. The clean laundry had to be rinsed in buckets of water and then they worked in pairs to squeeze out water from their laundry by holding each end of towels, sheets and tablecloths and twisting in opposite directions. The clean washing was then hung on washing lines set up in the playground and fastened with wooden pegs. From this experience, the children began to get some idea of the hard labour and length of time entailed in doing the weekly wash before the coming of electrical appliances.

History through drama

The children learn a lot about history from enactments. Every year, the younger children help to dramatize the story of the Irish Potato Famines and the emigration of many Irish people to America and the rest of the United Kingdom. The staff group take the lead roles (of absentee landlords, agents, members of parliament, Irish poor, the Prime Minister) and the Year 2 children are traditionally the children who died from starvation and sickness. One member of staff is the narrator who keeps the storyline moving, and no words are ever scripted although they are prepared in detail; both the children and staff speak in role as they wish. Actors and audience take these sorts of home-spun historical drama very seriously, and the stories are always keenly remembered.

Another favourite drama is the re-enactment of the Gunpowder Plot of 1605 when Guido Fawkes and his co-conspirators attempted to blow up the Houses of Parliament in London. We divide the children into two groups: those espousing Guido Fawkes's ideas about the freedom of Roman Catholics to worship as they chose, and those who supported King James the First and his Protestant views. Adults lead each group of children and the plot unfolds. There are simple dressing up clothes: hats, shawls and resources such as candles, Bibles, and crucifix. The school hall is divided into two areas: the Houses of Parliament with MPs in session with King James, and the cellar of the Houses of Parliament where the conspirators attempt to detonate their barrels of gunpowder. Classrooms are used as bases for the two opposing groups of children and their adults. At the end of the dramatic reconstruction (fortunately the plot is foiled and there is no explosion!), a teacher leads a discussion with the children, looking at the plot from the two opposing viewpoints and trying to understand each other's stance.

Fire of London

In the Autumn term when we traditionally study fire and the effects of heat in a 3-week block, the younger children help us to re-enact the story of the Great Plague of 1665 and the Great Fire of London of 1666. Part of the half-term homework is for the children to make a model of a mediaeval building at home with the help of their parents and carers. The models can be as simple or as complex as the children and their parents wish, but they do need to look architecturally accurate and in period. We put on a height and size limit: no buildings should be more than adult knee high. During the course of a weekend, a group of staff and parents create a map of the old city of London using authentic maps to help them. We use pieces of carpet, which we stitch together with trussing needles and string and then cover the joins with carpet tape. The base for the map usually covers half of our hall space.

The roads and alleys are chalked onto the map and then we set about painting the map using any pots of emulsion paint that parents and staff have spare. We mix several colours together in order to get large quantities of one shade, and we use rollers and large brushes to colour the roads, river Thames and the land on which the buildings stood tightly packed together. When the map is dry, we write in the names of the streets and alleyways using thick tipped indelible markers. The children bring their models into the hall and put them on the map in a site of their own choosing. The number of buildings that the children make mean that the model takes on an air of some reality: the buildings are back to back in high density, the old city of London takes shape. For 2 weeks, the children use the large-scale model to support their work in several areas of the curriculum.

We teach the children the old street cries of London: 'Hot Cross Buns! Hot Cross Buns!', 'Who'll buy my sweet lavender?', 'Cherries red, cherries ripe', 'Chairs to Mend' and we walk around the model singing these and making up some of our own cries. Rat catchers go to work: paper bag rats are hidden among the buildings, and the children hunt them out. For every rat they bring to the Mayor, they receive payment and they are asked to work out how much they are owed. We use real money for this and everyone is in role for this mathematics activity.

We consider the Great Plague of 1665 that spread rapidly in London due to the cramped and insanitary conditions and the high population of flea infested rats. The children pretend to be rats. While the lights are on, they hide themselves on the model and when the lights are turned off, out they come squeaking and scurrying

around the streets on all fours. We then ask the children to change role and become citizens of London who fall ill with the plague bacillus and die. Members of staff and Year 6 children are the burial parties. They walk around the model ringing a bell and calling out 'Bring out your dead!' One by one the plague victims are carried off the model and gently placed in pretend burial pits on the hall floor. The children take this very seriously, and we usually preface the activity by talking to them about keeping each other safe, carrying younger children carefully and respectfully and looking after each other. The burial parties then cover the bodies with invisible quicklime and soil.

Once the drama has ended, we talk with the children about the number of people who died throughout Europe at this time because of the plague. We tell them the story of the village of Eyam in Derbyshire and its Rector, William Mompesson who prevented the spread of plague in the area by completely isolating the village from the outside world. We reflect on changes in hygiene, health care and medicines available to us today.

After 2 weeks of use indoors, the children take their models off the map and we carry the map outside onto a gravelled area at the edge of the school field. The children bring their models outside and replace them on the map. We spread sawdust in the roads and alleys, and a fire is set at the bakery on Pudding Lane.

We make sure that the children are standing safely back from the burning model and we have at least six fire wardens with buckets of water. We are always surprised at how quickly the fire spreads, and how within the space of a few minutes all that is

left is a smouldering ruin. Most parents come to school early in the afternoon to be part of the experience. We record the fire in photographs and video and these images are used in the following days to recall the experience. The impact of experiences such as this is high and the children remember the fine detail of the whole project for a long time.

Viking funeral

The older children in the school had a different large-scale fire experience. As part of their study of the Vikings, the Year 6 children constructed a large Viking long ship using hessian and wood. Other children in the school made sails, shields, helmets, jewellery and Viking artefacts. They then went on to re-enact the burial of a Viking warrior. The long ship was taken outdoors onto the gravelled area and a model warrior was ceremonially carried by some of the children at the head of a procession of mourners and was carefully placed in the long ship. Mourners surrounded the corpse with a range of objects that would traditionally accompany the warrior on his last journey to Valhalla. The long ship was usually put to sea and then fired. Following this custom, a fire was started on our vessel and the long ship and the warrior were ceremonially cremated. Almost a year on from this, the children remember the event and comment that 'history came alive'.

Geography

Aerial views

Our school grounds give us a good starting point for the study of geography. Over the years we have changed the topology of the site and created a range of microhabitats for different natural creatures. Making refuges for individuals and groups to work outside has been part of the plan for the school from the outset. The immediate need was to establish windbreaks to shelter the children and suit the garden. Embankments and low mounds were raised and this natural solution made other choices possible. Children and teachers had on offer elevated views of their site and an outlook stretching to distant woodland and an old public footpath. This is part an explanation of neighbourhood and part a visual proof of life outside school. When turning through 360° it shows other children at work and play across an animated landscape. The view has many similarities with the pictorial guides of city centres, theme parks and forest trails. It is the ideal position for understanding such guides and to begin designs for school-based ones. Scale is not important. It is the fun in representing features that are important to the individual.

Occasionally we try to get hold of aerial views of the school and the grounds. Sometimes these are provided by commercial companies, and at other times we turn to different providers. We have a tradition of helicopters landing on the playing field. Our parent group help to source the machines for us. Whenever a visit from a helicopter is planned, we track the route from departure to arrival, check air distance and use maps. We also ask for photographs to be taken from the air. In other years, we have had visits from hot air balloons, whose crew will often be willing to take a member of staff with a camera up in the basket.

The development of Microsoft Multimap and Google Earth has made it easier to get good quality aerial views and print these off. Such views help children to identify landscape features and make comparisons between these and earlier photographs. This type of bird's eye view is important for children but is not a replacement for direct experience. The aerial photographs tie in to work on maps and follow and accompany illustrated plan drawing. Children can use china graph pencils on laminated pictures to mark other features or to personalize the topography.

Maps and map making

We use a map of the school site drawn for us some years by a parent who was a professional cartographer. This has been updated and children refer to these maps: to find their current location on it, or to walk to a certain landscape feature or mark in details relevant to their study. The younger children tour the grounds in search of messages in plastic bottles that have been hidden there. The discoveries are recorded on a photocopied map. Other searches could be for letters of the alphabet hidden in the playground or along the pathways at different heights and again, the children will mark a copy of the map with the letter found there. Through activities such as these, the children enjoy the use of maps and are more likely to be able to read a map accurately. Comparing the maps with aerial photographs can help the children to relate the connection between the landscape and a conventional map.

Knowing the school site

Use of materials gathered from the gardens helps environmental awareness and sustainability. Natural materials cost very little and vary from plants gathered to test their suitability for dyeing cloth to soup making. We cut willow sticks and make them into bundles of ten to reinforce the teaching of place value. When teachers lead children to explore and find such resources, the school site is felt to be a place with a variety of detail and meanings. It is also part of a geographical perspective to know where to locate these things on the site. We regularly collect clay from the grounds to use in a variety of ways. Clay is the distinguishing stratum of our area and the local brickworks depended on it. Knowledge about the environment is casually picked up and it gets woven into whatever is being taught.

Children are inclined to value the environment because it supplies them with things that they need. Smooth round pebbles are ready to hand in the borders around the building and integrated with the bark chippings in sections of the paths. Most of these pebbles have been set in the gardens by children and teachers after use as classroom equipment. Easily rediscovered, the pebbles are made into rings to enclose art ephemera arrangements or to make artistic statements by themselves. Stones found on the site were not local to it; they arrived with the builders in huge piles of gravel and better quality stones were bought as cobbles and pebbles in 50 kg bags from the garden centre. The children can still find pieces of flint with sharpened edges that can be used as a cutting tool.

Transport: People and places

Transport, journeys, sightseeing, the open road and similar ideas have been the focus for many themes and projects. For a period of five consecutive years, a traditional traveller came onto the school site with his dog, his horse-drawn painted caravan and a pair of chickens in a mobile coop on the back. Alan always stayed two or three nights and described his expeditions in search of casual labour and his traveller's tales to the children. We marked his progress from the daffodil fields in Lincolnshire, fruit harvesting in the Evesham Valley, hop picking in Kent and potato lifting in Suffolk. We matched the work to places, checked the travelling involved (usually 15 miles a day) and reflected on the movement of people to where there was work in the past.

Triangular journeys involving a hired coach, the local train and a bus route between Reading railway station and Arborfield village impressed everyone. Many children travel only by car and to board a train and a bus had novelty and gave them some understanding of other forms of transport. The children had to follow timetables, mark routes on a map and make comparisons about each leg of the journey. We contrasted distances, costs and convenience but in all cases, the train was the preferred means of travel and was the experience of greatest worth to the children.

Christmas puddings

Every year the children make their own Christmas puddings to eat at the school Christmas dinner.

Seen from a cultural point of view, a Christmas pudding is a very British food. However, when the children trace the origins of the ingredients they find links to countries across the world. Every pack of ingredients is investigated and a world map is marked. The children plot the journeys needed to bring dates from Tunisia, sultanas from Australia, flour from Canada, sugar from Barbados, oranges and lemons from Spain and so on. We buy eggs and milk from a local farm shop and the apples are Bramleys harvested from our own trees. The bread to be crumbed was cooked in-store at the local supermarket. A query by telephone to the bakery department reversed the children's first view of home grown ingredients: the flour was sourced from the United States, the yeast was produced in Hungary then dried and exported. It turned out that our traditional pudding is an international fusion and dependent on international trade. We asked the children to think of the reasons for this and they made many suggestions: 'people like to swap and sell things', 'these days we've got ships to make long journeys', 'we can get their summer things when it's winter here', 'it keeps us all meeting each other and trying new things', 'it gives people work to do'. Tracking the raw materials back to their separate beginnings makes the most of the whole adventure.

Geography through story and drama

The children enjoy retelling stories out of doors. One of the tree houses in the playground might serve as the home of Hansel and Gretel.[2] The children re-enact the story and take small pebbles to mark their path. After dropping their pebbles they gather them up on their way back. They then set out again, this time carrying crumbs of bread to mark their pathway. The following day they check the route and find that the crumbs have mainly disappeared, eaten by birds or other night visitors and there are no trails to follow. Later the children and the teacher plot the routes taken in the story they have just re-enacted. Another suitable story with a good geographical element is The Three Little Pigs.[3] The teacher leads the telling of the story and the group search the environment and collect straw, sticks and stones to represent the three houses built by the pigs. Back indoors the teacher and children map where they found the building materials.

The ditch that runs underneath the covered bridge is used as a hiding place so that the story of the Three Billy Goats Gruff[4] can be acted out. Such work promotes a sense of surroundings and their potential for imaginative play. Children discover how the landscape features are linked together by paths. They are secure in their knowledge about the features of the site: the paths, the steeper hilly parts of the site, the boundaries and where the clumps of flowers bloom in their season. Working in our outdoor environment translates directly into a child's sense of places and spaces that is fundamental to an appreciation of geography.

Once a year we bring to life an old English tradition of 'Beating the Bounds'. This ceremony dates back to the time when a local parish would be held responsible for the care of its poor and needy folk. In this custom, knowledge of the parish boundaries was beaten into the children as they were led around them by church elders wielding sticks. In some parishes this tradition is observed as a fun walk and in the same vein we do it at school. Each child and adult has a large stick that has been coppiced from hazels on our site. On the chosen day, children meet in the playground to practice the beating and singing of an accompanying song. Each class has a different starting point for the inner perimeter journey. During their visit they keep account of the differences in boundaries north, south, east and west. Moss and lichens predominate along the northern pathway. The southern boundary runs parallel to a road and is much noisier. The boundaries all have their characteristics and on one path there is a refreshment stop where the children get a drink and biscuit. All the boundaries are beaten by the children and when they have completed the circuit they might chart the features they passed and do other recording back in the classroom.

Other events like the Epiphany have an important geographical element. When the children visit the Food Inn, they taste food from the southern and eastern Mediterranean region. In the Fragrance Inn, they smell the fragrances associated with the east: green tea, coffee, curry, spices and incense and a journey between all the Inns is incorporated into the project. The whole idea lends itself to an imaginative journey, and the children carry their blankets and packages with them as they travel around the grounds.

In the winter months, we sometimes set up lantern walks in the woodland areas. We put candles into transparent containers that are strung up in the trees on the wooded pathways. When it is dark the children walk the routes by candlelight. The following day the teacher might show the digital images she has taken on the interactive whiteboard and the children see familiar places in a different light.

International links

The international links we have forged over the years with the United States, People's Republic of China, Scandinavia, West Africa, South Korea and France impact on the way we teach geography. Whenever we have visitors from these countries, we ask them to share a traditional story or sing in their native tongue or describe their home environment. The children pick up details from this sort of informal link and it helps to keep them curious. We have an ongoing contact with The Gambia in West Africa, and several members of staff have visited this country and brought back a lot of resources including toys, cooking implements, recipes, clothing and swathes of brightly coloured material from indigenous markets. Two members of staff have a smattering of Mandinka that they use to greet the children at register time. The teachers build and use three-stone fires to cook rice and a spicy tomato sauce (benachin) and the children take part in this. In these ways, the children can start to get a glimpse of a different culture, climate and language.

We routinely ask parents to represent their culture for the benefit of the children. Recently, Kamlesh, Shankar, Shanti, Shruti and Kala demonstrated Indian cooking, Indian instrumental music, singing and dance and showed the children how to put on a sari. They also help us to celebrate Diwali and other Hindu festivals. Our Jewish parents give us similar support and help us to celebrate their festivals. The parents are the best examples of multiculturalism and they have a vested interest in helping us value a society where differences are positively appreciated.

Sustainable living and recycling

We think that children need lots of practical detail and elaboration to make meaning of these big ideas. A presentation of one week's rubbish drawn from two households each having four in the family, can be significant and slightly alarming. Accuracy in this kind of presentation means making visible usually concealed evidence about the way in which we live and it helps our children to consider the facts. We also own up to the origins of the rubbish exhibited because there is a personal narrative in the waste. The most recent presentation was drawn from the households of a school governor, Pat, and a teacher, Ray. The actual examples spread on tough sheets of builders' plastic are spaced so that minor details can be identified. Among the discarded waste were some boxes of outgrown shoes, old clothes and bric-a-brac. The complexity of the waste disposal problem is revealed in the way that representing it with cans, bottles and cartons cannot portray. Families were thorough about saving things for examination: There were birthday remnants, a heap of mussel shells, all the supermarket packaging, fish bones, meat bones, egg shells and lots of vegetable waste. We are scrupulous about the hygiene aspects. There should be a smell. This is one of the ways we can be helped to empathise with the vital workers who collect our rubbish every week.

The children make a survey of the presentation, think about the possible reduction of packaging, note the compostable items, think about converting some of the materials into new products and consider further uses for other items. Finally the items are sorted. The children separate second-hand stuff such as outgrown shoes before wearing disposable gloves to sort and remove the compostable material. Paper, card and any other recycling items are put in appropriately marked containers. Finally we consider the ratio between the original amount in the presentation and the quantity remaining. This practical exploration presents a problem that is in large part solvable and the children see the visual evidence of this. We aim to shift the children's perception of what constitutes rubbish. Discussions on the contents of our rubbish bins touches on our dependence on landfill sites. We also think about the contamination by plastics and chemicals of water in our rivers and seas. To some extent these problems are a personal responsibility.

Sustainability is a global issue that only gets its meaning when it can be understood in concrete, personal terms. Children's daily experience of composting fruit and vegetable waste from their snacks and packed lunches makes a good foundation for a recycling commitment that needs to become a lifelong habit. There is a lot of life in the compost area showing the children how organisms exploit favourable conditions. Exposing some of this life is clear proof that compost is providing nutrients to the soil and adding to biodiversity.

Music

Music underpins all the work of our school: it adds another dimension to our teaching and learning programme and provides extension opportunities in all subject areas. Music can be a mood setter, an enticer of attention, a signal, a calming influence, a joyful celebration or a backdrop to cognitive development and thought. The link between music and mathematics has been well researched,[5] and the 'Mozart Effect' – that exposure to certain types of music, especially exposure to early classical music, very early in life can lead to improved performance on test scores including tests of spatial visualization, abstract reasoning and so on – still elicits discussion.[6] In our experience, children write better when they are listening to quiet, gentle music and music can be used to aid concentration or to set a tone for the learning environment. When we walk our large labyrinth together early in the Autumn term, Gabriella often plays her cello in the heart of the labyrinth and we find that this adds another dimension to the experience as well as helping the children to remain silent as they walk.

Rhythm work

Our music specialist, Gill, has inspired us all to use music in our teaching: she has composed songs which help the children when they are learning phonics, songs that help the children when they are learning number facts and songs to accompany many of our annual traditions.[7] For instance, when we celebrate the Beating of the Bounds, the children tap out the rhythm of a song which Gill has taught us with their long sticks – 'The children beat the bounds with a stick, they beat them slow and they beat them quick; they beat them forward and they beat them back, they beat them 'til the stick goes crack!'

Gill has also developed a series of rhythm activities using both short sticks (commercially produced claves or 12 inch long sticks cut from our site) and metre (or more) lengths of stick cut from our hazel or willow trees. The activities depend on collaboration and keen eyes and ears: many of them are passing on games and others depend upon the children copying a leader in moving the stick up and down, forwards and back, to each side and so on. The children led by their teacher tap out different patterns, or the children echo the pattern played by the adult or by another child. Many of the rhythmic games have their origins in the chants of Native American Indians, and it was an American Professor of Music, Randall Moore who introduced these to the school many years ago. The sticks are also used to support learning in mathematics (learning tables, counting backwards and forwards, directional commands, using specific vocabulary).

In literacy-oriented sessions, the children play the rhythm of the syllables against the beat of a song: they tap a table edge or the floor with their sticks. Descriptive language is also practised with the sticks. The children are asked to put their sticks flat on the floor pointing towards the centre of a circle, and are then asked what they look like. Responses are varied – 'sunrays', 'a volcano that a giant stood on', 'if you stand them up it will make a cage', 'put them halfway up one of us and we'll have a skirt on' and the sticks are rearranged into another pattern.

Around the world in music

Music is also used to support geography work. The children are taught songs from around the world and these are plotted on a world map. Many of the songs are in the local language and the children enjoy the unfamiliarity of the language. Whenever we have visitors from overseas, we ask them to sing for us and our collection now ranges from countries as diverse as Holland, Trinidad, New Zealand, Sweden, West Africa, China and Australia. We also have an extensive collection of instruments from around the world that is used to support an understanding of world geography.

Movement and music

Short periods of physical activity are an aid to concentration in the classroom, and for our Foundation Stage and Key Stage 1 children there is a short music and movement session three times a week led by Gill in the school hall. The first session concentrates on encouraging listening skills. The children listen for melodies, they move like the animals that the music represents, they listen for rhythm such as marching, walking and tiptoeing, they stamp out an ostenato, they listen for beat or pitch (high to low, middle, ascending, descending, staying on a same note) and respond with their movements around the hall.

The children are also encouraged to react to the different moods of music – happy, sad, angry, thoughtful – with their bodies. The second session will often focus on singing games that are so essential in all cultures. The games require everyone's concentration, awareness of each other, turn-taking and cooperation. Some games can also tell a story such as the 'Bear Hunt' where the children make up the sounds for each locality: when they cross the field of nettles there are 'ows and ouches!' and when they meet a muddy bank there are squelching sounds. The games develop gross motor skills and enhance the children's social development. Singing games are very important: they depend upon collaboration and concentration and we use them a lot with the children. They take the children back in time (many of the games are of Elizabethan or earlier origin) and into history: for instance, 'Ring a ring o' roses' dates back to the Great Plague of 1665, when the disease started with a red rash set in a ring pattern.

The pattern of concentric circles painted in our playground make an ideal place for music activities. The painted circles help the children to keep the shape of the circle as they sing and move together: without them, young children find it very difficult to maintain a circle or its size. The children get squeezed up together as the circle size decreases and it becomes very difficult to maintain the movement or the game. By playing on the painted circles, these difficulties are avoided.

Live performance

Whenever we can, we give the children opportunities to enjoy performances of live music by talented musicians. Many of these concerts will take place out of doors and the music has quite a different sound when heard in the open air. Several times a year, for instance on St Andrew's Day, a bagpiper comes to play for us (St Andrew is the patron Saint of Scotland). We listen to him play in the school hall, and then we all move outside to listen to him play there. String quartets, brass ensembles, woodwind groups, steel bands and the like play for us indoors and then, weather permitting, outdoors as well.

Our amphitheatre makes a wonderful venue for a concert and we use it as often as we can. It was created on a sloping edge of the field when a bank of earth was built up with surplus soil from the theatre itself and from a pond construction nearby. The soil was heaped up to form a semi-circular bank and it was then planted with masses of willow wands. There are three entrance points, as well as two in the bowl of the performance area. The staging area has a backdrop of a high wooden fence that serves as a sounding board.

The band of the Royal Electrical and Mechanical Engineers, based at Arborfield Garrison, present regular marching band concerts for us, and our large playing field makes an ideal setting for this. We also ask the band to play indoors as well, so that the children hear the music in a very different setting. Whenever we can we ask the Gurkha Band to play for us and the children can compare the different styles of music as well as the speed of the Gurkha marches.

Drumming workshops

One of our Key Stage 2 teachers, Shirley, has a great interest in West African drumming and she has learned to play the drums herself. She leads the children in drumming workshops that are held in the outdoor landscape. A flight of steps in the younger children's playground makes an ideal venue for this. The school has a good collection of drums from around the world, and our local authority also has a bank of 30 djembe from West Africa that they loan to schools free of charge. During a drumming session, it is important that each child in the class has his or her own drum, and that there is no waiting around to have a turn.

Gill has built up a collection of musical instruments from all over the world, and the children have many opportunities to use these indoors and outside. Gill also gets the children to find their own instruments from the natural environment: sticks, stones, seeds put in a sealed container or sea shells in a paper bag can all be used to make music and these simple instruments give the children a great deal of pleasure.

Musical challenges

In her music programme Gill sets high expectations and challenge. The Year 2 children learn to write 4:4 rhythmic patterns, they put in their own time signatures and bar lines and use conventional rhythmic notation including semibreves, minims, crotchets, semi-quavers and quavers. She also encourages the children to write their own compositions.

When studying fire, the children use bubble-wrap to make popping sounds, crumpling plastic or paper to represent crackling flames or stones in a plastic bottle to emulate whooshing sounds. She gives the children a wide experience of every aspect of music. In singing, the children sing in unison, four part rounds, they partner up songs and learn some simple two-part singing. In composing and recording, they use conventional as well as invented notation.

Listening to music is important and we use both recorded material as well as live performance in which the children have opportunities to take part. Whenever a harpist plays for us, the children come up a few at a time and get as close as possible to the wooden frame of the harp. They feel the vibrations of the music through the wooden floor and the wooden frame and we like the children to draw as they listen. In instrumental work the children use a wide variety of both tuned and untuned percussion. Many of the children learn to play the recorder and we also have a set of handbells for the children to use.

Drama

Drama and dance run as connecting threads through the whole curriculum. Drama in particular can be a powerful tool for teaching and learning and aspects of this have been described in several chapters. We acknowledge a debt to Annette Cotterill and Learning Through Action.[8] This is a group that has its roots in the learning strategies pioneered by Professor Reg Revan[9] in the 1960s and 1970s. Its programmes are varied but all rely on the children actively being in role. We have adopted aspects of this style in our teaching.

We use drama to bring stories, history and traditions alive for the children by using participation stories that are more likely to be remembered. On the feast day of St George, the patron saint of England, we re-enact the legend. The teachers wear simple costumes and use improvised speech. They always involve groups of children in the production that is unrehearsed. In the autumn we act out John Vernon Lord's story 'The Giant Jam Sandwich'.[10] The adult group take the part of the main characters and the Year 2 children are the wasps. We make a giant slice of bread by laying a white parachute over the hall floor and spread red carpet tiles on top to represent the jam. The action takes place while the narrator reads the poem, and we rehearse the children in their role as wasps so that they know when to appear (and disappear) in the story. If the weather is fine, we take the drama outside onto the field as well as performing in the hall. The activity always ends with us feasting on jam sandwiches, made with jam that the children have prepared after their harvests from the grounds and eaten together as a whole school.

Dance

The children have many opportunities to dance: dragon dancing for Chinese New Year, maypole dancing during the summer term, country dancing, line dancing, interpretative dancing and most importantly the ceremonial dance which happens at the beginning and end of each term. These are important elements of our school year. We also invite dancers into school. An Irish dance group from a nearby secondary school join us for St Patrick's Day celebrations, and around the time of St George's Day, the Hurst Morris group demonstrate and teach us their traditional dances using scarves and sticks. Recently we have also welcomed a Spanish Flamenco dancer, capoiera dancers, street dancers and ballroom dancers. Every now and then we are fortunate enough to watch and take part in Hindu dance. Whenever possible, we ask the dancers to perform outside in the playground as well as in the school hall.

Four classes of older children explored new ideas through dance in the large painted labyrinth on the field. Some used exaggerated machine movements to progress along the lanes, switched into reverse and danced back. Percussion sounds mirrored the movement and in pairs and fours children danced the choreography they had originated. Other children interpreted music and expressed their entry to the labyrinth as

a first time 'follow the sun' into the unknown. These groups challenged the way the rest of us had perceived the labyrinth (concentrating on our unique thoughts while moving together). Inventing movements and shapes, repeatedly practising them with the intention of sharing them different from any previous use of the labyrinth and watching the children as they danced was an experience that stayed with us.

Visits from the Hurst Morris Dancers are always eagerly anticipated. They demonstrate the ancient English dances as well as the music of the fiddle and squeeze box or accordion. They typically visit us on St George's Day when we think of particularly English traditions, and we gather to watch them perform in the school hall as well as in the playground. After demonstrations of several dances, some using sticks and others using scarves, the group then teaches the children some simple moves and we all dance together. The children regularly enjoy Maypole dancing as well as learning a range of traditional country dances. These encourage the children to work with different partners and with partners of the opposite gender. The children learn to follow instructions, develop gross motor skills, count in patterns of four or eight, and consolidate mathematical terms (forwards, backwards, diagonal, opposite, square, circle).

Physical education

Our first Physical education (PE) specialist, Jenny laid the foundations of a comprehensive Physical Education programme at Key Stage 1 and in the Nursery and ensured that it would be responsive to the themes running through the school and curriculum and would also be innovative and creative. Chris, Deina and Matt our current PE coordinators manage a range of sports and physical activities during and after school. They teach all aspects of the Primary PE National Curriculum and are always looking for ways to extend the children's sports experiences and enjoyment. The pathways through the grounds are used as cross-country running tracks, the slopes and woodland making ideal conditions for this. There is agreement about the care needed to prevent any unnecessary loss of habitat and generally everybody is very responsible. We created a new pathway running parallel to the Bluebell Woods path specifically for the use of the cross-country runners. This alternative path goes wide of the bluebells growing along the edge of the woodland path that are very susceptible to compaction. Deina also runs a before school walking club for older children who want to get fit or who lead a more sedentary lifestyle.

During Olympics Games years we always hold our own Olympics. Each class represents a country of its choice and the children research their country prior to the games. The children parade to the school field dressed in the colours of their country's flags and accompanied by their national anthem played over the loudspeaker system. They watch as an ex-Olympic athlete runs in with a burning torch and lights the Olympic flame (a charcoal fuelled brazier that is fenced off for safety. The flame is kept burning throughout the games. Our Chair of Governors Chris makes a speech and leads us in the Olympics prayer and the children take the Olympic Oath. The programme includes swimming, track and field events, gymnastics, ball skills and games and marathon running. There are also challenges of balance and controlled breathing using feathers and exercises using chiffon scarves. An adjournment based on the Olympic custom brings the 2 days to a close and every child is presented with a commemorative medallion. Previously all the children had made their own clay medallions stamped with the school logo and fired in our kiln.

Jenny had started a tradition for an annual sports day that was based on the children progressing around a series of sporting challenges on the school field, in the playground and car park and in the school hall and classrooms. This was not a competitive day with traditional races but involved some tough challenges for the children where they were encouraged to improve on their scores of the skills they had practised throughout the year. Our Key Stage 2 team also had a tradition of sports days and we combined the two events to have a 1- or 2-day event for the whole school.

Recently Chris led his class in work inspired by the Wimbledon Lawn Tennis championships. The children watched selected matches on the interactive white board and Chris taught them the scoring system as a mathematical activity. Outside the children practised tennis skills. He, Deina and Matt have also brought in fencers, golf players and a number of sportspeople with specialist talents to work with the children and introduce them to new skills and new activities. Matt has continued to develop the full PE curriculum and established a diversity of pre- and after-school PE clubs.

Working with parachutes is a team activity for groups of children in and out of doors. It can stimulate cooperative responses as well as being a keen physical activity. We have developed a series of exercises with the children and the parachute that provide experiences based on the nature of trapped air and offer a deeper understanding of the principles involved. On their first experience of working with a parachute the children want to grab it and start to shake it. We let them do this so that they can get to know the feel of the thing.

We then introduce protocols for safety purposes and given practice, the children learn not to step onto the parachute until it is flat on the ground and other social considerations. One favourite activity is 'lift and release'. The teacher asks the children to stretch the parachute tight at waist level and then lift it as high as possible. On the signal 'let go' the children release the parachute and do not touch it as it falls. The pattern of fall is exciting as the floating roof comes down over some or all of the children's heads. In another routine, small groups of children are invited to go underneath the parachute when it is first lifted and to lie prone on their backs and keep still. The rest of the group lift the parachute and let it go on a signal from the teacher. The parachute falls gently down over the 'sleeping' children, unless someone has kept hold of the parachute longer than the rest of the group.[11]

For the first 2 weeks of every term we offer social and cooperative exercises to help the groups to re-establish themselves after a break and to offer some physical challenges based on cooperation and team work. Many of the exercises will involve the use of mats, cushions, carpet tiles and large balls as well as the parachute.[12]

We target National Curriculum goals with lots of contrasting activities. Many of these are usually physically challenging because we believe that the whole range of developing skills fit together; our daily programme always contains elements of activity and physical engagement. Together with the dance sessions led by Kim and Gill's music and movement sessions for the younger children, our PE programme is very diverse. The children move between the outdoor and indoor spaces and much of the teaching and learning will contain kinaesthetic elements.

French

Children in Key Stage 2 study a modern foreign language (in our case, French) from Year 3 onwards, but some years ago, Anne our Special Educational Needs Coordinator (SENCO) suggested that this programme should start in Foundation Stage 2 or at the latest in Year 1. Anne has a good understanding of the French language and French culture and she was the obvious person to teach the language to very young children. Using games and activities, songs, traditional French rhymes and singing game she gives the children a good foundation on which their future foreign language acquisition will grow. By the end of Year 2, the children have a basic vocabulary, can respond to instructions or answer simple questions in French.

We draw on the children's knowledge of French for the celebration of Bastille Day on July 14 (or as close to that date as we can get). A pavement café is organized in the playground, the tables decked out with tricolours and children arrive to a French welcome. They are served croissants and hot chocolate while Gill strolls about playing the piano accordion. Entry to the street scene is prefaced with a brief history of the French Revolution and the Storming of the Bastille and we sing the Marseillaise.

Our Key Stage 2 team led the older children through a range of activities with a French flavour. As well as visiting their café they made truffles with Gill, built models of the Eiffel Tower with Neil, took part in a Tour de France on static bikes with Mark, practised French handwriting style with Carole, enjoyed French song and dance with

Hannah, listened to a French story with Claire and in ICT worked with Bridget on a variety of puzzles with a French origin. Deina taught the children how to play Boules, and they experimented with pointillism in the style of Seurat. Assembling a day's timetable with this interdisciplinary approach is holistic. The children become immersed in all things French and the concentration levels are maintained. At other appropriate times, the children cook and eat traditionally French foods such as snails in garlic, bouillabaisse, baguettes and croques monsieur.

We engross the children in French language stories: the Babar series by Jean de Brunhoff, Herge's Adventures of Tin Tin, Rene Goscinny's Asterix, Ludwig Bemelman's Madeline, Antoine de Saint-Exupery's The Little Prince and other stories written in French are shared in English and we tell the stories of the Count of Monte Cristo, Les Miserables and the Three Musketeers. Our intention is to give children an insight into French culture and the French language.

Design technology

Design and technology is generally perceived to be one of the more difficult areas of the curriculum to teach in the early years and is often presented at a fairly low cognitive level: designing and making a tool kit for a teddy bear with cardboard boxes is hardly a real challenge, nor a credible scenario. We prefer to anchor design and technology to activities that will be truly meaningful. We look for the technological elements of all our activities and themes and highlight these for the children. When our flock of four sheep is sheared, the children use simple looms that they have helped to make to weave wool and they learn how to make felt. We follow these activities by giving the children the opportunity to weave with other materials such as beaten nettle stems (this recalls the wonderful Grimm fairy tale of the 'Princess and the Seven Swans'[13] where a young princess saves her brothers by weaving them shirts of nettle). The children look for rounded stones to use as pestles, and they help their teachers to harvest nettles (taking care not to pick any which have ladybirds or their eggs on them). Next they strip the leaves from the nettles, wearing gloves of course, and use their stones to separate the stems into fibres. The children weave the fibres on a simple loom, each of them adding a row or two of nettle fibre.

Changing the school landscape

Whenever we have workmen on site, we encourage the children to observe and to ask questions. Most changes take place at school with the direct involvement of the children. When the school has building work in progress, we arrange with the contractors that the children will be watching every stage of the work from the digging out of the foundations, through the laying of bricks, the erection of the roof, the installation of the plumbing and electrics and the plastering of the walls. Before concrete is poured into the foundations, the children fill a time capsule for future historians. Everyone contributes a piece of writing or picture, and we add that day's newspaper, a few coins and other items of interest. This is then buried in the foundations. In one major change, the children watched bricklayers at work and talked to them about the tools of the job, the mixing of the mortar and the laying of the bricks. The builders donated bricks, cement powder, trowels and spirit levels. We gave the children the ingredients to make their own mortar and to construct their own wall. The children used all the resources from the builder to build their own wall on a plywood sheet. Next, we got the children to mix their own plaster and gave them sheets of plasterboard: these were anchored and secured with wire against a wall before the children set to work with plastering tools.

Building techniques

When we were studying the Tudor period, some of the children studied the building techniques of the time. We coppiced our hazel because the children planned to convert the hazel wands into wattle hurdles and to build their own wattle and daub walls. Strong hazel rods were used as uprights and the hazel trimmings were woven through them. The daub was made only with what could be found on the site – clay, sand, fleece, hair and animal droppings. The children mixed the daub mortar on work boards. On their first try, they added far too much water: as the daub dried it was full of holes. Mark suggested using only sufficient water to make the plaster flexible in order to make a successful daub. This was then forced into both sides of the woven hazel so that there would be depth and good bonding. The wall was then left to dry.

Forces, pulleys and levers

When the children were studying the forces of push and pull, Patrick asked a carpenter friend to construct huge wooden boxes the size of the building blocks of the Egyptian pyramids. The boxes were very heavy and could not easily be moved. He then went on to lead the children in the rediscovery of ropes and rollers to shift the enormous wooden blocks. We have done a lot of work with pulleys and levers. Using the story of 'Rapunzel'[14] as a starting point, the children constructed a pulley system that could carry food up to the stranded Rapunzel in her tower (one of the tree houses).

On another occasion we re-enacted the story of 'The Lighthouse Keeper's Lunch' by Ronda and David Armitage:[15] again, the children used pulleys and ropes to deliver lunch to the stranded lighthouse keeper (again, in one of the tree houses). The children were introduced to pole lathe working: they saw the effects of force and it led us to having our own pole lathe. When a parent or friend brings a small digger to school, he or she explains the mechanics of the telescopic arm and how the machine is stabilized as the children watch him dig out a trench for our autumn bulb planting programme or collect clay from our grounds to be used as a modelling or construction material.

Food technology

The preparation and cooking of food plays a big part in our technology work. The children use a range of tools and cooking methods and learn how to evaluate them. When we make our pancake batter, the children test out the use of forks, whisks, rotary whisks and electric mixers and compare them to find which mixes the smoothest batter in the shortest amount of time. When we bake bread we use various methods such as the clay oven, biscuit tin ovens set in a fire, a conventional oven and electric bread makers. The children also have a go at making damper bread: twists of dough wrapped around the end of a long stick and cooked over a fire.

One of the most exciting experiences is the use of fire to cook food. One of our members of staff shows the children how to construct a traditional African three-stone fire and the children help her to prepare maize porridge or a spicy tomato sauce to serve with rice. We eat in the open air from shared bowls and using our right hands only as spoons. We make flat bread that can be cooked on hot stones in the Indian tradition. The children find rounded stones between which they can grind small quantities of flour from wheat seeds (or grass heads). By re-introducing these age-old methods of food preparation, the children get a sense of historical perspective and a better understanding of modern technology that can simplify or speed up tasks.[16] We reflect on the benefits of the easy availability of electricity and gas, and on the differences in lifestyle of people living in the developed world and those in the developing world. It also reminds us that cooking over fire (such as barbecues) is attractive and alluring and in good weather as effective as other methods.

Art and craft

We emphasize process and individuality in art and craft. As well as teaching art as a separate subject, it is seen as an integral part of the whole curriculum. The use of colour and shape by artists such as Mondrian or Kandinsky can be the stimulus for some artwork that will take place as part of the children's mathematical study of shape and space. One of the children's favourite art activities is to go outside with a small rectangle of card across which is stuck a length of double-sided sticky tape. The children collect small samples of colour from the natural environment (leaf parts, a piece of petal, a little sample of bark, a grass seed head) that they attach to the sticky tape: their colour collections (or 'colour walks' as we call them) can be based on a single colour, shades and tones of green, or a random colour pattern of the child's own choosing.

Artists in residence

We are keen to work alongside artists in residence: some of these are former pupils like Claire who is a sculptor; others are talented professionals like Susie Stallard. The children have the chance to watch an expert at work as well as to have a go themselves. We like the children to come into contact with professional illustrators, and we have been fortunate to welcome people such as Toni Goffe, Stephen Cartwright and John Richardson. Talent is home-grown as well: Jo is our art coordinator and it is she who inspires us all with fresh ideas and new techniques and processes. She ensures that we all give the children the widest range of opportunities to develop artistic flair and a sense of colour or pattern. It is Jo who has the children working on large canvases with acrylic paints or mixed media or using watercolours on suitable paper.

Work in the style of Andy Goldsworthy, Archimboldo, Antony Gormley and Richard Long

Another member of staff, Carol introduced us many years ago to the work of Andy Goldsworthy, an artist who uses found materials in the natural world to create ephemeral works of art and to the work of Archimboldo the Italian artist who used fruit and vegetables to create pictures. We were also drawn to the work of Richard Long[17] and particularly to his work with stones in the landscape and to his sculptures. The children, inspired by these artists, have their own work recorded digitally. Art ephemera in every season is always beautiful. In the autumn, the children collect leaves of different shapes and colours and arrange these in patterns on a canvas or on the hall floor. They create pathways of colour which they can intersperse with pebbles or small pieces of wood. We get the children working in 3D as well as two dimensionally, and features in our landscape are used as part of their work.

The work of Antony Gormley[18] has also been inspirational to us. We have used his style to create exhibitions of simple clay sculptures featuring the work of every child and adult in the school. One of the more memorable of these whole school community projects was setting our models of rabbits across a section of the school field. On another occasion, the children made clay heads that were set en masse on the slabs of Cornish granite at the edge of the field.

Pavement art

We enjoy pavement art and we often give the children chalks or charcoal to work on the hard surfaces all around the school (but never on the walls of the building). Making marks in the environment is an age-old tradition that dates back into pre-history, and satisfies a primitive urge in all of us. The advantage of using chalk or charcoal is that these will have a very limited life, unlike the spray paints used by graffiti artists. With the first shower of rain or the wear of feet, the work is gone. When we harvest our sunflowers, the children each bring a sunflower from the back paddocks around to the front car park and they use chalk and charcoal to draw their harvested plant. When many works of art are viewed together they have a big impact and it is fundamental to take all the children to view the exhibition in situ at its best. We also encourage the children to take their parents at the end of the school day to see their work.

The outdoor studio and gallery

The outdoor spaces of our school and the range of habitats and structures there lend themselves to becoming a unique art gallery. One memorable occasion was the trans-formation of our geology trail. Each class adopted one of the rock installations as a setting and they worked within their shape, colour and form to make a piece of art-work in the style of a chosen artist. Artists such as Andy Goldsworthy, Clarice Cliff, Gaudi, Rousseau, Dali, Magritte and Kandinsky were chosen and the children and their teachers transformed their rock backdrop.

Light deprivation

Depriving grass of light can give remarkable effects. We used builders' plastic sheeting anchored with pegs into the ground to make the shape of the petals of a huge sun-flower on the small field. The seed head in the centre of the flower was made using tyres and large stones. The plastic, tyres and stones were left in situ on the grass for 2 or 3 weeks and then the children helped us to uncover the design. The result was star-tling because deprived of light, the grass had turned bright yellow. This technique was also used to create a simple labyrinth design and in a third experiment the covers stayed in the garden until the grass died. We then filled the inserts with bags of saw-dust. On the following occasion, we took the Angel of the North as our example and spread a huge silhouette on the ground. It was covered until the grass had died and because we revealed the surface clay, when it rained it looked as though the design had been varnished. It is important to ensure that thick plastic is used: thin black plastic such as that found in bin liners is not opaque enough and some light will come through it, making the results less vivid. Another idea is to use a carpet and to cut out huge letters (for the school's name, a motto or suchlike). Left in place, grass will eventually grow up and there will be writing in living grass.

Notes

1. Elementary Education Act 1870 drafted by William Forster and known as the Forster Education Act.

2. A traditional German tale by the Brothers Grimm.

3. Three Little Pigs is a fairy tale featuring talking animals. Printed versions date back to the 1840s but the story itself is thought to be much older.

4. Three Billy Goats Gruff (Norwegian: De tre bukkene Bruse) is a famous Norwegian fairy tale in which three goats cross a bridge, under which lives a mighty troll.

5. A web search will indicate thousands of related sites.

6. See www.mozarteffect.com

7. See Appendix 2 for a selection of these.

8. Learning Through Action formed in 1983 by Annette Cotterill. Gained Trust status in 1991. www.learning-through-action.org.uk

9. Reg Revan introduced action learning in the mid-1940s as Director of Education for the British National Coal Board, and continued to develop and promote its principles until his death in 2003. It is used by a broad range of organizations, for-profit and non-profit, national and global.

10. John Vernon Lord, *The Giant Jam Sandwich*. Piper Picture Books: London, 1972.

11. For details of the parachute games we play refer to S. Rowe and S. Humphries. 1994.

12. See again S. Rowe and S. Humphries. 1994.

13. A traditional tale by the Brothers Grimm.

14. Rapunzel: a story written by the Brothers Grimm first published in 1812.

15. R. Armitage and D. Armitage. *The Lighthouse Keeper's Lunch*. Deutsch: London, 1977.

16. See Chapter 6.

17. Richard Long: a British artist, sculptor and photographer born in 1945 with a passion for art made by walking in landscapes and for marking the pathways with his work.

18. Antony Gormley: see Note 3 Chapter 6.

9   School traditions

When our school opened 40 years ago, the founding members of staff wanted to set a tone for it, to give it its own unique personality and feel. Central to our educational beliefs was the children came first, that we would have children at heart and in mind in everything that we did. We also wanted to be working in partnership with the children's parents and families, involving them as closely as possible in our work. Many of the children's parents were (and still are) members of the British Armed Forces; some of them based at the nearby Garrison for a very short term. We wanted these children and their families to have the sense of belonging to a community, to be part of a place where they could put down roots albeit for a short time.

Open door policy

In the early days, there was not a great deal of pressure on schools to control access into the buildings. However, following the Hungerford and Dunblane tragedies there was increasing central government and local authority pressure to restrict admittance to schools. The pressure on us to lock all points of entry to the school throughout the day was intense but with the parents as our allies, we withstood it. We did not want our children to feel in any way that they were being locked in to an institution nor did we want the parents to feel they were locked out. NSPCC and Childline statistics show that children are at most risk of harm from the adults that they know in their home environment. We recognized that a good life is about trust, acceptable risk and caring adults. In our view, a maniac intent on causing harm in any community would not be stopped by locks and security pads. He or she would gain entry in other ways. Because our teaching and learning programme takes place in the outdoors nearly as much as it does in the classrooms, it was vital that we maintain easy and open access to inside and outside. All schools take this risk – in outdoor games sessions, at playtime and in planned learning in the landscape.

We are aware of the risks of having an open door policy and we take the necessary precautions to protect the children. We watch them carefully, we monitor where they are, we are alert to strangers and make direct contact with them, we ensure that there is a responsible adult with every group of children outside. Our parents were very supportive and they worked with us to check the business of any 'stranger'. This worked to everyone's advantage. It gave visitors and prospective parents the chance to talk to people whose children were enrolled and who had an opinion about the system.[1]

Curriculum planning

The way in which we have set our curriculum in all subject areas to follow the pattern of the year also helps to give our school a particular character and this is described in earlier chapters. We have a programme of future events and the children and their families can build up a sense of the whole year. They also have things to look forward to and to compare year on year. There are also rites of passage for particular year groups. Our Year 2 children know that they will have the responsibility for making dragon costumes for Chinese New Year and that it will be they who perform dragon dances for the rest of the school. Our Year 4 children can look forward to a 3-day field trip to an outdoor activity centre in the Spring term and our Year 6 children anticipate their week-long stay at a centre in Somerset. All the children look forward to the pancake parlour that marks Shrove Tuesday as well as to the French breakfast on Bastille Day each year. The predictability of a programme of annual events helps to add to the flavour of the school year for all members of our community.

A spiral curriculum

While it is important to have a dependable timetable of events, it is important to see that each year there are subtle differences in approach. In this way we keep the curriculum fresh and invigorating and we ensure that there is challenge for the children as they move through the different year groups. Nothing is ever identical to a previous year and each cohort meets the red letter days with differently. We are often asked how we prevent the children from becoming blasé with the pattern of events. Our response is that there is always variety and progression in the academic programme and in methodology to implement the teaching of the children.

A creative dynamic

Integrated with the learning cycle described are other events that are not predictable, that are innovatory and meet a particular need or focus. Each term and over the course of a year, previous work is evaluated and analysed in staff workshops. It may be that the team agree that Design Technology needs more emphasis or that music should dominate the next bit of the curriculum or that we need to do more work for history or geography. Evaluation and guidance from each other keeps our approach fresh. One person's idea for a curriculum challenge will lead to the whole group adding to it and selecting from it. The staff group will brainstorm for a new project, will share individual talents or interests and will look for creative ways in which to meet curriculum needs.

It may seem that this is rather an ad hoc way to go about curriculum planning. We believe that it is this creative dynamic, referring to the views of everyone that best supports the children. The energy this generates is central to the idea of sustainability and keeps us all moving into the less familiar or the unknown. None of our projects is set in stone. One idea will lead to the next or point us in another direction. We always try to be the drivers of the curriculum rather than letting it drive us and we are ready to go down unfamiliar paths. We also never lose sight of central government curriculum requirements and we are mindful that although a democratic debate produces alternatives in matters of methodology, our goals are set for us to a large extent.

Tasting the curriculum

The growing of food, the harvesting of it, the preparation of it and the eating of it is a particular characteristic of our school. We reinforce the children's understanding of a healthy, balanced diet and of the need to care for our teeth but at the same time we are great believers in the notion of 'eating our learning'. We know that particular tastes will be remembered for much longer than the event of which they are part. Most subject areas and particular themes will have a food element running through that will add extra interest or novelty. A phonics session focusing on the 'ch' phoneme will be more memorable if the children get tastes of chestnuts, chipolatas or cherries. Chinese New Year will be remembered as much for the flavours of the orient as other details; year on year, the children can recall their use of unfamiliar chopsticks or the taste of a freshly made stir fry. The Jewish festival of Hannukah will be remembered for the doughnuts so generously donated by our Jewish parents as well as for the origins of this festival of light. The celebration of Diwali will stand out because of the curry and chapattis we have tasted as well as for the paths of light that we all walked.

Eating, drinking and smelling is making links to learning and we encourage the children to become 'food adventurers'. We ask the children to approach an unfamiliar food as an explorer and to taste just a little in that frame of mind. In our experience, the children are usually ready to taste something different in tiny amounts if the food is given an enthusiastic introduction by the teacher and if they see all the class trying it. When we eat food together for a Passover meal, even the youngest children will know that they are expected to taste a little of each ritual part of the meal, and they will be urged to go home and talk through the experience with their families.

When the children make chutneys from surplus or specked fruit from our trees, the sharp smell of spiced vinegar and fruit permeates the school for several days. Around St Andrew's Day in November the children dissect fish in their science lessons and then cook and eat it together reminding themselves that fish is one of our primary food sources. Eating together is an important means of social bonding and we look for every opportunity to enjoy the experience.

Ceremonies

We use a range of ceremonies to express our togetherness and set us as one school community. For many years, the Infant School has used ceremonial dance to start and to end each term. Our now retired PE specialist Jenny Poore continues to devise and lead whole school dances that will bring children and staff group moving together. The expectation is that we will all dance in silence, listening to the music of Pachelbel, Grieg or Enya, that we will be respectful of each other and that all individuals are as important as each other no matter what age or gender. These ceremonial dances are immensely emotive; they represent a community moving as one body, remembering the events of a term and marking its closure or looking forward to new beginnings as a term starts. We anticipate extending dance into our Years 3–6 groups and ultimately to dancing as a whole school together once we have a hall large enough for it.

Grandparents' and family days

Once a term it has become customary to welcome grandparents and other members of the children's families to share a day at school with the children. These family days usually occur on the Friday preceding the half-term break, so that members of the family who may have travelled some distance have the opportunity of sharing the whole or part of the half-term holiday. Attendance at these events is good. There is usually a specific topic and the children in their class groups take their visitors from one themed activity back to their class base for work in context and then on to another activity.

For the family day in February, the theme is usually 'love' – thus ties in with Valentine's Day. Peter Hearn, a highly talented storyteller and singer, will tell stories around the theme and teach the children and their guests some friendship songs. Jenny or Deina will lead us through a session of aerobics (to look after our hearts) with our teddy bears, hence the name Bearobics. Gill, our music specialist or Neil and Mark will lead us in a medley of songs about love as well as related rhythm work with big sticks or percussion instruments. There will also be a slide show or power point presentation deriving from the activities of the children over the preceding months, and there will be an art activity to work on together. On one occasion, our participating visitors were cutting hearts from folded paper with a special focus on symmetry. They then went on to help the children enjoy the regularity of symmetry in the chains of people cut from folded paper. Children need the fun of discovering variety in cut paperwork that the extra adults make possible.

In our view, it is vital to invite the extended family and particularly our grandparent group to work alongside the children and to give them a flavour of our work and approach to education. The third generation can have a particular relationship with their grandchildren that is special. Those children who do not have a grandparent or substitute family member attending will be adopted for the day by the guests of other children and so will have a similar involvement. We provide tea and coffee for our visitors throughout the day and we invite them to bring along a packed lunch so that they can eat alongside the children at lunchtime. The feedback from these days is positive. The families get to know more about how the school works and they also have the chance to share specific moments and build up a family history that involves the children's school years. Of course there is more work for all the staff and particularly for the teachers who have an extended class to look after but there is a vast amount of school philosophy contained in these days' experiences.

A scheme for the grandparents' day is drawn up by the staff group. The day will be a part of the current topic with the addition of a substantial citizenship, shared learning and cross-generational approach. Visiting specialists bring a third perspective to the day's programme in which active involvement is seen as the catalyst to understanding. The specialists' role might be to make a chair from a standing tree; it could be to take apart a bicycle and reassemble it, or a mime workshop. The idea is to showcase possibilities that have an affinity with the topic. Groups return to their class base to discuss and record or come up with their own creations in collaboration with their visitors. A range of workshops is ongoing through the day and last approximately 30 min per group. The schedule for the day has changes of pace and show a variety of teaching styles.

Drama, role-play and mime

Drama and role-play are frequently used as part of our teaching and learning programme. Prepared but unrehearsed drama such as the story of Johnny Appleseed, the legend of St George, the life of Sir Isaac Newton or a retelling of Each Peach Pear Plum is used as a teaching tool. A narrator guides the plot and the actors are members of staff helped by the children. These dramas encourage active engagement and they are more forceful than a story simply told. Costumes are basic: a hat or a cloak support the role. Drama is used in curriculum lessons and children are involved in mime and the retelling of stories. Members of staff have developed a style of talk to deal with negative behaviour that does not involve the children except as listeners. The support assistant might challenge the teacher about treading on her feet without an apology and together they will make the point that certain skills are needed to protect relationships.

Mime can be a fresh approach to story but its spark depends on more than one performance. The adult will offer the mime: at first, the children tend to call out, vocalizing their impressions and guesses which can make it awkward for the children who are quietly trying to work out what is being revealed. It takes practice for all the children to learn to watch carefully. In mime, two adults raise a problem in mime, taking the parts of an adult and child. The story goes that a child wants a pet,

child visits a pet shop and comes back with a dog. Adult mimes that dog is too big, child returns next time with a cat. Adult mimes allergy to cats, child comes back with a snake. Adult indicates that snake should be liberated. Adult and child visit per shop and return with two mice in a cage.

Sometimes we use the idea of flea circuses where there is a little talking but the acts of the fleas are all imagined. In these scenes, the children 'see' fleas leaping into the air, double somersaulting and diving into a saucer of water. There are a range of other circus style acts. All are imagined and all require the suspension of reality as the children interpret the happening in their own ways. Sometimes ideas are about journeys where tigers are held at bay, sandwiches can be drawn, picked off the paper and eaten.

In dog shows, pairs of children act the parts of dog and owner. Initially all the children are dogs – they demonstrate dog behaviours and most movingly become guide dogs for each other. In the main this sort of work is non-verbal or with minimum language. It sums up dependence on the spoken word as well as independence from it. All of this involves imagination, problem solving and empathy building with short, sharp action to be felt. This kind of stimulus uses few props; it is an artistic expression with negotiation and cooperation that gives value to the children's own ideas. At times, we make token dogs from scraps of different fabrics that are tied to a piece of cord (the lead). The fabric dogs take on their own personalities and often the children become so attached to them that they want to take them home. The qualities we observe and admire in dogs are often values we want to own in ourselves – loyalty, trust, forgiveness and a wish to play.

There are many ways to make puppets and in our experience, sock puppets are good promoters of dialogue. They can show an interconnection between craft, art and language and children can be very creative with their design and use. Shadow puppets are not as spontaneous, they need a great deal of careful preparation and manipulation. We use them as part of topics about light or to look at multicultural art forms.

Badges and tokens

In 1978 a lion cub came to school. It arrived as the result of a goodwill visit from an 'ethical' circus that relied on acts from ponies, dogs and a pair of camels. The circus owner told us that the lion and its cub had come from another circus that was being disbanded and that negotiations were in place to re-home the lions in a reputable zoo. The children met the lion cub in small groups. They thought he was beautiful and he was.

The lion became a springboard for thinking about animals and birds in captivity. We looked for models to help us express some principles in a systematic way and we established some new traditions as a result. One was the regular release of homing pigeons, another concentrated on rearing animals such as sheep, chickens and ducks and a third focussed on growing wild life corridors through the grounds to create eco-consciousness and species movement. Such actions were beneficial in helping us relate to non-human needs and there were intrinsic rewards both aesthetic and spiritual.

In an effort to help the children hold on to ideals that involve our relationships with each other and our relationships with nature, we started giving the children small tokens. These souvenirs are generally made of wood and are distributed about three times a year. The badges are an expression of regard for the children and they help to fix in the memory a pattern of beliefs and care arising from a particular interest or topic. In the case of the lion cub's visit a wooden shape followed an examination of ethically based work with lions: Joy Adams and Elsa, a lion in the fantasy world of the intimidated child in Philippa Pearce's story Lion at School and in Shel Silverstein's story of Lafcadio The Lion Who Shot Back. These examples were starting points for assemblies where the lion was the nucleus of the story and the lion's view was central to the retelling. The people of Ghana have a saying, 'Until the lion learns to write, the hunter will always tell the story of the hunt' and this is also a springboard for an assembly.

One of the children's fathers cut a wooden lion for every child and the lions were hidden in different places outside. The children were asked to pass on any lion they found to a person without one. This forestalled the possibility of children drifting round the gardens without a lion keepsake or with more than one. The shape marked our first wooden badge.

Badge designing, painting, lettering and threading draws on the talent and time of many people. All those involved see it in the context of a love and care response to the children that is stated artistically. In our attempt to help children hold on to ideas that involve our relationships with each other and our relationship with nature we given the children these small wooden tokens as an expression of regard for the children and they help to fix in the memory a pattern of beliefs and care arising from a particular interest or topic.

There is no norm for these mementoes and one year we gave the children decorated wooden spoons to mark Shrove Tuesday. The pilgrim's symbol, a scallop shell, is given to everyone after walking the perimeter path and the labyrinth at the start of a new academic year. Horseshoes are given to the children after they have visited the farrier during the Epiphany celebrations and in the Autumn term all the children and adults receive a sunflower badge to mark the success of the seed to seed cycle.

Frogs, ladybirds, deer, hearts, doves, sheep, fish, robins, trees and flowers have been the subject of badges. The folk art style is typical of all badges that are painted, sanded, printed and varnished as artistic creations. A group of parents known as the 'Coombes Badgers' led by Sarah and Jo has helped us with the preparation of the badges, and three members of staff print the children's names, the year and a short message on each.

Badges are presented at a special ceremony. When the adults fasten a badge onto each child they both share a hug. By the end of their time at school, most children will have received about 24 badges to form a personalized collection. Each badge is unique and no design is ever exactly repeated.

Wooden books

Over the years we have taken the idea of wooden badges one step further and we now have a collection of our own wooden books. The books are illustrated by artists within our school community and hand-printed by two members of staff. They represent long hours of work and each is beautiful to read and to handle.

Photographs

Photographs play an essential role in describing learning to the learner. This has a bearing on the child seeing him or herself in the conditions that govern learning, socializing and discovering. Pictures of the garden displayed through the school corridors are an impetus to rediscover a location for oneself. The photograph tends to put a value on the happening and the place. Photographs clarify the differences between inside and outside and they help children to consider the things they have been taught. The pictures are key to encouraging discussion with other children and with adults so it is bound to affect the quality of learning.

Some concepts about teaching and learning styles are presented to the children and parents through photographs. We try to capture natural moments when creativity and new ideas are being demonstrated. Photographs of these moments are displayed in the corridors and classrooms. Images of this kind are also a vital part of the learning platform and are kept as current as possible. Information carried this way is personal and details the life of the school with its events and traditions.

Individuals see themselves in different settings or experiencing new ideas. In school, at the local church, in the natural environment shaping and managing their landscape, visiting a construction site or generally engaged at work and play. The visual message is about serious learning in a social context where individuals are valued. Single portraits of children are easier to capture but the pictures with the basic message show groups at work in which most of the individuals are recognizable. Since photographs are so suitable for presenting a view of the children and teachers to themselves, we ask parents to sign a permission slip so that we can record at will. Every so often a parent will request no exposure to cameras for their child. This need for privacy is respected and we make adjustments through the view finder or when editing, so that this request is honoured. Access to our learning platform is password protected and we have a comprehensive e-safety policy in place.

The photographs, videos and colour slides are shared with parents, grandparents, governors and the wider community and they are basic to the records that we keep. Above all the pictures are for the children.

School calendars

Photographs of groups of children at work are used in the school calendars and these pictures are supported by text that give explanation about the work and the ideas that underpins it. Each year the calendar focuses on a particular aspect of the children's learning experiences, but every publication is about the children learning through practical experiences. One of the calendars, published in the past five years, records the range of trees in our arboretum and includes the class groups at work with different challenges. Another is a monthly guide to the collection of wild flowers with children and teachers capturing the essence of the environment developed for its ecology.

A third calendar is a presentation of our geology trail, demonstrating creative play and study around the rocks. Two other calendars detail aspects of the curriculum being taught out of doors to different age groups of children. Innovation in the natural space is easier to manage and recognize and these calendars aim to capture the spirit of our recently combined schools at work together. It is a rewarding challenge to produce a high-quality calendar every year that is aimed at becoming part of the backdrop to events reviewed at home.

A former governor, Sue Coffey and her partner Andrew Evans keep the editing and production in house. This back up of creative designers gives our calendars a well-presented look and makes each edition worth keeping as a souvenir. The photographs are laden with memories and the text is a brief guide to our shared philosophy. The calendars are a recognition of many shared talents and reflect our school as a learning community working together.

Visits to the school

The practice of inviting professional actors, musicians and dancers to perform at school through the year gives the children a sense of what it is like to be part of a live audience. Our children are used to television, DVD and computer images, but fewer of them have the chance to enjoy live performance. The experiences need to be regular and of high quality so we canvas parents and friends to find gifted amateurs. Every year accomplished Irish dancers from a nearby secondary school dance for us on St Patrick's Day and are often accompanied by an expert Aeolian harpist. On Burns Night and St Andrew's Day, pipers play for us in the hall and then again in the playground. A harp maker, Keith Beechey has become a friend of the school and visits us to celebrate St David's Day and Welsh culture and traditions. As well as playing for groups of children, he describes his harp making and shows a harp in parts. In turn the children touch the harp as Keith plays to feel the vibrating strings and they also catch the resonance of the music when they put an ear on the hall's wooden floor. The children bring pencils and paper to make instant visual records of their experience and they lie on the floor to work, rather than sitting in formal groups.

School birthday

Community is felt rather than explained by words: the school's birthday is a day that is apt for the children as it celebrates a birthday in which they are the centre. We display photographs, news items and first plans of the building, and also get former pupils to talk to the children about what they remember. We examine the process of change by walking through the school interior and then follow the outside walls around the building. In the afternoon we cut a birthday cake. This will usually be a cake we can sit alongside. On the school's 25th anniversary, we made a 25-m-long cake by joining swiss rolls together with icing. The cake is set on a narrow roll of foil or paper. We generally eat on the grass: we sing, blow out the candles and help ourselves to a piece of the celebration cake.

Christmas dinner

This meal carries a lot of symbolism and is meant to express the values of the school family. Puddings made earlier by the children in the classrooms are steamed then stored and reheated on the day. Friends who have helped the school (other than parents) and former members of staff are invited to have dinner with us and sit among the children. The children make placemats for themselves and their guests and we eat by candlelight. A piper plays the children and their guests to their seats, there is a formal grace and all the adults collect the turkey and vegetables and serve the first course. The adults are offered pre-prandial drinks and the children have juice at the table. When the first course is finished we have some community fun. Some adults gather around the piano to sing and mime the Twelve Days of Christmas song led by Gill with help from the children. The remaining adults clear the tables ready for the Christmas pudding service. Everyone then sings the Figgy pudding song and two flaming puddings are carried out of the kitchen and paraded around the tables to the sound of the singing. After this short drama, puddings are served and eaten, the kitchen staff are brought out to be thanked and applauded and the children go to their classrooms to take off their character hats and have a play outside with some of the adults.

The children's hats relate to characters in an adapted story that will come together in the afternoon. It is reworked so that it is brimming with action to be shared by each class in turn. The staff group are the main actors and one member of staff is the narrator who keeps the plot going. There are no rehearsals – the action needs to unfold in stages. Some role play, mime, movement or song has been practiced in advance by each class so that there can be a guarantee of dependable reactions from the children. The whole entertainment lasts approximately 80 min, feels spontaneous and guarantees that everyone will take part. Guests at dinner often stay for the afternoon but this is ad hoc and sometimes people not intending to stay find themselves included in the afternoon's entertainment.

Museum education

Examples of our commitment to museum education have been given throughout the book and the idea is fundamental to our educational philosophy. The exhibitions offer the stimulation of hands-on experiences. Touching an object even if its purpose is unknown is important – in the context of a textiles exhibition one of the children guessed that a round mallet could well have been used for knocking shape into felt. There are opportunities for the children to develop good reasoning and inference skills when they are encouraged to touch the exhibits and use their senses to explore them.

Museums containing artefacts collected from the school community give opportunities for parental involvement and have a lot of meaning for the children. The museums are linked to themes: it may be Victoriana if we have been thinking about Victorian history; it could be examples of transport through the ages if we have been studying the laws of motion and the forces of push and pull. One simple theme was a museum that specialized in arachnids. We asked the children to collect spiders from around their home environment. They were kept in containers with transparent lids and the children were asked to bring in labels staring time, place and method of capture. Children not able to bring in a spider from home were helped to find one at school.

A specialist in arachnids brought in some of his own collection and shared his knowledge and enthusiasm with the children. As a centrepiece in the school hall, we constructed a floor-to-ceiling spider's web using white yarn and anchoring it to points in the ceiling and on the floor. As part of the museum opening, the children stepped up and through the middle of the web in an interactive kinetic art activity. Children were curators to their own spider exhibit and gave anecdotal information. This museum took a few days to set up and intrigued the children and families who visited before and after school said that they were seeing spiders in a different light. We plan for the children to have at least two visits to each museum. There is always an adult curator to set the tone and check the exhibits. The hall is set with tables and cloths and with different heights to suit the display, recognizing that behaviour and outcomes are affected by the quality of presentation.

Tree and bulb planting

Greening the school grounds has been in progress for many years and physically involving children and staff in planting trees every autumn renews our dream to have a school set in a wood. The trees we have around us are living references to the tree planting of the past and they tell us different stories. Most reflect the annual class plantings; others are memorials such as Carole's copper beech planted in memory of her mother, or Annabel's silver birches, Alastair and Helen's aspens and Patrick's mulberry. Many of the trees have a narrative: in 1997 Sarah organized leavers gifts of trees that were set in a line down the length of the field. An acorn from the Boscobel oak in which King Charles sheltered from Cromwell's troops was nurtured by John's mother and then planted in the gardens. Cedars of Lebanon came from friends of the school.

Woodland demonstrates one of nature's great flows through leaf production to leaf litter and on to the production of new soil in preparation for emerging life. Teachers demonstrate this with the children by raking up soil and examining the particles in it.

In late October every year, the children plant narcissus bulbs around the gardens. This activity is integrated with the story of Narcissus who fell in love with himself and pined away beside his reflection in a pool. The story is used to examine the sense of responsibility we have for ourselves and for each other and ends on a note of hope. That he would be remembered by all those who admire the flowers named for him. Baskets of bulbs and posters of the types of narcissus we are going to plant provide information. We talk to the children about the construction of a bulb and its capacity to respond to particular conditions. At flowering time each boy and girl will pick a small bunch of daffodils for their mothers. The children gain from the results of the year-by-year planting programme that fills the grounds with flowers.

We replenish our native bluebells as these plants are so easily damaged by the pressure of feet on them. The common bluebell, once widespread in woods and old banks is Hyacinthoides Non-Scriptus. This bluebell should be the type chosen to naturalize in grassy places where there are native shrubs and trees. The Spanish bluebell Hyacinthoides Hispanka is a garden escapee and does not need any encouragement.

Authors and illustrators

One powerful element in our practice has been the regular visits of authors and illustrators. The teachers and children who had these experiences were able to absorb some of the best preparation for literacy from these visits. One result of having creative people as examples was the production of many big books. In interactive workshops with teachers and children, wholly original stories and poems were powerful outcomes. This material was made into outsize books that were read, shared and hefted about until they fell apart. Over many years and before we were able to build a library we regularly laid out all the big books on carpets in the hall, and the children came to read them, sharing one big book between two and with the children almost inside the book.

It is hard work to keep a steady stream of these books in production because they needed to be passed around the classrooms to optimize the creativity involved. Carolyn Dinan's work was typical: she used the children's lunch boxes to boost their immunity to fears such as her own personal one where her monster was controlled in the lunch box. She helped every group by drawing hybrid monsters to represent the individual fears. Using humour to help the children talk about and then use their own powers and by leaving extensive material for us she supported the children emotionally and in their development of literacy.

Guided tours

Unless children get a good model for guiding each other and visitors around the school their efforts will not be rewarding for them or those depending on them. The best support for doing this job comes from the teachers whose purpose it is to give the children a secure foundation on which to talk comfortably and knowledgeably about their landscape. The following experience is typical of the teaching style begun in and out of doors.

In Carol's class, snowdrops and hazel catkins were passed around the group. The plant parts were identified by Carol and in pairs the children took a snowdrop apart and studied its features. This was repeated with the hazel twigs, their catkins and leaf buds. Carol told the children that they were going outside to see great quantities of hazel and snowdrop and that they would be examining them without taking them apart. She explained that we depend on the snowdrops to seed and the hazel to set nuts for birds and mice. The children went outside – the established rule is that the teacher goes first setting the pace. The children walked informally to the hazel/snowdrop copse that was in full flower. The children touched and smelled, lifting up some snowdrop heads and they vibrated the catkins to see the pollen scatter. They wandered around the edge of the copse while Carol moved about asking questions and getting impressions. She was helping the children to see the relationship between the plants and the spaces they occupied. She asked the children why there were so many flowers and wondered how they had spread. The clues given in the classroom guaranteed a lot of answers. Talk and informality was key to the experience where content and method is fused into scientific, social and environmental objectives. This style of delivery repeated many times in many venues becomes the basis for children teaching each other and visitors during guided walks: it is method in action.

Awareness of the landscape

Developing a consciousness of the landscape in which the children interact during free play involves the teachers regularly working outside with groups of children. A group's experience of sketching the earthworks around the grounds or collecting photographic evidence of the embankments, mounds and sunken pathways and measuring them, may be a prelude to a map-making exercise. Equally it could stem from an investigation on growth governed by light and shade or the children may have been directed to think about why early people with handtools changed the landscape to include so many vast earth structures. These are activities that blur the margins between curricular disciplines and encourage children to apply thinking they develop via learning out of doors.

Learning through art with the garden as a setting can reinforce creative energy. Parts of out teaching are planned so that children learn curriculum essentials through artistic expression. Activities range from teaching about photosynthesis from pattern-making on grass, lots of writing and recording on paving and playground becomes graffiti art, successive addition using lines of flowers in the grass is art ephemera, signatures made through marking shadow length through the day is recording by diagram. Map making on the sport that refers directly to the immediate context can be a useful introduction to reading plans of the school. Features on the children's maps often indicate the things they prefer by the degree of attention to size and detail. Outline drawing of features depicts relationships of features to spaces. In these early maps, chalk outlines of the features are drawn as the children attempt to organize what they know and see into a guide of the area.

The children who share these activities with their teachers tend to remember them because they have been using all their senses. Attention paid to trees, wild flowers and small creatures as well as for each other gradually builds up layers of messages that are processed and internalized. The children are feeling their way towards relationships with nature and each other and their surroundings need to be planned so that they are aware of constant possibilities. There is real choice during playtimes: the children can jump on and off stepping stones, climb on logs, run up and down steps, make arrangements of flowers, leaves and pebbles. During free play they can deal with big spaces and small measures of risk and uncertainty.

Earth works

Once or twice every year we return to our original plan to change or reshape our school site. We make 'ground breaking' opportunities as described in Chapter 4. Nothing makes this notion more powerful than when it becomes a tradition. The school's history holds many moments of children watching diggers and their drivers excavating clay, shifting donated topsoil, cutting pathways and dressing the labyrinth site with wood chip. Like other traditions it is often a signature piece for new projects and changes in design. Usually the digger driver is a parent or grandparent who owns the machine and is connected with the school community. Earth moving exposes soil profiles for study, the machines are of great interest in themselves and the operators stop the machines to explain the handling and the power of their model and to describe safety protocols.

Simply moving earth in large quantities reshapes the land. Creating high banks and hills can be a protection against the wind but most strikingly it alters the way outside areas are viewed and used. A parent, Tina Parker said, 'The grounds make you feel together but separated. When you are in there you turn a corner and find another group of children at work and you didn't know they were there.' Getting to know the grounds should mean moving into them. iIn order to understand them it is necessary to go into them. The general lay-out of the site emphasizes the child as an explorer.

The trickiest part of any hill, bank or similar creation is getting it to look good. Mass planting of willow cuttings provides food and shelter for wildlife in its second year: the roots lock the soil and the willows leaf early in spring. Depending on how they are planted, willow cuttings can mark the semi-formal routes through the gardens.

Note

1. The issue of health and safety and safeguarding is discussed more fully in Chapters 2 and 10.

10 In conclusion

Evaluating our work

In 1996 the BBC made a film about our school for the Open University's In-Service programmes for teachers. We saw ourselves teaching the children and watched the children's reactions to us and to each other. The sharing and debating of ideas during planning meetings was also recorded. When we viewed the film we thought it captured the essence of our school and described our competencies. It seemed that the value we put on the collaborative judgement of each other's work and that the aspirations we had hammered out together had largely become the way we worked.

Film has the potential to expose weaknesses but it can also evince a sense of school relationships and their nature. The children filmed were relaxed and connected to their work; they were neither exceptional nor mediocre but their independence and creative attitudes were plain to see. This was not providential because the children are always ready to deal with a camera collecting data for individual records, personalizing journals and recording the interactive thematic work for display. When the children are pictured working they interpret the observations as a sign that their efforts are appreciated. The teachers refer to the camera as an invisible eye and advise the children that they should just get on with what they are doing so that we can film a working situation. Looking good for the camera simply means getting on with their jobs. Our staff group is also accustomed to being photographed or filmed.

Teachers seeing each other at work is also a formalized system in our school. The interpretation of the observer during the course of a half-day session is fed back to the class teacher on the day. It is not a bland surveillance because the aim is to help a colleague become aware of shortcomings and respond positively. Half of the feedback is positive reinforcement but our purpose is to give support, advice and criticism. Being mentors for each other is an important tool in striving for the school to become a learning community. Professional development is nothing to do with line management – every teacher is a research worker. Democracy is a gate-keeper of creativity and if there is too much control then creativity is hobbled.

Fault-finding is a serious responsibility and if the receiving teacher thinks a criticism is wrongly applied he or she can claim to have been misunderstood. Assessments must be justified. They are reciprocal but the partnerships alter regularly so that awareness of one another's weaknesses and abilities are factors for change in the whole group. Occasionally there are nuggets of inspiration in these mutual exchanges but only when positive and negative feedback is balanced. Any curb on criticism hobbles the process and is seen as a defensive reaction against moving towards a better teaching style. This last consideration tends to favour the rationale for performance management to be a top-down model displacing the idea of giving and doing equally in return for a deeper understanding. We prefer the mutual plan and it always worked well during the many times we engaged in it. Many teachers would argue that management powers are not necessarily in the hands of gifted teachers because management can be about many different things. In the top-down model merit is seen in the conditions that were choices in the classroom of the evaluator: it is easy to rate highly what was successful for yourself. There are dangers in being observed and assessed by only one evaluator and we believe that it is preferable to have a rolling programme where teachers are seen at work by different colleagues and where the roles are interchangeable.

We are all teaching the children: all looking for better solutions and all coming to terms with issues around behaviour, motivation and attainment measures. Added to these is the impact of technology and changes in society to acknowledge. Each teacher depends on others as partners and on parents as associates to bring the school to life so that children can enjoy education and get the fullest advantages from it. Vitality in and around the school was to be braced by each other's needs and opinions, those of the children and parents and crucially through teachers working in a coalition. Each individual is a committed professional in different stages of tackling methods, weighing proposal and personal growth.

Other people's evaluations

When schools open their doors to parents, grandparents, trainee teachers and visiting colleagues it is hoped that the school has become an interesting model for study. Like it or not, the school has also allowed people with mixed agendas to look at the self-confidence of pupils and teachers, get a measure of the physical and emotional release of pupils and judge the intellectual stimulus of the place. It is not just the knowledge of their child's teacher or how special needs children cross the gap to become enfranchised as writers: all kinds of knowledge is picked up from contact with and listening to the children and their teachers. Evaluations are a large part of every visitor's unspoken brief. Whatever judgements are made about the school we believe that it is right to open the doors and welcome democracy and accountability.

In the safe confines of a well-aware society there are rewards for the children in having extra adults. It can mean learning alongside each other or being guided by an adult with a different approach. We ask all our visitors to get involved in case they are unaware of the myriad ways in which their interest can benefit the children.[1] The essence of what they have come to see is best experienced by sitting with the children as a child themselves and doing what the children do. This is a genuine shortcut to understanding from the child's viewpoint. The children get a lot of satisfaction from seeing adults learning with them and it reinforces their pleasure in learning.

The gradual addition to children's knowledge about a world elsewhere that is interested in them can help the children question their choices in the far future. It can certainly bring an immediate sense of the connections between school society and society outside. Children field questions from visitors about their interests, how they make sense of the natural world and why they do what they do: all this and more helps the children to define their situation in school. Guided tours are another aspect of school life shared with visitors.[2] Adults seek the views of children and ask relevant questions. These dig into the different fields of study the children have followed and their knowledge is related to what they say during their walks. Explanations are given from one to the other and this also upholds a democratic approach.

Using video for evaluation

Our presentation of assembly times was not always as we imagined it. A lot goes by unnoticed: teachers or parents move through the hall, there may be noises such as the clatter from the adjacent school kitchen or the teacher's intention is poorly realized. This will impact on the atmosphere but not necessarily stop the children from concentrating. We asked Robert Howe, one of our governors, to make video films of some of our assemblies in order to assess the children's level of concentration, our choice of content, our presentational style and the overall quality. The staff group was also asked to give us honest, critical feedback that we could use to improve our assemblies. Some members of the team then went on to have their teaching filmed for a similar purpose.

Choice

The children should face choices at some time every day: in this way, they learn to ask questions and think about options. Choice is about evaluation, information gathering and risk taking; by making choices the children begin to build up the life skills that result in critically considered judgements. Starting points may be as simple as 'what shall I wear today?', 'which pen should I choose for this job?', 'where shall I sit?'. We build in activities that will lead to choice-making because personal choices matter so much. Children have the right to be a unique individual in a socially cohesive group.

Modelling behaviour

Our adult group model conduct for the children: we are seen to collaborate, to share problems and to give each other honest feedback. We work together to brainstorm ideas and describe our preparation for lessons to the children. Setting out these models, we hope to encourage similar behaviours in them. Diversity is a fact of life going beyond mere tolerance. Respecting difference and the right to be different is fundamental and we do a lot of work to help the children to understand this. It cannot be taught in one or two lessons but rather has to be absorbed into the culture of the school and be evident in daily practice and in the way we relate to each other. Howard Gardner talks of the 'respectful mind'[3]: there is a big difference between being tolerant of differences and respecting them. Real respect, he argues, is much more than that and it is our role as educators to cultivate respect as well as emotional and interpersonal intelligence. As Gardner says, the future will need citizens and workers who can 'think out of the box' to solve tomorrow's ever more complex challenges. The 'respectful' mind will actively welcome differences between people and cultures and will respond constructively to them. Our world has become a small place with the development of technology and travel and the ability to understand and respect other people is increasingly important. We need perspectives other than our own and to afford them the same importance as our own. Socially adept and emotionally intelligent adulthood has its roots in the foundations of childhood.

Multi-sensory experiences

Experiences contain the essence of life. They are the pieces of the story that make us who we are as we begin to understand how the world works, our own place in it and our own potential. Experiences evoke possibilities, new approaches and new ideas. Like Bronowski[4] we recognize that the hands are the cutting edge of the mind. Being an active participant in an activity rather than having a merely vicarious experience will set the children on the path to understanding and skills development. 'I hear and I forget. I see and I remember. I do and I understand.'[5] By purposely engaging all our senses, we internalize the learning and start to make sense of it: it is remembered through the whole body. Children record things in the brain through smell and touch as well as through the ears and eyes. Internalized experiences are something of a blueprint on which the children will draw in later years. In recent years some schools have had the effect of suppressing creativity and experiential learning in favour of rote learning and conformity. The children in these schools pay a high price for this. Instead of being the raison d'etre for school-based teaching and learning, they have taken second place to standardized test scores, punitive health and safety directives and a monotonous teaching diet.

Providing challenge for more able children

Seen from the point of view of the parents and grandparents, all their children are gifted and talented, and they are right. Our brief is to identify any talent in a child and help those with gifts to define and improve what they have. It also seems reasonable to encourage every child so that they might triumph in some field or other.

Experiences are generalized at many different levels and experiential education favours children who are devoted to learning as much as motivating children who opt out easily. Topic work requires the collection of evidence. This research can lead to a degree of self-sufficiency in order to be more successful. From the perspective of an accomplished child, progress can be in the fast track and the next set of details can be handled.

We advocate shared teaching roles to model cooperation and extend the pool of expertise available to the children. We plan that the children experience a number of adults as experts in residence or as a friend in need to solve a problem. Drawing on opinion, knowledge and guidance from a group of teachers and other adults should give added strength to the learning and expose the children to contrasting styles of teaching.

Our planned museums introduce children to collections of pieces, fossils, first editions, tools of a trade, fungi, looms, hemp, jute, tweed and many of the items that lie within the heart of a theme. Such articles are a persuasive and subtle inducement to gather more information, become a collector and to check up on the things that carry a personal appeal. Most importantly, museum education is an introduction to visit exhibitions and art galleries and to use the computer to download street art or look at National Trust gardens or historic houses. There are manifold ways of sharing such pleasures that stretch understanding and are intriguing in their own right. It is not about appreciating high style, it is simply about seeing many layers of a fulfilling life.

We have tried to leave no stone unturned in the search for satisfactory teaching methods to suit all the children and this research is ongoing. Arguably, the defining aspect of success is hard work and purposefulness combined with a sense of responsibility towards self and others. The naturally gifted do not always develop this understanding and when this happens their gift might be described as a wasted talent.

Children's preferences in the outdoor environment

We were interested to find out what the children's preferences in the outdoor environment were in order to see it through their eyes. Over four consecutive years, we asked the children to draw what they liked best outside the school building. The children worked in the hall because the larger area gave each child a discrete space to lie on the floor and sketch. We closed the curtains so that the children were detached from the outside and we asked for ten parent volunteers to help us. As the children began to draw using pencils, the adults marked their first drawing with a number 1, the second with number 2 and so on. The children were asked to put down at least three but preferably more places or things they liked outside. They were given 20 min to complete their sketches, and some of the older children labeled their own drawings. The adults asked each child about their drawings to expand the meaning and notes taken from the talk were clipped to the research.

On a large grid marked with the many features outside the school, a member of staff ticked the relevant box whenever a feature was drawn. Results for each class, for boys and girls and for the whole school were collated. There were interesting findings: over the course of the 4 years, the most preferred feature for the whole school over that period was the trees. Closely second to the trees were flowers and plants. Third came the tunnel ('somewhere to hide') followed by the large logs for climbing on in the playground. Walls to sit on was next and then followed the various pieces of playground furniture – the saddle, the stepping stones, the concrete blocks and the hump-back bridge. The ponds and the newts, toads and frogs in them scored highly throughout the year.

We went on to more sophisticated scoring by showing the first, second, third and fourth preferences for each child for each outdoor feature. This was a much more complex process but the results still clearly showed that trees, plants and flowers, the logs and the tunnel were by far the most popular features for the children.

In a second activity, we asked the children what they would like to see in the outdoor setting and although trees and flowers still featured strongly, the children also suggested roundabouts, slides, cycle tracks – much more the stuff of parks, funfairs and civic amenities.

Talking to the children after the research and getting them to respond more generally about the outdoor features, the children liked having places to sit down, places to hide in and high spots where 'you could be the tallest person outside'. They liked being able to sit under trees, look at flowers and squeeze herbs. Children put value on a varied landscape in which to work and play and by involving them in the planting of trees, flowers, herbs and vegetables, these things become even more interesting and pleasurable. The boys often commented that the school garden gave them opportunities for climbing, hiding in and for games they could invent.

Health and safety issues

A person who does not have the capacity to feel fear cannot survive for very long. Having too little fear can mean personal and group levels of safety fall, accidents happen and there are damaging psychological impacts. The other side of the same coin is when individuals live in such a state of apprehension that risk and possibilities are a threat. This is so desperate that life is limited and cannot be lived on equal terms with others. Such a condition blocks decisions and has equally bleak psychological prospects. These states are the extreme ends of a continuum. We all live somewhere between these points in an ebb and flow of boldness and caution. Our position keeps changing depending mostly on experience and on such factors as encouragement received, personal strength, friendships and abilities. Adults can make children distrustful and uncomprehending when they give recurring directives such as 'keep safe', 'stay clean', 'don't speak to strangers', 'no climbing', 'play near a grown-up' and children struggle to reconcile all this with the teacher's directions at school 'go and explore the nursery garden: our visitors Kim and Russell have hung some bells in the trees: we'll know you have found them when we hear them ring'.

At school, we lay the foundations for trial and error learning in the playground by providing the means for this. We encourage climbing on the PE apparatus emphasizing the successful feelings of getting part-way up the rope. When we cook we broach the subject of germs, we impress on the children the dangers of high heat and we pond dip and bring home to the children the dangers of water and notions of water safety.

The possibility of being lost in the nursery garden among a dozen trees and a few bushes totally enclosed by a secure fence is almost impossible but the conceptual understanding about finding the way back to the teacher is imprinted by the confident adult. She knows that her children can manage this. Developing safety competence should come from this perspective and we argue from the need not to undermine the children's emerging independence and common sense.

All of this is a balance. Each risk is carefully negotiated as a step towards understanding and having a positive view about life. Intelligent care does not trivialize safety issues and it seeks to establish both trust and caution. Where the children are on the continuum cannot be fixed, they have to discover it each time, as do adults.

There is much debate from the standpoint of health and safety officers and parents about the dangers posed to the children from the community. The fact that people with psychopathic tendencies can target children in school may not be a good argument for making schools off-limits to the community. Aberrant behaviour is played out across society and for all the world to see as a clearly apparent problem. Measures taken for security purposes are high fencing, locked gates and an office/guardroom at the entrance to the building as well as keypad entry systems on other access points. This is separation and withdrawal at penitentiary levels. Naturally schools shelter their children but basic rights are just as much about avoiding an outlook where fear and suspicion is tangible from the security precautions.

International links

There is nothing like being able to think about your own school from a distance. By examining provision in another country we extend all our terms of reference. Two members of staff were invited by Dr Carol Vukelich to lead workshops for American teachers during the summer holidays at the University of Delaware. One of these workshops required the students to renew their knowledge of heritage sites as part of the course. We organized a tour of historic houses in old New Castle in Delaware for the students and visited the old church and churchyard there to make connections between the early settlers and their life expectancy. Back in the classroom, graphs were drawn up, a large model of the historic area was planned and the plants and trees of the gardens and parks were logged. Although we were leading the course, we also took a lot from it that influenced our reading and writing work back in the United Kingdom. Members of the US group of teachers planned their writing together – they read each other's work aloud from a 'writer's chair' and they used Donald Graves's[6] conventions for creative writing. These were still in their early days at the time but we imagined our children at The Coombes working in a similar way.

Since then members of our team have visited schools in several countries in order to discover more about lifestyles and the schools there. One teacher, Celia undertook a year-long exchange with a colleague in an Australian school and there were mutual benefits from this. Our experience suggests that matching visits and longer term relationships between the staff groups of two schools can more directly involve the children. We started a long-term exchange link with children and staff at Tunaskolan in Lund. This led to Stina and Kerstin from Tunaskolan bringing a class of 25 9-year-old children for a 5-day study visit to The Coombes. Until her retirement, Stina and several of her colleagues visited our school at least once a year and many members of our team went to Tunaskolan in return. We also benefited from having other Swedish teachers perform a St Lucia parade in December and at midsummer others helped the children to decorate our own Midsommar Stong and to dance around it.

We offer experience in our school to teachers and trainees from around the world. An initial visit from colleagues at Pabo Arnhem in The Netherlands has resulted in groups of four or five trainee teachers at a time working for 12 weeks with us. This programme has continued for 5 years. We have also welcomed trainee teachers from France, Sweden and from Boston, Oregon and Delaware in the United States.

Standing on new ground claims your attention. Teachers visiting our school are referring the characteristics of their own settings and rearranging their thinking. This is something we have in common with them when we are the observers elsewhere. As a spectator you are taking stock of your accepted patterns of working and positioning yourself for hypothetical change. Awareness of the need to alter a system is just that and being able to follow through markedly harder. Every time working patterns are called into question there is a degree of unease. Some of us would argue that the pace and scale of change in schools needs to accelerate greatly if we are going to raise levels of teaching for peace, for fairness and for an ecologically sustainable future. Developing wisdom in these fields should be a priority but at this point in time such ideas are not in the order of national reforms.

Some visitors to The Coombes have been regularly viewing our work over a period of years. Dr Petter Akerblom from the Swedish University of Agricultural Sciences in Uppsala has been bringing groups of Swedish professionals to focus on the children at work and play in the gardens. These educators direct detailed questions to all of us about what they see and ask for explanations. Justification for our work is partly crystallized through the scrutiny and questioning of others. Levels of discussion from visiting specialists cannot go forward from shallow responses: much longer versions of the philosophy are required to analyse the developments seen during a series of visits.

Another dialogue about the school's programmes for music and spiritual awareness was begun with Dr Roger Nickerson. His interest in music and spiritual development has brought him to the school over a period of 20 years. He led assemblies during his visits and he examined our needs and judged our work towards satisfying them. As a

Christian he works within a belief system but he is a member of a very broad church and has supplied us with much food for thought.

We welcome all visitors to join our children at work.[7] Many of them are interested in the ways in which we spread our teaching from the inside to the outside and back again and in seeing social goals and wider possibilities for their own pupils. Visitors from the United Kingdom tend to want to see how we deliver the National Curriculum in a different way and they also share their own school's philosophical evolution to its current point.

Creativity

We try to teach creatively. So much of what we are mandated to teach by central government is dismal stuff. The national curriculum and national strategies with their measurable outcomes sweep creativity sideways. As a force creativity remains and it is talked about quite often; it is rarely an anchor or a mainspring for what happens. If the children are to recognize creativity and feel confident in displaying it, we teachers need to be the people who demonstrate its value. By speculating on what makes a 'human' human we bounced some ideas off each other and then drew up a list of indispensable needs. Creativity and the appetite for experiences were clearly identifiable. To teach creatively we went back to basics and were able to see that it was possible. Creativity is part of our human blueprint and our belief in ourselves. We know these things empirically; in fact there is a great deal of information about the value of experience and its ties to creativity. During a lifetime's learning people discover creative powers by drawing on diverse experiences. Experience and learning are fused together – the second drawing insight from the first. Sometimes, experiences can be lived through dreams or by daydreaming. They can also be found in story, theatre, TV and interactions with friends. In all of these ways, spiritual and emotional energy helps to germinate creativity. The influence of what has happened is brought to succeeding experiences so that they get connected and reshape our deductions.

So much of our teaching is structured around creativity and children's experiences. The ideas woven into the topics and the techniques are on view in the displays in our classrooms and corridors and in the outdoor setting. Most crucially they are on view as interactions among children, between teachers and as transparent attitudes to learning.

A child absorbs the experiences available and slowly builds on these happenings to construct formulas to deal with life. We design experiences to serve teaching aims and believe that when a topic can unfold through them there is the potential to learn more than what we had intended the experience to teach. Creative achievement is individual, interdependent and intergenerational.

The value of play

Play is the most creative state. We all play and through it we explore ideas about making sense of the world. We endeavour to put playful ideas into the curriculum because we perceive play to be a serious approach to learning. Play is a celebration of life, a healing time, a reawakening and always at the high end of what we do. We all need to play and for children, play is deeply significant. There is so much growth and development that flows from play and yet we have not found a way of testing and classifying it to suit school practices. Play is not generally seen as *the* efficient tool for learning except during the Foundation Stage; perhaps it is simply too much fun or we are all suffering from play blindness.

Play still works knowingly or unknowingly on behalf of the children and in some measure through the subject teaching. It is the position of the authors that there must be fun in learning and that learning should be a pleasure. To illustrate creative play, we use the example of sessions based on playing with water. A class went outside with their teacher. Each child was given approximately the same amount of water in a plastic bowl and the teacher asked them to play with the water for 5 min – no top ups and nothing but plain water.

During the first experience, the children flicked it, drank it, splashed it or watered the plants with it. The second time they trickled the water through their fingers to make patterns, they floated sticks and leaves in it and five children worked together to saturate a part of the bank and watched a channel being formed by the running water. The third time all the children went to the bank to play and make channels. On the following day, they repeated this and then started to try to catch some of the water as it reached the bottom of the bank, dash back to the top of the bank and release it again so that the stream would keep flowing.

All of this represents the value to learning of play, shows how repeated experiences gain cohesion and the power of group wisdom. There is a mutual exchange between the child with water wetting the ground and the action being repeated. It all happened with very little teacher intervention although the teacher was encouraging of the activities and she helped the children to draw conclusions about water finding the lowest point, erosion and patterns of flow. Undirected and partly directed activity can free energy and the brain operates differently. This is playful learning remembered and internalized and it can be a driver for learning.

Playing in the natural environment where there are few limits on space and the children can use the slopes, the trees, the rocks and the grass is one of the best quality experiences we can give them. The implicit invitation to duck into a quiet space and 'disappear' for a minute, the discovery of small creatures inhabiting the play area, the smell of fresh air, the absence of artificial elements, these attributes combine to make ideal conditions for children and adults.

Too many children experience school as a by-road to nowhere. The fact that for them so much of the teaching and learning was unmemorable means that they have wasted a lot of their time. Tedium served up daily can prejudice the children's view of education and we have done all in our power to avoid it.

Notes

1. Refer as well to Chapter 2.
2. Guided Tours are discussed more fully in Chapter 10.
3. H. Gardner. *Five Minds For The Future*. Harvard Business School Press: Cambridge, MA, 2007.
4. Jacob Bronowski: 1908–1974. Mathematician, Biologist, Science Historian. Author of *The Ascent of Man*. 1974. Made into a BBC TV series of 13 programmes 1974.
5. A saying attributed to Confucius, and bedrock philosophy of the Nuffield Foundation.
6. Donald Graves: American educationist who had a profound impact on teaching writing. More than 26 published works chief of which are *Writing: Teachers and Children at Work*. Heinemann: New York. Reprinted 2003 (original book published 1983) and *A Fresh Look at Writing*. Heinemann: New York, 1994.
7. The tensions associated with welcoming visitors is dealt with more fully in Chapter 2.

Calendar of events

These events form the structure of the year. Other projects are slotted in through the whole year.

January	
	● Epiphany journey: visiting different inns, gift-giving in the form of childrens' charitable donations to a worthy cause
	● Visit of mobile planetarium: stars and planets
	● Planting mistletoe: the Norse legend of Baldur
	● Burns Night – piper and haggis eating
	● Chinese New Year: restaurant, dragon dancing and story
February	
	● Candlemas: candlelit procession; snowdrops
	● Shrove Tuesday: pancake parlour
	● Valentine's Day: badge ceremony, science work, Bearobics
March	
	● St David's Day – story of Bedd Gelert, story of St David, welsh cakes
	● Focus on frogs, toads and newts – new life
	● Mothers' Day: history, pick daffodils to take home
	● St Patrick's Day: Irish potato famine drama, Irish dancing
	● Purim – Jewish festival, Story of Esther
April	
	● Easter celebrations: Moses/Exodus, Passover feast, Palm Sunday re-enactment, foot washing, Last Supper, hot cross buns, nest building and visit of Easter rabbit
	● St George's Day – Morris dancers, story of St George and the dragon
May	
	● Wesak: Vesakhaa Puja stories, Buddhism
	● Planting crops
	● Birth of lambs
	● Incubation and hatching of eggs, rearing of chicks
	● Beating the Bounds
June	
	● Sheep shearing
	● School birthday celebrations
	● Continue planting programme – sunflowers
	● Working with clay

July	• Silent walks (Steve von Matre)
	• Sports celebrations
September	• Labyrinth: walking the large painted labyrinth
	• Release of doves of peace (homing pigeons)
	• Plum harvest – Each Peach Pear Plum drama
	• Sunflower harvest: work of great artists, picking the flowers and parading them, chalking flowers outside, badge giving ceremony
	• Apple harvest – apple stories, apple barn, picking apples from school trees and eating fresh and cooked. Making jams, jellies and chutneys, dramas of Johnny Appleseed and Isaac Newton
	• Visits to local churches
October	• Harvests continue: pears, potatoes, blackberries, pumpkins
	• Fungus forays in grounds
	• Focus on art ephemera using leaves, fruit and nuts
	• Diwali: story of Rama and Sita, walking the path of light, dance
	• Tree planting and bulb planting
November	• Fire projects: the drama of the Phoenix, Matilda drama, Great Fire of London re-enactment
	• Work with leaves – hibernation, soil production
	• St Andrew's Day: story of St Andrew, visit of piper, cooking and eating fish, porridge, oatcakes
	• Remembrance: laying poppies on cross in hall, cornet player playing Last Post and Reveille, working with poppies in library
December	• Harvest Christmas tree from gardens
	• Swag making to decorate school hall using evergreens harvested from school gardens
	• St Nicholas: re-enactment of story of the gift giver and badge giving
	• Hannukah: Jewish festival of light, eating doughnuts
	• Christingle: making Christingles, ceremony of light
	• Nativity story: reenactments with each class
	• Mummers' Play
	• Handbell ringers
	• Christmas dinner
	• St Francis story using small wooden figures

Index